EDUCATION AND EQUALITY
IN JAPAN

EDUCATION AND EQUALITY
IN JAPAN

William K. Cummings

PRINCETON UNIVERSITY PRESS

To "The Folks" in Raleigh
and my wife's family in Kyoto, in appreciation of
their continuing support.

Contents

This is a study about schools, and how, under the favorable conditions present in Japan after World War II, they can both promote greater equality in the skills, motivations, and values of their pupils and contribute to leveling the social structures that youth enter. The Japanese experience may be exceptional among the advanced societies. In the United States, following World War II, schools were asked to promote greater social equality. Major efforts were devoted to desegregating school facilities, to improving the quality of schools in backward areas, and to improving the quality of guidance available to pupils. Yet several studies that have evaluated these reforms challenge their efficacy. Christopher Jencks and his colleagues in *Inequality* conclude: "There is no evidence that school reform can substantially reduce the extent of cognitive inequality, as measured by tests of verbal fluency, reading comprehension, or mathematical skill. . . . None of the evidence we have reviewed suggests that school reform can be expected to bring about significant social changes outside of the schools" (1972:255).

I maintain that recent Japanese experience totally contradicts these conclusions. Distinctive changes in postwar Japanese education have substantially contributed to the emergence of an exceptional degree of equality in adult institutions ranging from the family to the work place.

My thesis on the potency of Japanese schools will certainly surprise many readers. It has been my experience that many otherwise well-informed people do not have a balanced perception of the Japanese situation. For example, they think that Japan is characterized by great inequalities in income, power, and wealth; this is true, but Japan's inequalities are less than America's and have been decreasing over the past twenty years. They may have learned about Japan's highly competitive examination system and how it chains so many unhappy youths to their studies; yet they do not know about the happy Japanese primary school where children form loving friendships, appreciate music, develop aesthetic sensitivity, and also learn to read, write, and calculate. Hoping to correct some of these misconceptions, I have attempted in this study to provide a rich detailed description of Japanese education, particularly as it is practiced in the primary school. At the same time I demonstrate how

xiii

the Japanese educational process is promoting egalitarian social change.

Several years ago when I began this study, I had no idea it would take its present form. Originally I viewed education simply as an indicator of social status and intended to investigate how its contribution to the Japanese process of status attainment was similar to or differed from the experience of other societies.

In this connection, I collected, coded, analyzed status attainment data, and participated in Japan's 1975 national social mobility survey organized by Saburo Yasuda and Kenichi Tominaga of the University of Tokyo. I have published some of the results of my investigations on education's role in status attainment elsewhere (Cummings and Naoi, 1974; Cummings, 1977) and other findings are reported in this book. In addition, I urge readers to look at an excellent Ph.D. dissertation by Hidenori Fujita (Department of Education, Stanford University, 1978) that provides a thorough analysis of Japanese data on status attainment.

However, the more I worked on status attainment, the more I was disturbed by the limitations of the underlying "meritocratic" paradigm. Although I became convinced that education in Japan was an important engine of social mobility, I did not feel this was the entire story. Rather, I became increasingly intrigued with education's role in transforming postwar Japan, pushing it toward greater equality in the distribution of challenge, responsibility, prestige, power, and income. Finally, I decided to make this larger story the focus of my research.

Various factors in my personal background also influenced the shift in focus. In ways that are too complex to relate here, I appreciate how my childhood in the state of North Carolina, the most egalitarian of the Deep South states, has always sensitized me to questions of equity and human feelings. These innate concerns surfaced as I became more familiar with the Japanese story. My wife, who was educated in Japan and also taught for several years in a Kyoto high school, possibly influenced me to devote more attention to Japanese schooling. Conversations with Benjamin Bloom, Charles Bidwell, Mary Jean Bowman, and other colleagues at the University of Chicago also played an important role. It was Bloom, in particular, who sensitized me to the plight of the slow pupil and helped me to understand and value the processes in the Japanese classroom that enable this often neglected being to master the curriculum and to develop self-respect. I am grateful to these individuals for leading me onto a new road.

I have followed this road as far as possible, given the limitations of time and the pressure of other duties. Two themes that I have not been able to treat adequately are Japanese education's role in transforming the status of indigenous minority groups and in reducing sex differentiation. I provide some information on these themes, but there is need for additional research on them.

With regard to the format, three explanations are in order:

1. Both to conserve space and to increase reader accessibility to references, I have adopted a special system of footnoting. All the sources cited in the text are listed in the bibliography at the end. Where the main objective of a reference is to indicate the source of information, I have not created a special footnote. Instead, I have simply placed the author's last name, the date of publication, and when appropriate, the page number in parentheses in the text. Only where the objective was to clarify procedures or amplify some point made in the text have I prepared a footnote.

2. The second explanation concerns Japanese names. Japanese people normally place their family names before the given name; because the text is written in the English language where the convention is to place family names last, I have observed this latter convention in writing Japanese names.

3. Finally, in the Japanese language some vowels are short and others long. When the Japanese language is transliterated into the roman script, the long vowels are sometimes indicated by drawing a line above them (e.g. ō instead of o). However, linguists are not always in agreement on whether a particular vowel is long or short. In the face of these ambiguities and also to ease reading for those who have not studied the Japanese language, I have decided to write all vowels, whether long or short, without the line. Readers are advised to keep this in mind when turning to a dictionary or card catalog.

In carrying out this research I have incurred many debts. Through the major period of this study, I was the recipient of a grant from the National Institute of Education, U.S. Office of Education, and benefited from the support of my project directors, Robert Pruitt and Nevzer Stacey. My year of actual fieldwork in Japan was supported by the U.S. Educational Commission in Japan (also known as the Fulbright Commission). I will always appreciate the hospitality of Tetsuya Kobayashi and the Faculty of Education at Kyoto University, who were my local sponsors, as well as of the principals, teachers, and pupils of the schools I visited and observed. I wish to thank the following individuals who generously shared their insights and in some instances their as yet unpublished data with me: Atsushi Naoi and Kenichi Tominaga of the University of Tokyo; Ikuo Amano, Morikazu Ushiogi, and Hidenori Fujita of Nagoya University; Makoto Aso and Yasumasa Tomoda of Osaka University; Michiya Shinbori and Kazuyuki Kitamura of Hiroshima University. I would also like to thank the several individuals who have played a key role in helping to compile information or otherwise assist in the development of this study: Noritsugu Ishido of Kyoto University, Michael Barnas, Osamu Kusatsu, Miranda Ferrell, Robert Burns, Kenneth Egusa, Karen Pittman, Gary Thiesen, and Earline Franklin of the University of Chicago. Thomas Rohlen, Koya Azumi, and Herbert Passin deserve special thanks for their thoughtful critiques of my first draft. Finally, I am grateful to Morris Janowitz, William J. Wilson, Philip Foster, Edward Laumann, and Tetsuo Najita for their support over the difficult period during which I completed the first draft. The final draft was completed in Jakarta, Indonesia where I have been working with the Ford Foundation as a consultant in educational research to the Indonesian government. I thank the foundation office for facilitating the preparation of the final manuscript, and especially Joyce Kansil who performed the honors.

EDUCATION AND EQUALITY
IN JAPAN

Chapter One.

TRANSFORMING SOCIETY BY
EDUCATION

How can education promote egalitarian social change? Much of the current thinking on this matter is concerned with decreasing the impact of social background on academic and socioeconomic achievement. This conventional meritocratic approach assumes a continuation of the established inequalities between the powerful and the weak, the rich and the poor, the respected and the rest. The goal is to alter the conditions that determine who assumes these unequal positions. Based on the meritocratic value premise that the most able products of the schools should be selected for the most important positions in society, this conventional approach results in reforms to promote greater equality of opportunity.

The meritocratic approach is outdated. Its concern with reducing the impact of social background can be applauded, but it becomes increasingly difficult to assess progress in this effort as the schools receive the full cohort of young people and promote them, irrespective of performance, until the completion of high school. In school young people are tested and graded into "differential ability" groups for subsequent channeling into stratified educational careers. Compensatory educational programs are developed to improve the school performance of children from deprived backgrounds and elevate them to the higher educational tracks. These compensatory programs do not seem to work. But even if they did, would the improved school performance of these children do them much good? For in today's overeducated society we witness the anomaly of unemployed Ph.D.s and college graduates working as waiters, while high school educated electricians enjoy a princely life-style (Freedman, 1976). Children from lower class backgrounds may, thanks to the compensatory programs, do well in school only to find out that they are destined to do poorly in society.

In contrast with the meritocratic approach is the transformationist approach. It focuses first on structures rather than on the flow of people through these structures.[1] The transformationist ap-

[1] The term "transformational" is taken from the "Introduction" to the 1974

3

proach challenges the established hierarchies, urging that they be leveled. Rather than concern itself with reducing the effect of social background on individual learning, it attempts to realize a situation where all can learn; rather than have pupils learn those skills and knowledge that will help them to fit into the existing hierarchies, the transformationist approach urges that pupils develop a critical attitude to these hierarchies. Today's critical children will be tomorrow's adults, working in positions where they can level the hierarchies. As the hierarchies become more equal, so will the opportunities.

NEITHER RADICAL NOR CONSERVATIVE

Current thinking about the transformationist approach is intimately related to the present politico-ideological debates. Most proponents of the meritocratic approach are political conservatives or liberals who believe egalitarian change can be achieved through working "within the system." Most proponents of the transformationist approach are political radicals who believe egalitarian change can be achieved only if the system is simultaneously changed. Radicals assume that the meritocratic approach is necessarily intertwined with liberal ideology, and liberals assume that the transformation approach is an expression of radical ideology. We believe that the approaches can be dissociated from these prevailing ideologies and maintain that the theory of transformation through education is neither radical nor conservative.

Indeed, in several of the recent cases where education has been used to transform society, politics was simultaneously pushing in the same direction. That is, a political revolution was carried out first by political elites, egalitarian social reforms were then introduced, and education was mobilized to support these reforms. The cases to which we refer are China, Cuba, and Tanzania. In these instances, it cannot be said that education acted as an independently transforming force but rather as one of several mutually reinforcing component forces. This empirical association between revolution and education as an agent of transformation leads the political radicals to theorize that there can be no other way.

We maintain that the radical "theoretical" position is too pes-

---

World Year Book of Education (Foster and Sheffield, 1973). Hutchins (1968) and Bell (1973:402-455) present two visionary analyses.

simistic. Propitious political developments may be necessary if education is to promote an egalitarian transformation, but we do not believe these events need be so momentous as to equal revolution. Only some arrangement whereby the educational system and educators achieve a degree of autonomy is required. We appreciate but are not convinced by Bourdieu and Passeron's (1977) contention that educational systems, even in revolutionary societies, enjoy considerable autonomy from the polity. Relative degree of autonomy cannot be theoretically deduced; it is an empirically verifiable variable. To the extent that an educational system is autonomous, its opportunities for promoting a transformation increase.

Postwar Japan As an Example

Looking to education to transform society is not a new approach. Aristotle, Rousseau, and Dewey are only three among many social thinkers who have looked to education as a transformative agent. But for over two decades the mainstream of American social thought has ignored this tradition, or at least viewed it as too Utopian for America. On the one hand, America's reformers have emphasized change within the framework of the meritocratic tradition. On the other hand, America's radicals have, especially recently, expressed a renewed interest in the transformationist approach, but they doubt its applicability to America or to any other advanced industrial capitalist society. Rather they are most appreciative of the utility of the transformationist approach for interpreting events in developing societies where the "system" is more changeable.

But is education's transformative potency necessarily tied to a society's level of economic development? To answer this question we can turn either to theory or to the real world. In this book we choose the latter strategy. Postwar Japan, we maintain, constitutes an example of a society that has been transformed by education. This book attempts to illustrate and explain how.

Immediately following World War II, extensive reforms were introduced in the Japanese educational system with the explicit hope that these would contribute to an egalitarian social transformation as the crucial background for a democratic form of government. But almost as soon as the reforms were introduced, a conservative political regime emerged, and under the circumstances few would have predicted that education might transform society.

The conservative regime worked to reverse the postwar reforms, but these efforts were stubbornly resisted by the Japan Teachers' Union (Nikkyoso). The union and apparently some elements in the government actually favored the "democratic" goals of the new education and worked for their realization, and gradually their efforts to gain acceptance for these goals acquired momentum. Over the postwar years increasing proportions of young people were exposed to an egalitarian educational routine with the result that cognitive achievements became more equal. Indeed, Japan's distribution of cognitive skills is probably more equal than that of any other contemporary society (see Chapter Six). At the same time, an egalitarian sentiment became more widely internalized.[2]

As these youths passed from schools into society, they exerted egalitarian pressure on adult institutions, which inevitably had to introduce changes in order to accommodate them. For example, work places enriched work routines, delegated authority, and equalized pay. The result was a transformation of Japanese society so that it is today one of the world's most equal in terms of a wide variety of indicators (see Chapter Nine). That education is transforming the system of at least one advanced capitalist society implies that its potency is not deterred by level of socioeconomic complexity. It is conceivable that education, given favorable circumstances, could have similar transformative effects on the systems of other advanced societies, including America.

THE DISTINCTIVE CHARACTERISTICS OF JAPANESE EDUCATION

Japan is an especially relevant case for Americans to examine, for the two nations have so much in common. Both are advanced capitalist societies with a democratic political system. Japan's population is slightly more than half of that of the United States with an adult educational level that is, as in the American case, comparatively high. Since World War II, the formal structure of the educational system has resembled that found in many American school districts, that is, a single track structure partitioned into a six-year

---

[2] The egalitarian sentiment is defined in greater detail in Chapter Seven. A number of surveys and anthropological studies suggest that the members of Japan's younger generation are more egalitarian, individualistic, and critical of authority than their parents. The first general report documenting this trend is by Matsumoto (1960).

primary school, a three-year middle school, a three-year high school, and a diverse program of post-secondary educational institutions centered in the university. Today, the Japanese system offers as great an opportunity to young people for post-secondary education as the American system.

However, Japan is markedly different. The nation is more centralized, more densely populated, and more racially homogeneous. Its cultural heritage is more complex, being based on diverse Asian traditions as well as on modern Western culture from which it has profusely borrowed over the last hundred years. Finally, there are a number of specific ways in which Japanese education differs from the United States. The following differences stand out as being of great importance in our effort to explain the success of Japanese education in transforming society.

1. *Diverse interests in Japan are concerned with education.* Japan, as a late developer, was one of the first societies to treat education as a tool for national development. The central governmental and business elites look upon education as a means for training a skilled labor force and highly qualified manpower, for identifying prospective elites, and for teaching a common culture.

Over the postwar period, the powerful Japan Teachers' Union has emerged to challenge the ruling elite's traditional educational policies. The union emphasizes the educational system's capacity for developing rich personalities and critical abilities; in alliance with progressive political parties, the union has repeatedly sought the support of rank-and-file teachers in political efforts aimed at toppling the ruling conservative regime. These battles at the central level, extensively covered by the mass media, serve to sharpen public understanding of education and its supposed consequences.

The public is disturbed by this highly competitive nature of postcompulsory education and tends to believe that government policies are responsible for this situation. Thus, there is considerable popular approval of the teachers' union with its emphasis on the humanistic and self-actualizing goals of education. At the same time, however, the public believes that individual success in education leads to personal advancement. Thus, families invest enormous amounts of time and energy in promoting the educational success of their own children. The responses to the educational system by its many participants are diverse and often contradictory. Yet out of this confusion emerges an impressive level of interest in education.

2. *Japanese schools are inexpensive.* Educational costs to the Japa-

nese taxpayer are comparatively small in relation to the high standards it has achieved. In 1973, Japan's public expenditures for education comprised only 4.9 percent of the national income. In contrast,
the expenditures relative to national income for the Soviet Union,
the United States, and the United Kingdom were 8.3 percent, 7.0
percent, and 7.8 percent, respectively. Among the advanced
societies, only France spent a smaller proportion (4.6 percent) of her
national income on public education (Mombusho, 1975:145).
Moreover, despite Japan's relatively small proportion of national
income devoted to public education, a comparatively large proportion of actual expenditures were allotted for new buildings and
equipment, while personnel expenditures were modest (see Table
1.1).

TABLE 1.1
DISTRIBUTION OF PUBLIC PRIMARY AND MIDDLE SCHOOL
EXPENDITURES AND STUDENT-TEACHER RATIO

	Personnel (Teachers' Expenditures and Salaries— Percentage of Total Expenditures)	Capital Investment (Debt Service on Investments— Percentage of Total Expenditures)	Students per Teacher
Japan (1973)	46.5	28.7	27
United States (1971)	58.6	12.1	22
England (1972)	50.2	24.6	28
France (1973)	79.1	9.8	23

SOURCE: Mombusho, *Wagakuni no Kyoiku Suijun* (Educational Standards in Japan),
    1975, pp. 149, 94.

Higher student-teacher ratios are part of the explanation for the
modest proportion of Japanese educational expenditures devoted to
personnel. In addition, it should be noted that Japanese schools hire
relatively few auxiliary personnel. Students and teachers perform
services that are likely to be discharged by specialized personnel in
other societies. Regular teachers perform many of the clerical and
counseling activities that are handled by specialists in the United
States. Students deliver and serve lunches, clean the classrooms and
grounds, and operate school facilities such as the library and public
address system. This unpaid labor significantly cuts down on costs.
Consequently, Japanese schools have relatively more money available for plant investment.

3. *Japanese schools are equal.* The postwar public concern with education has placed pressure on the central government to reduce inequalities in educational expenditures per student. Today, at the compulsory level, there is virtually no variation between prefectures in annual operating expenditures per student. While some areas lead and others lag in the introduction of the latest educational technology, such as color televisions, language laboratories, and the like, remarkable equality in distribution has been established with respect to the essentials.[3] Similarly, teachers tend universally to have similar qualifications; the major exceptions are those prefectures that have lost population to the large cities. In these prefectures few new teachers have been hired for several years and, hence, the teacher age distribution is older.

Some of the government's equalizing measures are directed at disadvantaged social groups. For example, one law subsidizes children from low income families to pay for school lunches, excursions, and other regular activities. Another law includes provisions aimed at equalizing the educational conditions of children in remote areas: the law provides transport subsidies to enable children living on small islands to ride boats to mainland schools, and it authorizes hardship salary supplements so as to induce skilled teachers to take positions in these areas (Ministry of Education, 1971:92-109). Recently, the government began to put additional funds into the schools that receive children from the "outcaste" *burakimin* community. As these outcaste children traditionally have done poorly in schools, the supplements are used to pay for tutoring after school and other compensatory programs. The programs are so intensive that expenditures per student for outcaste children are three times as great as the expenditures for the other children.

The system of finance for Japanese education greatly facilitates the realization of equal expenditures. Japanese school boards are not dependent on local property taxes as are their American counter-

---

[3] Extensive data by prefecture on educational expenses are found in the basic educational statistics collected by the Ministry of Education and published periodically. From these total operating expenses per primary school student by prefecture for 1972 were computed. Forty of the forty-six prefectures spent between 135,000 yen and 170,000 yen per student or varied within a range of 30 percent. The most extravagant prefecture, Tokyo, spent 208,700 yen per student, or 56 percent more on operating expenses than Kumamoto, with 133,333 yen per student. Within prefectures, operating expenses per student were adjusted to take account of the scale of schools. As for capital expenditures, most prefectures spent more per student in rural and isolated schools.

parts. School districts in Japan tend to be much larger, which facilitates access to a wide variety of local tax sources. Moreover, for most categories of educational expenditures such as salaries, texts, and lunches, the central government is required by law to pay up to half of the expenses required to realize the national standard. The national laws on educational expenditures also include equalizing measures to help prefectures that, due to special features of geography, population structure, or industrial composition, experience difficulty in collecting sufficient tax revenues.

4. *Japanese schools are demanding.* The central government's role in providing a large share of educational revenues enables it to exert considerable leverage over certain aspects of the educational process.

The central government drafts a detailed course of study prescribing the contents of the curriculum and inspects commercial texts to insure that they conform to the official standard. One virtue of this procedure is that children throughout the nation are exposed to a common body of knowledge in an identical sequence.

At the same time, the curriculum is demanding. It covers a wider range of subjects and pursues these in greater depth than is the case for the curriculum of a typical U.S. school district. The differences are evident from the first grade of primary school. Young Japanese pupils spend a larger proportion of their time in subjects such as art, music, and physical education than do American students (Ministry of Education, 1971:56-63). Whereas many American schools do not offer a science curriculum at the primary school level, this is offered in Japan from the first grade. In arithmetic, a subject central to both the Japanese and American curricula, the Japanese texts move faster than a typical American text.

In order to cover the demanding curriculum, the government requires each school to operate an educational program for at least 240 days each year, in contrast with 180 days for American schools. In most cases, this means that children attend school six days a week for over forty weeks. School occupies a very central place in the lives of Japanese children.

5. *The school is the educational unit.* The foreign observer is impressed with the extent to which schools rather than individual grade levels and classes constitute the basic unit for integrating Japanese education. At the primary level, one finds an orderly progression from preparation for schooling in the early years to intense and

disciplined cognitive training toward the end. Teachers, while in charge of a particular class, feel a responsibility to speak to students from other classes when they see these children misbehaving in the halls or on the grounds. Most teachers eventually gain experience in teaching at several different grade levels.

The faculty meeting, as the basic decision-making body of the school, works to realize the school's integrated program. Each spring, it decides on an educational objective for the entire school and plans a schedule of school events around this objective. The faculty reassesses the school's progress periodically. In these general reviews, as in discussions on specific pedagogical issues, there is considerable communication between teachers responsible for different grade levels and specialties. Other aspects of school life from the weekly *chorei* (early morning school assembly) to club activities and festive occasions, such as sports day, reflect the emphasis on the school as the basic educational unit.

6. *Japanese teachers are secure.* Teaching in Japan is a respected profession. Teachers receive social status and a reasonable salary. Most teachers expect to spend their complete working life as teachers. As public servants, they automatically receive tenure upon initial employment, providing no special circumstances intervene. In the past, one possible circumstance that could have led to a teacher's dismissal was the feeling by a local elite or official that a teacher was not performing his job in a satisfactory manner. But today, in most areas of Japan, teachers do not have to fear dismissal on this basis. Roughly three fourths of all teachers belong to the strong Japan Teachers' Union, which is prepared to fight for each teacher's right to employment. In the past, too, the union saved the jobs of a number of teachers at much embarrassment to local governments. Thus, teachers do not fear the governments that employ them.

When employers make unreasonable requests, teachers sometimes express their reservations. In other instances, teachers ignore or prevent the implementation of official requests. For example, when the central government passed a law requiring school principals to fill out job-performance evaluations for each teacher under their authority, teachers in most areas persuaded the principals to ignore the regulation, arguing that it would destroy staff harmony. Likewise, teachers feel secure enough to stand up against pressure exerted by powerful parents. At the same time, teachers do not always comply with the requests of their union. Many teachers who

are members of the union do not support the union's explicit politically oriented protests such as the outbursts it organized against
American involvement in the Vietnam War.

The security that teachers enjoy enables them to run their schools
without excessive influence from any outside body. Teachers spend
a large amount of time each year deciding what their school should
attempt to accomplish. This discussion takes account of the various
external pressures, but is unlikely to submit to any of them. Balanc-
ing the external demands, the teachers collectively agree on the
program that they want to pursue for their school. Over the course
of the year, they then do their best to realize it. They are at once
autonomous from external power and responsive to these pressures. It is because the egalitarian line of the teachers' union is
among the more credible of the external influences that it has such a
significant impact on the policies of individual schools.

7. *Japanese teachers are conscientious.* A number of mechanisms are
built into the school routine to induce teachers to do their best. In
each school, teachers spend a surprising amount of time discussing
teaching in general—at the morning and weekly faculty meetings,
the biweekly research meetings, and the quarterly public research
seminars. In addition, the teachers who teach a common grade level
share desks and frequently consult with each other on ways to solve
specific problems. This interaction establishes a collective expectation for good teaching within each school that individual teachers
feel constrained to live up to. Moreover, local school boards and the
Japan Teachers' Union arrange pedagogical seminars that many attend.

To enhance communication with parents, teachers make a point
of visiting each pupil's home to meet the pupil's parents at least
once each school year. These visits also help teachers learn about
the home circumstances of their pupils. Many teachers make adjustments, based on this information, in their routine to provide
better in-school opportunities for those children who lack favorable
home situations. Parents are officially invited to the school once a
month to watch their children in the classroom. Once every quarter, parents have an opportunity to discuss their child's progress
with teachers. Parents are given the telephone numbers of their
children's teachers and encouraged to call if there is any special
problem. The concerned eye of the ordinary parent is another factor inducing teacher conscientiousness.

It is sometimes charged that teachers today are not as dedicated as
previous generations. They go home earlier, spend less time after

school in review sessions with problem students, and are less likely to invite pupils to their homes for tea and talk. It is difficult to evaluate these charges. Perhaps the critics also forget some of the postwar trends that impinge upon the schedules of both teacher and student. The contemporary curriculum is more demanding, requiring teachers to set aside more time for preparation. School days are at least a half hour longer than before the war. Due to urbanization, the teacher must spend a considerable amount of time commuting to school. Finally, many pupils do not want to spend after-school time with their teachers as the pupils have their own heavy schedules of after-school activities, including piano lessons, extra-study schools, and athletics.

8. *Japanese teachers believe in "whole-person" education.* The specter of exam competition and the concern many parents express for their child's cognitive development have been mentioned. Japanese teachers recognize these demands and do their best to respond. However, they feel that their most important task is to develop well-rounded "whole people," not just intellects.

Teachers at one of the schools visited selected the following goals to guide their work during the year of our observation: to develop children with pure and rich hearts; to build up strong and healthy bodies; to promote the spirit of curiosity and intellectual achievement; to encourage the will to endure in whatever is attempted; to help each child to understand how his strengths complement those of his classmates.

The willingness of Japanese teachers to develop whole people is a crucial factor in Japanese education's capacity to promote change. In teaching values to their pupils, the teachers influence the way these young people respond to established patterns of behavior.

The officially prescribed curriculum provides an important vehicle for whole-person education. Along with the standard academic subjects, the curriculum also sets aside a substantial amount of time for systematic instruction in art, music, physical education, and moral education. Teachers seem to be as conscientious in their attention to these subjects as to the standard academic ones.

The concern with whole-person education is especially evident in the early years of primary school where teachers work hard to establish order and to induce their pupils to perform in the classroom. During these early years, teachers are more concerned with getting all their pupils involved in learning than with making progress through the curriculum. This concern with proper behavior and motivation yields important long-run dividends. For instance, orderly classrooms mean that most of the school time can be spent on learning. Due to the attention to pupil motivation, dropouts are exceedingly rare. Although some pupils fall behind, nearly all who are mentally able acquire a basic proficiency in reading, writing, public speaking, arithmetic, and graphics by the time they complete their compulsory education.

Another aspect of whole-person education is the effort teachers devote to moral education. Both through the moral education course and through a wide range of other activities, teachers try to convey certain moral principles to their pupils. They stress the egalitarian, individualistic, and participatory orientations that constitute the egalitarian sentiment; yet, at the same time, teachers try to teach conventional values of friendship, cordiality, cooperation, and discipline.

9. Japanese teaching is equitable. The embattled conditions in which Japan's teachers are trained and work help to make them ideologically mature. The continuing battle between the central government and the teachers' union highlights the implications of educational actions.

Given its traditional concern with education as a means for identifying and furthering talent, the central government has advocated tracking and ability-grouped instruction. However, the union has opposed these reforms arguing that they would destroy the harmony of classrooms and the collective feeling that exists among age-mates. A common phrase in the union's rhetoric of opposition is discrimination. Union leaders appreciate that tracking could end up with lower-class and minority group children being permanently assigned to low-ability tracks.

Teachers are sensitized by these debates, and this affects their behavior. In the classrooms, teachers show an impressive concern with eliciting the participation of each pupil, thereby building up a positive orientation to schoolwork. Few teachers openly show favoritism to their best pupils, nor do they denigrate the performance of the weak performers. Rather, the teachers do what they can, given the constraints of time and the curriculum, to guide all pupils through the program.

PLAN OF THE BOOK

The nine themes highlighted above all contribute to an explanation of postwar Japanese education's transformative potency and each receives further development in the course of the discussion. Chapters Two to Four provide a detailed analysis of the historical, political, and social background of postwar education. Chapter Three focuses on the class system and how the government and the union relate to it. Chapter Four discusses family structure and the orientation of different family types to education. With that background, the analysis of the educational process in the schools is taken up. Chapter Five provides a rich description of everyday school life at the primary and secondary level based largely on a year of field observation in Kyoto. In Chapter Six, data from the field report is organized, using the theory of mastery learning, to explain the high average cognitive achievement of Japanese school children and the surprising degree of equality in this achievement. Chapter Seven accounts for the eagerness of Japanese children to learn and the school's success in conveying egalitarian values. The primary school is explicitly organized to achieve these egalitarian effects, whereas higher levels of the school system are more concerned with other goals. Chapter Eight explores an interesting paradox: Japanese education is perhaps best known in international circles for the tremendous competition it induces in young people over examinations. In that competition has inegalitarian consequences—some end up ahead of others—how can this competition be reconciled with equality? Thus, we ask if youth are able to sustain their commitment to egalitarian values as they move from the compulsory educational system into the competition for entrance to prestigious high schools and universities. Chapter Nine examines the impact of the new youth with their egalitarian values on adult institutions.

Finally, Chapter Ten brings the findings together. Although this book is conceived largely as an effort to illustrate Japanese experience, the description is ordered by a series of propositions, and these are listed and their implications examined. Will Japanese education continue to transform society? What can America learn? What are the implications of this study for the ways in which educational research is conducted?

Chapter Two

THE BACKGROUND FOR
CHANGE

Japan is a densely populated nation located on several rugged mountainous islands off the coast of the Asian mainland. This setting enabled Japan to develop somewhat independently from its Far Eastern neighbors. Japan was strongly influenced by Far Eastern culture. Yet Japan, while influenced by the Far East, also, on more than one occasion, attempted to shut out this tradition.

From 1600 to 1868, the central Tokugawa regime enforced what was probably the most extreme isolationist policy in the history of large-scale societies. As a result, the nation enjoyed peace, but only modest development. Meanwhile, the West was rapidly industrializing and adopting new forms of economic and social organization. Japan knew very little about these developments until Commodore Perry's warships, puffing black smoke, steamed into the Edo Bay, and shot several warning shots from their cannons. Japan's upper class of samurai, who took great pride in their military prowess, were startled by the American military technology against which Japan seemed defenseless. Immediately, young samurai began to consider how the nation could respond to this challenge. Within a few years, these debates led to the toppling of the Tokugawa regime by a coalition of young samurai who were determined to modernize their nation. The new leaders, who assumed power when the Emperor Meiji was crowned, were determined to modernize Japan's institutions and avoid the fate of colonization. Exercising firm central leadership, they imposed a formula of "Western technology and Eastern spirit" on the Japanese people.

The Meiji regime introduced Western liberal reforms including the abolition of the feudal class system, the promulgation of a constitution, and the establishment of representative political institutions. At the same time, it sought to marshal the nation under firm central control, directing popular energies to the task of national development. The "educational revolution," establishing what is today known as the "old system," became an integral part of the young regime's effort to realize these ends. Although other Asian nations lost their independence and failed to develop, Japan did otherwise. It rapidly gained in national strength and unity. Ultimately, Japan felt sufficiently strong to challenge several of the Western nations as Germany's ally of World War II.

Following Japan's defeat in World War II, the American Occupation, in reaction against many of the characteristics of wartime Japan, carried out a massive program of reform. The Occupation's aim was to establish a new society committed to democracy and peace. This brought about a "second revolution" in Japan's educational institutions. As a background for the analysis of the postwar egalitarian trend, this chapter will outline several characteristics of the educational systems created by the two educational revolutions.

An Outline of the "Old System" of Education

The young warriors who in 1868 took control of Japan were deeply conscious of the prime importance of mass education and advanced knowledge in order to achieve modernization. In the Charter Oath issued soon after their accession to central power, they announced the need to "seek knowledge widely throughout the world" (Tsuneichi, 1958:643). Upon consolidating the traditional governmental units, they began in 1872 to affirmatively construct a modern educational system. The Fundamental Code of Education issued that year declared: "There shall, in the future, be no community with an illiterate family, nor a family with an illiterate person. Every guardian, acting in accordance with this, shall bring up his children with tender care, never failing to have them attend school" (Passin, 1965:209-211).

At this formative stage, the government looked to education as a means for forging a closer integration of the diverse feudal loyalties and for training a technical elite. However, factions in the government disagreed on the basic tenets to shape the educational philosophy. After a decade of unrewarding experimentation with Western liberal ideas, from the early 1880s the government shifted toward a more traditional elitist and pragmatic conception. Mori Arinori (Hall, I., 1973), who from 1885 to 1889 served as minister of education, played a key role in articulating the new policy that was to remain as the framework for Japanese education through World War II.

The main characteristics of Mori's educational system included:

1. *Spiritual training.* All youth throughout the nation were required to spend a minimum of four years in primary schools where they would learn both the basic cognitive skills and the principles of the national morality. Mori repeatedly emphasized the necessity of spiritual education. An opening paper presented for the consideration of the cabinet put forth the following rationale:

Civilization is gradually spreading as can be seen by the progressive changes in the objects we use for our daily activities. Is the spirit of our people sufficiently hardened and trained that they may withstand adversity, bear up and endure under pain, and shoulder the heavy burdens of the long road ahead? This must be doubted. Since the middle ages, in our country only the warriors (*bushi*) have performed civil and military (*bunbu*) duties. Now, as a result, only one portion of the people adequately understands and supports the modernization of the state. In contrast, the great majority are confused and may lack those qualities of strong character essential for guaranteeing the independence of the state.
. . . We have identified those general moral principles which we hope the educational system will instill in the people, but what is the detailed educational program that will realize these principles? Consider for a moment. Our country has never been subject to indignity from a foreign nation thanks to the authority of the Imperial Throne which has been occupied by an unbroken line of Emperors from ancient times. The people's traditional spirit of defending the fatherland and of total loyalty to the Emperor still remains firm. This is the essential foundation for national wealth and strength. If this is made the goal of education and the character of the people is advanced according to this spirit, there will be no need for fear. The people will feel a strong sense of loyalty to the Throne (*chukon*) and love for their country (*aikoku*); they will have strong character, and be pure in thought. We must establish through education the principle of abhoring those who are insulting and evil. If we are successful, there is no doubt that the people will be able to endure much difficulty and will be prepared to strive together to carry out their tasks. . . . This vitality if channeled into productive labor will develop the national wealth. There is not one element in advancing the fate of the state and casting away all danger which does not come from this vital spirit. The elderly pass this vital spirit to the young. Fathers and ancestors pass this vital spirit to posterity. From per-

son to person and household to household, all are made the same according to this vital spirit. The vital spirit of our nation becomes fixed, and the nation naturally becomes something of great strength (Mombusho, 1972:270-276).

In 1891, after extensive discussion within the government, the main themes to be stressed in the school's program of spiritual training were summarized in the Imperial Rescript on Education.

Know Ye, Our Subjects:

Our Imperial Ancestors have founded Our Empire on a basis broad and everlasting and have deeply and firmly implanted virtue; Our subjects ever united in loyalty and filial piety have from generation to generation illustrated the beauty thereof. This is the glory of the fundamental character of Our Empire, and herein also lies the source of Our education. Ye, Our subjects, be filial to your parents, affectionate to your brothers and sisters; as husbands and wives be harmonious, as friends true; bear yourselves in modesty and moderation; extend your benevolence to all; pursue learning and cultivate arts, and thereby develop intellectual faculties and perfect moral powers; furthermore advance public good and promote common interests; always respect the Constitution and observe the laws; should emergency arise, offer yourselves courageously to the State; and thus guard and maintain the prosperity of Our Imperial Throne coeval with heaven and earth. So shall ye not only be Our good and faithful subjects, but render illustrious the best traditions of your forefathers.

The Way here set forth is indeed the teaching bequeathed by Our Imperial Ancestors, to be observed alike by Their Descendants and the subjects, infallible for all ages and true in all places. It is Our wish to lay it to heart in all reverence, in common with you, Our subjects, that we may all thus attain to the same virtue (Hall, R., 1949:27-28).

Every school child was required to memorize and recite these short paragraphs, and they provided the foundation for the moral education curriculum.

Among the many themes emphasized in the morals curriculum were the respective ways in which men and women could contribute to the national purpose. While men were urged to energetically assume their place in the world of work, women were directed to the home. After completion of the second grade, the sexes were placed in different classrooms. From that point on, the curriculum for young girls emphasized domestic arts such as cooking, sewing, and flower arranging. Girls were discouraged from attending school beyond the compulsory level, and the educational opportunities that were available to them were not equal to those for men. One official report stated: "Our female high education may be said to have the object of forming character in women and of imparting knowledge well-calculated to make *good wives and wise mothers*, able to contribute to the peace and happiness of the family into which they marry" (Fujita, 1938:121). Through World War II, a Japanese woman could not seek a degree at most of the indigenous universities. The majority who studied beyond the compulsory level ended up as temporary teachers in primary schools.

2. *National integration*. Up to the time of the Meiji Restoration, the political power in Japan had been fragmented into nearly three hundred distinct units. The loyalties of the warriors and common people had been to their local lords rather than to the national government. Hence, one of the greatest challenges faced by the young Meiji government was to alter this pattern of local allegiances. The new curriculum of spiritual training, richly infused with centrist themes of loyalty to the emperor and allegiance to the national purpose, was a principal means toward this goal of national integration. To ensure that local areas received the message, the young government quickly moved to a system whereby the central government exercised extensive control over local schools: texts were authorized by the central government, school principals were government appointees, expenses in the compulsory schools were supported by central government subsidies, and central government inspectors made annual visits to each local school. In these ways the government directed local schools to adhere to national policy.

However, prior to the formation of this policy of state dominance, many private groups established modern schools, and among these were several reputable institutions supported by foreign Christian missions. To avoid antagonizing the Western nations, the Meiji government allowed these mission schools to carry on with their work, but after the turn of the century the government took a series of steps that significantly reduced the attractiveness of these private schools as places for young Japanese to study (Burnstein, 1967). Among these actions were provisions making it difficult for private school graduates to sit for the exams at higher-

level government schools and universities. Because graduation
from a government school or university was a requisite for many
civil service jobs, these actions restricted the career prospects of
private school students. As with the public schools, the government sent inspectors to private schools. Some private schools were
forced to dismiss personnel who were considered objectionable by
the government. In these various ways, the government sought to
realize a uniform educational program that would foster national
integration.

3. *Meritocratic selection of an elite*. At the top of the old system was
the Imperial University (after 1897, the reference is to Tokyo Imperial University), the function of which was to select the national
elite and provide them with the broad education appropriate to elite
roles. In contrast with the compulsory primary school, virtually no
restrictions were placed on the manner in which the members of
the Imperial University conducted their educational or research activities. The assumption was that those who gained admittance to
this institution would already have developed such a strong commitment to national goals that further indoctrination would be un-
necessary. Admission to this elite institution was to be based solely
on a competitive entrance examination that anyone with the appropriate level of educational achievement could take. Through the
nineteenth century, the Imperial University accepted less than one
person out of every thousand in a given age-group who attended
primary school. Even as late as the 1930s when several additional
Imperial Universities were established, the ratio of primary school
entrants to places at the Imperial Universities for new students remained over a hundred to one. The government restricted the scale
of the most prestigious higher educational institutions so that their
degrees would confer honor and advantageous career prospects.

4. *Technically competent labor force*. In between the primary schools
and the exalted Imperial University, Mori Arinori had established
the framework for the development of a diverse multitrack postcompulsory educational system. The most prestigious track led
through a middle school and higher school into an Imperial University. Other tracks pointed the way to various vocational schools,
normal schools, and technical and semiprofessional schools. Figure
2.1 illustrates the various paths as they had developed by 1937. In
general, once an individual began on one track, he could not transfer onto a different track; for example, an individual who started in

a secondary vocational school could not upon completion of its program compete for admission to a college, but would first have to go back to complete the middle school course.

Mori and others of the Meiji government highly evaluated the potential contribution of the various schools comprising this intermediate sector. They appreciated the great need that Japan would have for competent, trained specialists and skilled workers if the nation intended to succeed in its industrialization effort. At the same time, Mori was concerned that the students who attended the postcompulsory schools should continue to receive spiritual education. During his tenure as minister of education, he devoted particular attention to the curriculum of the normal schools where primary school teachers were trained. Special morals texts were designed for these schools, as was a spartan schedule that included early morning calisthenics conducted by military officers. Mori believed their exemplary presence would help in cultivating the loyal and disciplined character appropriate for teachers. In that the state maintained a monopoly of the teacher training schools, these provisions were certain to reinforce the official policy of providing systematic spiritual training to primary school students. Similar provisions for spiritual training were built into the curricula of the other intermediate schools.

STRAINS IN THE OLD SYSTEM

The educational policies to promote national integration, spiritual training, the development of a core of competent technicians, and the meritocratic selection of a national elite were established by the central government to serve the interests of the state and those social groups closest to the state. While Mori Arinori and others indicated their concern for the welfare of the common people, the policies they devised were not intended to respond to the "felt needs" of these people. Instead, the policies were designed to bend the people into conformity with the program established at the center. As Mori often indicated, "education is not for the sake of the student but for the sake of the state." The central elites believed that the ordinary Japanese subject was backward and needed to be guided into the modern world. In their opinion, the interests of each subject would best be served if all cooperated in realizing the goals of the state.

The central government retained its commitment to these basic

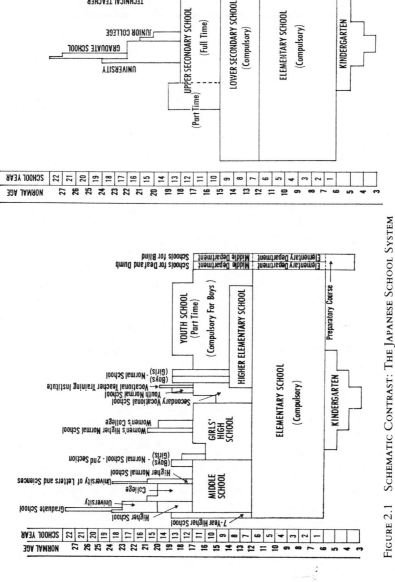

FIGURE 2.1 SCHEMATIC CONTRAST: THE JAPANESE SCHOOL SYSTEM

SOURCE: Herbert Passin, Society and Education in Japan, pp. 308–309.

policies through World War II. Yet vast internal social changes in
this period modified policy specifics. For example, with industrialization the demand for technically trained manpower increased.
Events following World War I encouraged a more militaristic national tone, and this led to an intensification of spiritual training.
Most historical accounts imply that the policies designed by the
government to cope with these social changes were successful. Yet
that was not always the case.

1. *Primary school enrollments.* While the central government declared as early as 1872 that it intended to achieve universal attendance in primary schools, this goal was not realized until circa 1910,
nearly forty years later (Mombusho, 1972:192 ff.). The government
initially required mandatory attendance and compelled parents to
pay the necessary fees. Upon realizing that these policies actually
caused a decline in enrollment, the government ordered local governments to collect the revenues to support compulsory education,
and at the same time, it allowed those localities facing fiscal
problems to forego an educational program. Only as the central
government began from the late 1880s to subsidize compulsory
education was there significant progress toward the realization of
universal enrollment. The growing popular recognition that education offered career alternatives also contributed to the increase in attendance.

2. *Spiritual training.* Although the central government was concerned from the beginning with introducing moral education into
the curriculum, it took time to develop acceptable texts. The views
of diverse traditions, including religious groups and the Meiji
oligarchs, differed substantially leading to long and divisive debate.
It was not until 1891 with the proclamation of the Imperial Rescript
on Education that some agreement was achieved. The early curriculum essentially emphasized the values of a nineteenth-century
liberal society committed to national development and the preser-
vation of familistic values. Over time, the compilers of the texts became increasingly zealous in their identification with the national
purpose. Thus, increasingly biased and nationalistic themes were
introduced. A favorite example of this trend concerns the treatment
of Socrates. In the earlier morals texts, Socrates was merely described as a wise man in ancient Greece who lived an aesthetic life
of the mind. However, by the 1930s, Socrates became a Greek sol-
dier who "went to war three times to fight bravely for his country"
(Hall, R., 1949:105). A fifth grade morals text describes Socrates'

trial and then Crito's attempt to persuade Socrates to escape. The story concludes with Socrates making a long speech revering law and nationhood:

> Crito, I am grateful for your kindness. However, as you know very well, up to this day I have followed the paths of virtue and have persuaded others to do likewise. How can I say that because my life is valuable [it is all right to go against my principles] and do even a single thing contrary to what is ordered by the national laws? If the citizens of a country did such unlawful things, the country would not be able to exist. My parents, my grandparents, and I have all grown to adulthood receiving the benefits of our country. We exist because of our country. Whatever the law orders, no matter what it is, we should obey. I love my country and I have gone to war three times at the risk of my life. Could I bring myself to trample on the sacred laws of the country which I love so dearly, and run away somewhere now? Crito, we must obey the laws.

Throughout the ethics texts of the 1930s, one finds explicit accounts of the bravery of soldiers, their willing sacrifice for the nation, and the benevolence of the emperor.

Despite these intensified efforts to use education in channeling the moral inclinations of the populace, many young people failed to conform with the official morality. Especially in the period from 1917 to the mid-1930s, there were frequent incidents of student protest, labor revolt, and other expressions of ideological deviance. The central government responded in a manner that would shock contemporary defenders of civil rights: teachers at all levels in the education system were relieved of their positions, and many intellectuals were imprisoned and subjected to brainwashing treatments. Christian schools were forbidden to teach doctrines that the state considered incompatible with its official ideology, and some Christians were persecuted. Communists, in particular, were subjected to intense harassment. It was only as Japan moved into full-scale war against the Allied Powers that the incidence of deviance and rebellion subsided.

3. *Technical training.* Despite the government's commitment to the development of technical manpower, implementation was slow and uneven. Industrial groups made repeated requests through the 1880s and 1890s, but it was not until 1903 that the government promulgated the specialized school order (*senmongakkorei*) and

began to systematize its program for training engineers and technicians. Official programs for training skilled workers were not established until even later. Many accounts of Japanese education marvel at the government's prescience in establishing those specialized schools and assume that the graduates from these schools played an important role in stimulating Japanese industrialization. However, investigators who have followed the careers of specialty school graduates provide evidence against this. In several instances, well over half the graduates went into fields that had little relation to their training (Iwauchi, 1972, 1973). The government tended to establish these schools in response to local demands. But by the time the government had established a school, the local area often found alternate means to satisfy the demand, thus rendering the schools useless for their intended purpose.

4. *The meritocracy.* The government was determined to make the Imperial University established in 1886 at Tokyo the foremost institution of learning in the nation. Thus, this institution was provided comparatively generous annual grants for its operation, and its graduates received favorable treatment in the competition for civil service jobs. As other sectors of society began to develop a need for highly trained manpower, they also turned to the Imperial University. Within a short period, this institution was supplying the personnel for a variety of elite careers.

Makoto Aso sampled several hundred elites from each of several editions of the *Jinji Koshin Roku* and investigated several of their background characteristics (see Table 2.1). In the earliest period, a majority of the elites had not attended a university; however, among those who had attended about half were Imperial University (Todai) graduates. The Todai graduates were especially numerous in the civil service, education, and business. The military, which had its own academy, was the one modern elite sector where Todai graduates failed to gain a significant proportion. Over time the number of elites who had attended a university increased, yet up to World War II nearly half of these continued to be graduates of Todai. The proportion of Todai graduates among the elite civil servants and educators declined only modestly. Since World War II, this proportion has declined somewhat but still represents a sizeable fraction in most of the elite fields. Considering all elite fields, the proportion who attended Todai increased from 12 percent in 1903 to 17 percent in 1964.

As ambitious youths came to appreciate the importance of at-

TABLE 2.1

JAPANESE ELITES ATTENDING THE UNIVERSITY OF TOKYO (TODAI), 1903–1964

	Todai Graduates as a Percent of All Elites Who Attended a Higher Educational Institution					
	1903	1915	1928	1939	1955	1964
National civil service	73	65	76	65	42	41
Business leaders	66	33	28	21	18	14
Land owners	0	0	0	0	—	—
Military	0	20	0	8	—	—
Educators, professors	88	88	52	63	45	36
Doctors	—	50	100	41	11	17
Lawyers	—	66	—	0	17	31
Artists	—	—	—	0	22	25
Religious leaders	—	0	—	0	0	50
Opinion leaders	—	—	—	0	0	20
Politicians	0	—	100	0	18	30
Noblemen	17	100	20	36	—	—
Other	50	0	0	9	8	—
Todai graduates as a percent of elites who attended a higher educational institution	55	44	36	46	34	21
Percent of elites who attended a higher educational institution	28	26	37	53	77	94
Todai graduates as a percent of all elites	12	14	17	19	19	17

SOURCE: Makoto Aso, *Erito to Kyoiku* (Elites and Education), pp. 217–219.

tending the Imperial University, increasing numbers began to set their sights on entrance to this institution. Because the government allowed only slight increases in Todai's size, many youths were destined to be disappointed. Still these youths committed themselves to the necessary preparation by attending a middle school and seeking entrance to a higher school. In that the Imperial University could not accommodate them, the youths and their families demanded alternative higher educational opportunities. The government's initial response was to establish several additional Imperial Universities in new locations—the second was established in Kyoto in 1897 and eventually came to rival Todai in its scale and eminence. Other Imperial Universities were established in Tohoku, Hokkaido, Kyushu, Nagoya, and Osaka. Still the public demand was not satisfied, so in 1918 the government promulgated a University Law that considerably liberalized the criteria for granting a university charter. Over the next years, many secondary institutions, including several in the private sector, upgraded their standards to achieve recognition as universities. By the time of the Great Depression, Japan had thirty universities serving approximately 40,000 university-level students and producing nearly 15,000 graduates each year. However, there was no way for the Japanese economy to absorb all of this highly trained manpower, at least in their chosen specialties. In the "softer" fields, well over half the graduates failed to secure a job even after several months of search (Kotschnig, 1937). These unemployed intellectuals provided the core leadership for certain rebellious movements noted earlier. Eventually these highly educated youths ended up in jobs that did not require their level of education. But because university graduates took up these jobs, the jobs came to be designated as suitable only for people with degrees, thus leading to additional stimulation of the demand for education. Ronald Dore (1976), reflecting on this situation, suggests that Japan was the first of the new nations to become infected with the "diploma disease."

Government leaders promoted the ideology of opportunity through education, and numerous examples of successful individuals rising from humble backgrounds were cited as evidence that the educational system provided opportunities to all, regardless of their background. But the opportunities were unequal. The state made certain that every child attended a primary school and, insofar as practical, attempted to spread secondary schools throughout the nation. However, the tuitions for these postcompulsory schools were substantial, and apart from the normal and military schools, scholarships were rare. In general, local primary schools reflected the hierarchy of their communities. Teachers, recognizing their obligations to the local elites (who as members of the local school board controlled appointments), often favored the children of the established families.[1] The children of the better homes were most

---

[1] This generalization provoked sharp criticism from two Western readers of the manuscript, yet Japanese reviewers accepted it more readily. Originally the generalization was based on reports from several autobiographical novels written by authors who went through the school system between about 1910 and 1940. Subsequently, more systematic accounts were consulted. For example, two leading Japanese educational sociologists, Aso and Amano, write about this period: "Schools constituted a means for reproducing the respective social strata. At the same time, because of their institutional openness, schools served as the ladder leading up to

likely to get high grades, pass examinations, and move up in the educational system.

Many poor youths living in rural villages resented the inequities promoted by the educational system. For them, going to a normal school or a military school was the only realistic postcompulsory educational opportunity. Dore (1950) has suggested that their feelings of class hostility help to explain their willingness, once they became adults and entered the military or assumed teacher roles, to blindly support those discontented ultranationalistic rebels who both opposed the privileged classes and urged an imperialistic war. According to this interpretation, Japan's involvement in World War II was a reflection of her domestic class warfare.

Background for the Occupation Reforms

Japanese society made impressive strides toward realizing the goals designated by the Meiji rebels. By the mid-1930s, the national institutions were effectively unified under a strong central regime. The economy was diversified, the military was strong, and the people were loyal. Education, despite its many shortcomings, had aided in each of these developments. If Japan had managed a more successful conclusion of World War II, the central government might have retained the old system in essentially unaltered form.

By September of 1945, Japan had no choice but to declare unconditional surrender. In anticipation of Japan's fall, the Allied Powers on July 26, 1945, issued the Potsdam Declaration, which declared their intent to remove "all obstacles to the survival and strengthening of democratic tendencies among the Japanese people. Freedom of speech, religion, and of thought, as well as respect for the fundamental rights shall be established" (Anderson, 1975:61). In addition, the Allies had given some consideration to the specific changes that would be introduced, but they could not fully prepare for the situation they encountered.

> The nation that had been so remarkably successful and had believed so implicitly in its own divinity and invincibility was defeated in 1945. It was physically devastated; its cities were de-

---

success in life for people of the lower middle and upper lower classes who had high ability and a strong desire to move upward" (1972:31). This account dwells more on inequality of results than of treatment. For this period more in-depth research is needed on the behavior of teachers toward children of different class backgrounds.

molished, its homes, temples, schools as well as industry were in
ruins. Its farms were exhausted from want of fertilizer, its fishing
fleets were destroyed. People were reduced to near starvation. An
estimated 1,850,000 Japanese were dead. Public morale had col-
lapsed. The citizens, nurtured in the Shinto faith that theirs was a
divine land under a divine Emperor, now felt these beliefs had
been proven false. The normally disciplined and determined Japanese were confused and dazed. Schools were closed and some 19
million schoolchildren were idle (Anderson, 1975:61).

Although Japan had surrendered to the Allied forces as a whole,
the actual task of implementing the spirit of the Potsdam Declaration was assumed by a U.S. Occupation government headed by
General Douglas MacArthur. The Occupation was instructed to
work through the existing Japanese government and emperor but
not to support them. In the early months, the Occupation issued a
number of directives to the Japanese government, and among these
were several intended to remove all militaristic and ultranationalistic influences. Thus, in the field of education, the courses of moral
education, geography, and Japanese history that were considered
supportive of the wartime ideology were temporarily suspended. A
purge of those educational officials and teachers who had played
key roles in promoting the wartime ideology was begun. Over
120,000 teachers, or one fourth of those in the profession, were
either purged or resigned in order to avoid the threat of a purge.
Similar steps were taken to remove officials and responsible individuals in all sectors of life from business to the arts. The removal
of these nationalistic elements from former positions of prominence and the appointment of "liberals" in their stead considerably
facilitated the Occupation's reform program.

One of the first major goals of the Occupation was to establish
the foundation for a more democratic mode of government. A special committee of the Diet was charged with the task of drafting a
new constitution, and when it faltered, the Occupation submitted
its own proposal. Ultimately, a version identical in most respects to
that proposed by the Occupation was ratified in November of 1946
by the Diet. The preamble clearly reflects its American authorship.

We, the Japanese people, acting through our duly elected representatives in the National Diet, determined that we shall secure
for ourselves and our posterity the fruits of peaceful cooperation
with all nations and the blessings of liberty throughout this land,
and resolved that never again shall we be visited with the horrors

of war through the action of government, do proclaim that sovereign power resides with the people and do firmly establish this Constitution. Government is a sacred trust of the people, the authority for which is derived from the people, the powers of which are exercised by the representatives of the people, and the benefits of which are enjoyed by the people. This is a universal principle of mankind upon which this Constitution is founded (Beckmann, 1962:673).

In contrast with the Meiji Constitution, several articles of the new "Peace Constitution" dealt with educational matters. Article 20 declared, "The State and its organs shall refrain from religious education." Article 23 stated, "Academic freedom is guaranteed." And Article 26 stated, "All people shall have the right to receive an equal education correspondent to their ability."

Whereas the old system had been created through a series of imperial decrees and administrative orders, the new educational system was based in the constitution and in laws that were debated and legislated by the national Diet. The change to a legislative basis in combination with the emergence of progressive political parties that developed an interest in educational policy resulted in a lively postwar educational dialog (see Chapter Three).

A NEW EDUCATIONAL PHILOSOPHY

To aid in the development of concrete proposals for educational reforms, the Occupation invited twenty-seven distinguished U.S. educators to Japan in March of 1947. These educators, known as the U.S. Education Mission to Japan, produced a report that provides the clearest statement of the philosophy underlying the subsequent reform. The opening statement echoed the Occupation's goal of helping Japan to develop a new education appropriate to a liberal democratic society. It urged the development of an educational philosophy that recognized "the worth and dignity of the individual" and that would "prepare the individual to become a responsible and cooperating member of society." The mission enumerated several weaknesses of the old system.

The Japanese system of education in its organization and curricular provisions would have been due for reform in accordance with modern theories of education even if there had not been injected into it ultranationalism and militarism. The system was based on a nineteenth century pattern which was highly centralized, providing one type of education for the masses and another for the privileged few. It held that at each level of instruction there is a fixed quantum of knowledge to be absorbed, and tended to disregard differences in the ability and interests of pupils. Through prescription, textbooks, examinations and inspection, the system lessened the opportunities of teachers to exercise professional freedom. The measure of efficiency was the degree to which standardization and uniformity were secured (U.S. Education Mission to Japan, 1946:4).

The mission then turned to a consideration of reforms that might alleviate these weaknesses. It is not necessary to consider them all, because many of them were never realized. However, as background for the subsequent discussion, it will be necessary to consider in some detail what happened to the mission's proposals for a new educational philosophy, a new single-track structure, a decentralization of control, and an improvement in the situation of teachers.

To translate the mission's recommendation into concrete reform proposals, an Educational Reform Council was established with official status equivalent to the Ministry of Education. As its first task, the council considered the development of a statement of the philosophy of the new system that might replace the old system's Imperial Rescript. The council ultimately decided that the specifics of the new education should be worked out by the local communities, school boards, and schools that were in closer contact with the desires of the people, and that it would be inappropriate to draft such statements from above. Nevertheless, in the Fundamental Law of Education, one of the first laws drafted by the council, the new aim of education is stated. "Education shall aim at the full development of personality, striving for the rearing of the people, sound in mind and body, who shall love truth and justice, esteem individual value, respect labour, and have a deep sense of responsibility, and be imbued with an independent spirit, as builders of a peaceful state and society" (Anderson, 1975:349).

THE STRUCTURE OF THE NEW SYSTEM

To realize the new democratic philosophy, the U.S. Education Mission urged a new structure for Japanese education. The key features included the following:

1. A six-year free compulsory primary school that "should prepare children to become healthy, active, thinking citizens eager to develop their innate abilities."

2. In contrast with the old system where several different non-compulsory tracks had opened up after the primary school, the mission recommended "that there be established for the next three years beyond the primary school, a 'lower secondary school' for all boys and girls, providing fundamentally the same type of curriculum for all with such adjustments as are necessary to meet individual needs. The main purposes should be similar to those of the primary school, with emphasis upon personal development, citizenship, and community life. Into this school should be introduced certain opportunities of an exploratory nature in the vocational field" (U.S. Education Mission to Japan 1946:18). In further contrast with the old system, the mission recommended that the lower secondary (middle) schools be free, compulsory, and coeducational.

3. Beyond the lower secondary schools, the "Report" recommended a free coeducational three-year high school "open to all who desired to attend" that was modeled, insofar as possible, along the lines of the American comprehensive high school, that is, the school should include the courses that would both enable students to prepare for college and to acquire vocational skills.

4. The "Report" emphasized the potential role of the university in fostering liberal thought, urged that this become "an opportunity for the many, not the few," and suggested that the university with its liberal atmosphere provide a more favorable setting for teacher education than the separate normal schools characteristic of the old system.

These recommendations, adopted virtually without modification in the School Education Law of 1947, required a massive reorganization of the existing school facilities. To comply with the new requirements for compulsory middle school education, many new institutions had to be established. Due to war, damage of existing facilities, and a shortage of revenues, educational administrators in most areas faced an extremely grave situation. Yet somehow by the end of the Occupation, these areas were able to achieve the necessary results. The structure of the new educational system is contrasted with the old in Figure 2.1.

In terms of the discussion here, two differences deserve special emphasis: by extending compulsory education from six to nine years, the new structure postponed the point at which pupils began their preparation for competitive entrance examinations; by placing all students on a single track and reducing tuition at public schools, it enabled a far greater proportion of youth to acquire the necessary academic background for attending a university or other higher educational institution. The response to these new opportunities was immediate, resulting in steady pressure for expansion of the postcompulsory educational facilities (see Chapter Eight).

Educational authorities have barely managed to keep up with the demand for places by allowing the establishment of numerous substandard institutions. However, in so doing, they have aggravated the long-standing problems of academic competition for entry to the highest quality postcompulsory institutions (see Chapter Eight for a detailed examination of this development).

DECENTRALIZATION OF CONTROL

Possibly the most persistent theme in the "Report" was the danger of concentrating too much authority in the hands of the central bureaucracy.

> An educational system, controlled by an entrenched bureaucracy recruited from a narrow group, which reduces the chances of promotion on merit, which provides little opportunity for investigation and research, and which refuses to tolerate criticism, deprives itself automatically of the means of progress. . . . Experience indicates that the centralized system is more vulnerable from the standpoint of manipulation and exploitation by powers either outside or inside the system. . . . The control of the instructional program should be more dispersed than at present; vertical lines of authority and responsibility should be definitely broken at certain levels of the system (U.S. Education Mission to Japan, 1946:4).

Along with the recommendation that more authority be shifted to local governments, the "Report" encouraged the formation of parent-teacher associations and other popular groups that serve as a check and as vehicles for generating new viewpoints on education. The "Report" urged the formation of professional associations for teachers and even approved the organization of teachers' unions, adding "no democratic principle is more crucial than the right to assemble for the extension of ideas."

The Occupation enthusiastically supported the mission's recommendation for a more decentralized educational system, and quickly took several steps to implement this change. The Ministry of Education was relieved of its power to censor textbooks; special funds were made available to support the formation of parent-teacher associations, and teachers' unions were allowed to organize at the expense of the pro-government teachers' association, which rapidly lost membership. However, as the Occupation began to press for additional ways of promoting decentralization, it encountered numerous obstacles. Among these was the Occupation's need to rely on the central government for the implementation of the complex reform programs. By the time the Educational Reform Council began drafting proposals for the decentralization of educational control, the domestic political climate had become more complicated and the national Diet more reluctant to approve Occupation-promoted reforms.

In the context of this new political situation, a Private School Law was passed. It gave private schools at all levels much greater autonomy than they had enjoyed under the old system. The U.S. Education Mission had urged such a reform in the hope of diversifying the types of educational opportunities available to Japanese youths. In addition, the mission, recognizing the serious financial situation of private schools, urged that some steps be taken to provide them with aid from public sources. Unfortunately, little action was taken to improve the finances of private schools, leading to a situation where many of these schools were forced to permanently reduce their academic standards.

Occupation officials hoped to see authority for the control of school education divided up among a large number of local school districts just as in the United States. However, the Educational Reform Council argued that most local areas lacked the financial resources, administrative experience, and political wisdom to manage their own schools. For different reasons, this judgment was supported by both the conservative government and the leadership of the progressive teachers' union. These differences threatened the likelihood of achieving Diet approval for bills detailing procedures for localized control and administration.

Finally in 1949 the Diet enacted a law turning over the control of education to locally elected school boards, but actual implementation was staggered over a six-year period. A parallel bill to remove control of national universities from the central government and place them in the hands of boards of trustees failed. Administrative orders were used to decentralize certain other responsibilities. Yet, all things considered, it would have to be concluded that far less than anticipated was achieved with respect to this particular reform theme.

THE SITUATION OF TEACHERS

Another recurrent concern in the U.S. Education Mission's "Report" was the oppressed and impoverished situation of teachers. The mission was obviously impressed with the dedication of many teachers, but felt that they had suffered from lack of autonomy. At several points, the "Report" criticized the intrusions of governmental authorities into the classroom.

> We have seen that the effects of the old regime are manifest in the teaching practices. Teachers have been told exactly what to teach and how to teach it. Teaching has been, by and large, formal and stereotyped. To prevent any deviation from the prescribed content and form, inspectors have been charged with the duty of seeing that printed instructions were followed to the letter. Such a system has the effect of putting teaching in a strait jacket.

> If the teacher is given sufficient freedom, he will make use of many facilities outside the school to enrich the learning of pupils. Farms, factories, offices, libraries, museums and hospitals provide educational opportunities. In some cases where classes are too large, a teacher skilled in democratic processes can call upon student leadership, breaking up the class into smaller groups under student chairmen (U.S. Education Mission to Japan, 1946:23).

The mission enthusiastically endorsed the need for teachers to form professional associations of their own, and emphasized that while governmental bodies might want to encourage such associations, "it is true that the most effective meetings of teachers are usually those which the teachers themselves organize." The mission suggested that the wartime government's heavy hand led to a situation where teachers lost confidence in the government. "The teachers of Japan, insofar as their views have been represented to the Mission, are critical and restless and are looking for leadership outside the Department of Education" (U.S. Education Mission to Japan, 1946:4).

Clearly the mission looked to teachers and their associations as major forces for building the new education. In response to these recommendations, the Occupation developed an extensive program to help Japanese teachers acquire democratic pedagogical techniques and provided considerable encouragement to fledgling teacher associations. Even when these associations took on some of the characteristics of a trade union, the Occupation looked on approvingly at first. "The working classes constitute, potentially, the strongest if not the only reliable base for a democratic regime in Japan. . . . Japanese labor holds the key to success or failure in the attempt to convert Japan from a dangerous enemy into a good neighbor" (Duke, 1973:52). The new constitution fully recognized the right of labor to organize, and the Occupation was initially disinclined to introduce any special qualifications for civil servants or teachers. As the U.S. Education Mission's "Report" indicated, Japan's teachers were grossly underpaid.

The Occupation's views were exceedingly liberal for that period. Even in the United States, teachers were not permitted to form unions. Moreover, the Occupation's position was at considerable variance with the preference of most Japanese government officials. The liberal Yoshishige Abe, who served as minister of education in 1946, questioned the propriety of allowing teachers to organize. Yet through the middle of 1947, the Occupation remained firm in its liberal position and union leaders made great progress in their organizing efforts. Well over half of all teachers had joined a union, and rival groups were moving toward some form of federation.

A number of factors, however, led the Occupation to retreat from this original liberal position. For instance, the U.S. government's perception of "international communism" was going through a significant transformation, and this led to suspicions about the relationship of Japan's union leadership to this worldwide "conspiracy." Also, in 1947, after the ineffectual performance of a coalition government in which the Socialist party participated, the Occupation developed greater respect for Japan's conservative political leaders.

The Occupation gradually came to feel that Japanese labor was demanding too much. For example, in early 1947 after the Occupation had already promised government employees a substantial wage increase, the unions representing these employees agreed to participate with private sector unions in a general strike. General MacArthur was so upset by this plan that he personally intervened.

Referring to the general strike as a deadly "social weapon in the present impoverished and emaciated condition of Japan," he ordered the unions to abandon their plans (Duke, 1973:63).

In the immediate aftermath of this particular confrontation, the unions modified their conflictual orientation. For the first time ever in Japanese history, the Ministry of Education agreed to enter into collective bargaining with Zenkyokyo, the most prominent teachers' union. As a result of the bargaining, teachers achieved many of the benefits promised by union leaders a year earlier.

The collective bargaining in early 1947 seemed to imply that the government had decided to recognize the rightful existence of unions. However, events over the next two years proved otherwise. In 1948 the Occupation refused to interfere as the Japanese government cleverly framed a series of laws and administrative orders concerning public employees that effectively deprived teachers' unions of their power to bargain with the central government. In 1949, the Occupation carried out a "red purge" that led to the imprisonment of a number of union leaders.

Thus, after appearing to recognize the right of teachers to organize, the government and the Occupation subsequently recanted. Surprisingly, these actions, rather than turning teachers away from their unions, seemed to increase their commitment. By the latter years of the Occupation, three quarters of Japan's teachers had joined unions. Most of these unions became federated in a single national organization known as Nikkyoso. In 1952 Nikkyoso proclaimed its "Code of Ethics for Teachers" (Duke, 1973:224-227), which, in fact, was a manifesto of goals for the union's postwar educational struggle. Included among these were the following:

—Teachers shall fight for equal opportunity in education.
—Teachers shall protect peace.
—Teachers shall allow no infringements on freedom in education.
—Teachers shall fight side by side with parents against corruption in society and shall create a new culture.

CONCLUSION

The Meiji government, through strong central leadership, laid the foundations for Japan's old system of education. This system was reasonably effective in developing a common national morality, in training technical manpower, and in selecting a talented central elite. Yet from the point of view of the U.S. Occupation following World War II, these achievements had contributed in significant ways to the extremist tendencies that led to Japan's involvement in the war. Thus, the Occupation contemplated a massive reform of the "old system." Reviewing several of the central concerns of the Occupation reformers, one finds that perhaps the Occupation's greatest legacy was the democratic and humanistic philosophy of education that, under its stewardship, became implanted in the constitution and the basic educational laws. Also, a new 6-3-3-4 structure was begun and steps were taken to improve the status and increase the autonomy of teachers. Other proposed reforms, particularly those concerning decentralization of authority, were less successful. While some domestic educational groups identified with these reforms, others strongly opposed them. Thus, when the Occupation left Japan in 1952 the fate of many of its reforms was uncertain. The domestic educational struggle would determine the ultimate outcome (see Chapter Three).

THE GOVERNMENT AND THE
TEACHERS' UNION

A number of studies have indicated the extent to which formal educational processes are influenced by and serve to reinforce established class alignments (Bowles and Gintis, 1976; Carnoy and Levin, 1976; Collins, 1977; Jencks, 1972; Karabel and Halsey, 1977). In this book a different point of view is presented: the schools are altering established class alignments or at least the magnitude of differences between them. However, before examining the link in Japan between education and the changing class system, it is necessary to clarify the principal characteristics of this system.

The discussion of Japan's class system will highlight the role of cultural commitments in shaping class alignments. On the one hand, there are those classes, led by the conservative government, that adhere to more traditional values. On the other are the middle and working classes of the modern sector that prefer a more progressive culture. The Japan Teachers' Union (Nikkyoso) is particularly important as an articulator of this progressive culture, and because the union believes the schools should be used to promote the progressive culture it has frequently clashed with the government. The second section of this chapter outlines the specific issues over which the government and the teachers' union have clashed.[1]

In these clashes, the union has done remarkably well. On a number of occasions, it successfully resisted government authority. Considering the extensive power the government frequently mobilized in these conflicts, the union's achievements seem all the more remarkable. Thus, the final section of the chapter explains how the union has been able to persist against government opposition. The tenacious efforts of the progressive union are a key factor behind recent egalitarian change.

---

[1] In preparing this chapter two excellent studies of the postwar educational struggle were consulted: Benjamin C. Duke, (1973), and Donald R. Thurston (1973).

An Outline of Japan's Class Structure

The Sector-Class Model

First, assumptions concerning the basic social groupings essential for analysis will be made explicit.

The orthodox analyses of Marx, Weber, Dahrendorf, and others identify classes as the relevant social groupings. These analyses define classes in terms of their relation to a single key social resource—be it property, authority, the command of knowledge, or whatever (Giddens, 1973:100–106). Also, orthodox analyses insist on emphasizing a dominant subordinate pair of classes while treating other classes as "transitional" and destined to fade away. These assumptions are too inflexible to cope with the social reality of modernizing Japan. For example, Japan's old middle class of small shopkeepers and small-scale industrialists has, rather than disappeared, maintained its numerical size and solidarity throughout the modernizing period even as the new middle class has increased in scale and significance. Similarly, while Japan's rural society has been significantly restructured, it continues as an important sector of the contemporary society.

For these reasons, in the discussion of social groupings the first step will be to consider an entirely different axis best described as the historical differentiation of distinctive sociocultural sectors. Within each of the sectors, unique hierarchies have evolved.

The basic groups that will be included in the model are identified in Figure 3.1. A problem arises about naming these groups. The term group does not seem appropriate, for distinctions are based on an objective analysis of common activities, not on observation of patterns of mutual interaction or some subjective criteria. Category is another alternative, but this has too much of a statistical connotation. Following Giddens' recent innovative study, the familiar term class has been chosen, though it is emphasized that the use of the term differs from the orthodox analyses. Class, when used below, refers to "a large-scale aggregate of individuals, comprised of impersonally defined relationships, and nominally 'open' in form" (Giddens, 1973:100).

First, the historical dimension of sectoral differentiation depicted across the horizontal axis of the diagram is discussed. Then, the classes that have evolved within each sector are considered, and finally, the alignments that have obtained between these classes, es-

FIGURE 3.1   MODEL OF JAPAN'S SYSTEM OF CLASSES

SECTORS

		Agricultural	Entrepreneurial	Large-scale Organizational
	Rulers	Large rural landowners	Successful heads of small enterprises	Executives, managers of private firms and government
CLASSES				
	Ruled	Owner farmers, fishermen	Family members and stable employees	New middle class of professional and white-collar workers
		Tenants and landless laborers		Grey-collar workers New blue-collar workers
			Marginal class of unemployed and unskilled workers	

pecially as these bear on the educational struggle, will be examined. The manner in which the Japanese class system is depicted builds on the pioneering work of contemporary researchers (Tominaga, 1970; Ohashi, 1971; Yasuda, 1973; Cummings and Naoi, 1974). If this book were on class alone, far more space would be devoted to definitions and supporting data. Thus, only a brief summary of the main features of the class system supplemented by a few pieces of illustrative data can be presented.

The Differentiation of Sectors

One of the more striking features of modern Japan's process of development was the emergence of a dualistic economy with the traditional sector centered around property and labor intensive operations and the modern sector centered around advanced technology and trained manpower (Sumiya, 1973; Lockwood, 1968). During the Tokugawa period, Japan had been divided along different lines—with a clean division between samurai and peasants (Smith, 1960; Moore, 1970). This traditional pattern was eroded during the early decades of modernization, but it was not until the 1920s that the new dualistic pattern crystallized.

The new pattern had complex links with its feudal predecessor. The leading force behind the development of the new order was the modern state, the principal architects of which came from the former samurai class. Most of the large industrial organizations of the modern sector were initially either developed by the state or received substantial business from the state (e.g. for public construction, the production of armaments, ships, and uniforms). As in the case of the government bureaus, these organizations recruited many of their staff from the former samuri class. In contrast, the traditional sector developed from the small-scale economic units that had been common in the Tokugawa period and continued to rely on kinship networks for the recruitment of personnel.

Within the two basic sectors, further distinctions are useful. Within the traditional sector, there are obvious differences between those enterprises engaged in agriculture and fishing and those located in the urban areas that specialize in small-scale production and the distribution of primarily indigenous goods. These small urban firms compose the "entrepreneurial sector." Turning to the modern sector, virtually all large-scale organizations are located in urban areas, so the rural-urban distinction is not useful. Moreover, despite wide differences in the types of goods and services produced, large organizations are remarkably similar in their education-oriented patterns of recruitment, their development of seniority-based wage and salary schedules, the level of pay provided employees, their emphasis on group and corporate spirit, and the various welfare benefits they offer employees (Abegglen, 1958; Dore, 1975). In that the large-scale organization is the most fundamental characteristic of the modern sector, it also can be referred to as the "organizational sector." While for analytical purposes, the organizational-entrepreneurial or large-small distinction is sufficient, as one turns to empirical data it is useful to establish an "intermediate sector" category in which organizations can be placed that mix traits of both the large- and small-scale prototypes.

In societies with high levels of interorganizational mobility, the types of distinctions on organizational types made above could be tangential in analyzing political interests or cultural differentiation. But in Japan, these distinctions are important. Japanese who enter the labor force tend to get locked into career lines at an early stage. Particularly in the organizational sector, most new recruits are obtained straight from school, and the vast majority of them stay with the particular organization they first join through most of their working life. In the entrepreneurial sector, a young person may move among several firms; however, the average number of firms where he might work would be only a fraction of the average for an American worker, and it is unlikely that he would move out of the sector where he first started to work. Because Japanese tend to stay in the sector where they begin their careers, their social networks tend to be specific to these sectors, they come to learn the values characteristic of these sectors, and they identify with the sector's special interests (Cummings and Kusatsu, 1975). For this reason, in the Japanese context, sectoral position is an important dimension of social and especially of cultural differentiation.

The secondary analysis of the Japanese National Character Survey helps to illustrate this point. This survey, which has been repeated every five years since 1953, is a remarkably sensitive means for identifying the patterns of attitudes and beliefs of major social groups.[2] The survey instrument asks respondents to indicate their orientations to a wide variety of traditional norms and beliefs—for example, the importance of filial piety and of repaying indebtedness (*on-gaeshi*) to others and willingness to adopt a child in order to maintain the lineage of the household (*ie*). For our analysis, we grouped respondents into three large groups that correspond closely with the aforementioned sectors; within the modern as well as the entrepreneurial sector further distinctions with respect to occupation that resemble but are not identical to the classes identified in Figure 3.1 were made. A sector-occupation classification with ten categories was established. This variable was cross-tabulated with all of the questions in the 1963 version of the National Character Survey in order to identify questions where respondents indicated substantial variation in their attitudes and beliefs. Eleven questions were selected, and then entered into a multiple scalar analysis, a computer technique which facilitates the identification of the dimensions underlying the between-group variation (McFarland and Brown, 1973).

The results, presented in Figure 3.2, indicate the significant impact of social sector on cultural disposition: the most interpretable dimension underlying this figure is the lineup from left to right of modern to traditional sector-occupation groups. The members of

---

[2] A full introduction to these surveys may be found in National Institute of Mathematics, *Nihonjin no Kokuminsei: Volume III* (The Japanese National Character) (Tokyo: Shiseido, 1975).

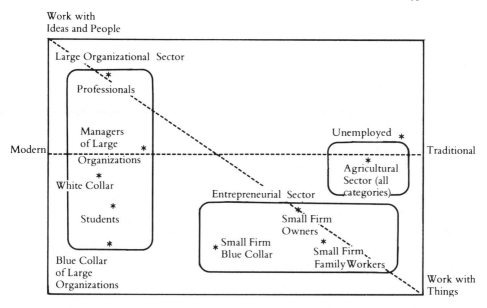

Work with
Ideas and People

Large Organizational Sector

Professionals

Managers
of Large   *
Organizations

*

White Collar

*

Students

*

Blue Collar
of Large
Organizations

Modern ─ Traditional

Unemployed *

*
Agricultural
Sector (all
categories)

Entrepreneurial Sector

*
Small Firm
Owners

* Small Firm   *
  Blue Collar   Small Firm
                   Family Workers

Work with
Things

FIGURE 3.2   TWO-DIMENSIONAL SOLUTION TO MULTIPLE-SCALAR ANALYSIS OF ELEVEN
QUESTIONS FROM THE 1963 JAPAN NATIONAL CHARACTER SURVEY

the modern groups—the managers, professionals, and white- and blue-collar workers of large organizations—are most approving of individuation, independence, and playful "post bourgeosie" values, whereas those of the traditional groups—farmers, housewives, and the owners and workers of small enterprises—emphasize filial piety, the importance of perpetuating the *ie* (household) through adoption, the value of a religious attitude, and the need to follow custom.[3] In general, the cultural distance between groups of a given sector is shorter than the distance between different sectors; this even applies to two groups of otherwise similar composition, the workers of large firms and those in small enterprises. These empirical results along with others following a similar pattern underline the critical importance of incorporating sectoral differences in an analysis of Japanese social structure (Cummings and Kusatsu, 1975:8).

[3] The concept of "post bourgeosie" is borrowed from the intriguing analysis of youth value trends by Ronald Inglehart (1977). For a critique of Inglehart based on the National Character Survey mentioned above, see Nobutaka Ike (1973).

Classes Within Sectors

It is only after recognizing the significance of sectoral differentiation that social class should be considered. Each of Japan's sectors is based on a distinct combination of resources, and hence each generates a somewhat distinctive class hierarchy. The critical resource in the agricultural sector is land, and thus historically large land-owners stood at the top and landless laborers at the bottom; the postwar land reforms significantly reduced but certainly did not eliminate the land-based inequalities of this sector. In the entrepreneurial sector, command over petty capital is the critical resource; those with capital own and manage small firms while those without capital work for the petty capitalists. Finally, in the organizational sector, educational qualifications are a critical minimum resource supplemented by individual achievement. In contrast with many other capitalist systems, relatively few Japanese families have accumulated substantial industrial fortunes that might enable their family members to assume top organizational positions without independent evidence of educational qualifications and achievements. Thus, at the top of the organizational sector, there exists an elite group who were trained at the most prestigious universities whereas the working and service classes have a high school education at best.

One way of illustrating intra-sector-class differences is to inspect empirical data on the average annual income earned by the members of each class as reported in the 1975 National Social Mobility Survey.[4] Before turning to this data, however, we need to indicate how it has been computed. Figure 3.1 presented a model of the Japanese class system. This model made precise distinctions between the respective sectors and classes; however, in the real world, these boundaries are not so distinct. When considering sectors, it is particularly difficult to establish a precise boundary between large and small organizations; to accommodate this difficulty in handling empirical data, the category of intermediate-scale organization was

[4] The 1975 National Social Mobility Survey, managed by Professor Kenichi Tominaga of the University of Tokyo, is composed of two parts. Survey A on social mobility was administered to 2,724 respondents from a national probability sample of 4,001 (68.1 percent response rate). Survey B on occupational prestige was administered to 1,296 respondents from a sample of 1,800 (72.0 percent response rate). The basic report is *1975-Nen SSM Chosa: Kiso Tokeihyo* (Report of Basic Statistics from the 1975 SSM Survey) (Tokyo: 1975-Nen SSM Zenkoku Chosa Iinkai Jimukyoku, 1976).

established and all individuals working in nongovernmental organizations of 10 to 999 employees were placed in it; this empirical strategy enables the differences between the small- and large-organization sectors to stand out more clearly. Second, for purposes of empirical analysis within each sector, not two but rather several classes, ranging from aggregates of the most powerful and privileged to those at the bottom, have been specified. The empirical categories created to make operational the analytical model of the Japanese class system are identified in Table 3.1.

Some of these categories require a special comment: professional

TABLE 3.1
CLASS DIFFERENCES IN INCOME, EDUCATIONAL ATTAINMENT, AND
SUPPORT OF LIBERAL DEMOCRATIC PARTY

Class	Average Personal Income (Millions of Yen)	Average Educational Attainment (Years)	Percent Supporting LDP in 1975 General Election
Large-Scale Organizational Sector			
Manager	4.1	14.4	65.7
Professional	2.6	15.0	16.1
White-collar	2.3	14.4	28.0
Gray-collar	2.3	11.7	53.1
Blue-collar	2.0	10.8	19.0
Intermediate-Scale Organizational Sector			
Manager	3.1	13.2	46.3
Professional	2.6	14.4	35.2
White-collar	2.1	13.2	36.0
Gray-collar	1.9	12.3	32.6
Blue-collar	1.7	10.2	29.2
Entrepreneurial Sector			
Owner	2.3	10.5	50.0
Family-worker	1.5	11.4	36.8
White-collar	1.9	12.9	46.7
Gray-collar	1.6	11.7	38.8
Blue-collar	1.6	9.6	34.4
Agricultural			
Owner-Farmer	1.7	9.3	63.6
Family-worker	1.7	10.8	50.0
Farm laborer	1.8	9.3	25.0
Marginal Class	1.5	10.2	28.9

SOURCE: 1975 Social Mobility Survey.

includes the established professions as well as other occupations requiring technical training such as lab technician, engineer, and, of
special significance for this study, teacher. Gray collar refers to various service occupations including the protective services, delivery
men, bill collectors, and others. In the more traditional sectors, family members of the owner often help in the operations; in view of
their special tie to the owner, family members constitute a distinct
class subordinate only to the owner class. Finally, there is a relatively small number of day laborers and unemployed who are marginal to the labor force and require a separate category.

   With this background, let us now turn to an examination of income data by sector and class. In the 1975 National Social Mobility
Survey, the respondents (all males between the ages of twenty and
sixty-nine) were asked to report their total annual personal income
for the previous year. The variation was from less than 250,000 yen
(roughly $1,000 at that time) to one respondent who reported 20
million yen (roughly $80,000) with the median at 2 million yen
($8,000). Table 3.1 presents the average of the incomes for all the
members of each class. As can be seen, managers of large-scale organizations have the highest average income (4.1 million) whereas
the average for the marginal class is lowest (1.5 million). The range
between these two averages is surprisingly low (see Chapter Nine).
For the present, the focus will be on the variation between classes.
As can be seen, with the exception of the agricultural sector, within
each sector average class income corresponds neatly with hierarchical position: for example, in the large-scale organization sector
managers have the highest average while the blue-collar class has
the lowest. The generalization does not apply to agriculture because
many of the members at the bottom of this class hold second jobs in
other sectors. It can also be seen from Table 3.1 that the average
incomes are highest for the organizational sector classes and lowest
for agriculture. The table clearly illustrates significant distinctions
between sectors as well as the class differences within sectors.

   Drawing on the same survey, the average years of educational attainment by class are presented in Table 3.1. Focusing on the modern sector, the ranking by class is similar to that for personal income except that professionals, as might be expected, have a
slightly higher average educational attainment than managers. The
averages for the classes of the organizational sector are highest,
whereas those for the agricultural sector are the lowest. Again, both
sector and class differences are striking.

Other surveys mentioned below indicate that the particular classes differ significantly in their orientations to education. The new middle class and the modern managers evidence the greatest concern with education. On the one hand, these classes clearly view education as a means to achieve social status. New middle-class parents promote their children through the academic course in secondary schools and spend relatively large proportions of their household income for various education-related expenses. On the other hand, the other classes tend to be partial to vocational courses and to be unwilling to devote as much income for education. All social groups look to educational institutions to provide children with moral education. However, the moral concerns of the respective groupings differ. Generally speaking, the more traditional classes ask the schools to convey moral lessons reminiscent of an earlier period, such as loyalty, discipline and filial piety, whereas the modern classes are partial to the individualistic and humanistic values that characterized the Occupation's progressive educational reforms.

Relations between the Major Classes

For this study, not only the attributes of these different classes but also the links that have developed between them are of interest. The several classes of the contemporary system are joined in a great diversity of ways—through primordial ties, economic exchanges, political alliances. In each of these respects, the patterns are complex and certainly do not imply that any single class has a unique relation vis-à-vis all others. For example, in examining the social origins of the several classes, no class except the owners of agricultural enterprises has recruited as many as 50 percent of its members from families of identical class status. Indeed, for most of the classes, less than 10 percent of the recruits come from families of identical class position. The small incidence of class heredity is related to the extraordinary extent of change in Japan's occupational structure over the postwar period.

Turning to the pattern of economic exchanges, the productive and commercial enterprises operated by the modern sector classes increasingly exert an exceptionally strong influence. Whereas in the past the agricultural sector produced nearly half of the gross national product, today its contribution is modest and indeed, except for the noneconomic concern for self-sufficiency and the political survival of the ruling conservative regime, could largely be replaced by imports. Likewise, increasing proportions of the small enterprises are subcontractors to or franchises of the organizational sector. And as Vogel (1963:267) observed in his study of the new middle class, the overwhelming objective of economic production is to serve the tastes and needs of the households in the organizational sector.

Political relations are also significantly influenced today by the organizational sector, but here the situation is more complex. In the old system, the modernizing elites realized their control through a state mechanism that could operate relatively independently from the public will. In the Meiji period, parties and interest groups such as labor unions or associations of industrial enterprises were discouraged, and the franchise was limited to a small minority of the population. Over time, the rights to establish associations and to freely express opinions were opened somewhat, but never so wide as to allow a challenge to the leadership role of the modernizing elites.

The postwar Peace Constitution, through authorizing universal suffrage, the formation of labor unions and associations, and the establishment of political parties, completely altered this situation. The modernizing elites, whose ranks were thinned by the purges, faced a situation where their survival more than ever before depended on establishing alliances with other class groups (Fukutake, 1974: Chapter 9; Fukui, 1974). While the elites who commanded the large corporations and government bureaus were most concerned with rebuilding the productive capacity of the economy, the rank and file of their organizations were more concerned with welfare-oriented policies. As soon as permitted, labor unions formed to capitalize on these sentiments, and by the late 1940s, these unions had established firm alliances with the Socialist and Democratic Socialist parties. Likewise, some workers and intellectuals aligned themselves behind the small but highly active Communist party. While at the time the social base for these leftist parties was concentrated in the numerically small modern sector, the solidarity was impressive. Moreover, with industrialization and the expansion of the modern-sector working class, the left could look to a bright future.

The natural response of the modern elites was to forge links with those classes that had historically demonstrated loyalty to the state, namely the agricultural classes and the more traditional components of the urban entrepreneurial sector. The modern elites promised price supports for farm products, roads, favorable credit, and other benefits in exchange for the rural vote. Rural political bosses, through playing a mediating role in this exchange, perpetuated their prominent role in the political process.

Thus on one side of the postwar political arena an alliance emerged between the modern bureaucratic and corporate elites and the agricultural sector with the selective support of the urban entrepreneurial sector. These groups constituted what is sometimes referred to as the conservative camp and provided the popular base for the Liberal Democratic party. On the other side stood labor with its primary base in the rank-and-file workers (both blue- and white-collar) of the bureaus, corporations, and educational institutions of the organizational sector, though again with selective support from the entrepreneurial sector, especially from its working class. These groups made up what is often called the progressive camp and provided the base for the various opposition parties.

Table 3.1, based on data from the above-mentioned 1975 National Social Mobility Survey, also presents the proportion of respondents from each social group that supported the Liberal Democratic party in the 1975 general elections. Inspection of these proportions clearly illustrates the alignments. The party receives its strongest support from the managerial classes of the modern sector and the agricultural sector (except the numerically small class of agricultural laborers), and it receives moderate support from several of the classes in the entrepreneurial sector. In contrast, the progressive opposition receives its strongest support from the modern intellectuals, the modern white-collar workers, and the blue-collar and laboring classes of all sectors.

Whereas blue-collar workers might be expected to support the opposition, this same tendency in the modern professional and white-collar classes requires a special explanation. First, in Japan many of the members of these classes belong to unions affiliated with the leading opposition parties. In addition, political analysts such as Joji Watanuki (1967) suggest that the modern professional and white-collar classes support the opposition parties because the ideology of these parties corresponds more closely with their new values whereas the ideology of the Liberal Democratic party is considered to be too close to the values of the feudal ethos they want to see eradicated. Watanuki suggests that the cultural commitments of the white-collar and professional workers dominate the class interests that might otherwise orient them toward the conservative party. The competing factors of class interests and cultural commitments lead to a pattern of political alliances that, strictly speaking, cannot be summarized in terms of orthodox class categories. Japan's Liberal Democratic party has little difficulty recognizing this situation. However, two of the opposition parties derive their ideology from Marxism and thus often feel compelled to phrase their political rhetoric in Marxism's orthodox language of class alignment. As the Japanese class reality cannot be described effectively in terms of this orthodox language, these parties often fail to achieve clear communication with the electorate.

The political salience in Japan of cultural commitments has important implications for the remainder of the discussion in this chapter. The leaders of both the Liberal Democratic party and the progressive parties believe that what happens in the schools has important implications for the future of Japan's cultural development. Teachers in most societies hold similar views, but these opinions are not usually taken very seriously by the general public. However, in Japan where cultural commitments are a central political theme, the public evidences much interest in these opinions. Thus, the educational struggle, far from being carried out in a vacuum, attracts much public interest, and public opinion often influences the outcome.

The Changing Relative Size of the Sociopolitical Camps

Before actually turning to the educational struggle, there is one other background factor. In the immediate postwar period, when the above-mentioned political camps were being formed, Japan was still at a relatively early stage of economic development. Since that time, the economy has experienced a miraculous surge of growth, and this has necessarily been accompanied by massive changes in the employment structure. These changes have political implications.

One way to examine these implications is to look at the relative proportion of the labor force that work in classes that tend to be conservatively inclined and those that tend to be progressively inclined.[5] Table 3.2, though based on data from the Japanese census

[5] Working from census categories, Ohashi (1971:84–85) established four main classes (Capitalist, Protective Services, Old Middle Class, Working Class), and within these a total of fourteen more detailed categories. Within his working class are most of those aggregates identified in this book as the subordinates of the mod-

TABLE 3.2
POLITICAL TENDENCIES IN THE LABOR FORCE (PERCENTAGES)

	1950	1960	1970
Conservative inclined	61.8	49.5	39.9
Modern capitalist class	1.9	2.7	3.9
Protective services	.9	1.1	1.2
Old middle class (includes family workers)	14.4	15.1	16.7
Agricultural sector	44.6	30.6	18.1
Progressive inclined	38.2	50.5	60.1
New middle class	11.9	14.2	18.7
Productive workers	20.0	27.8	29.6
Nonproductive workers	4.3	7.8	10.5
Unemployed	2.0	.7	1.4
	100.0	100.0	100.0

SOURCE: *Population Census of Japan* for 1950, 1960, and 1970; categories for the analysis adapted from Ryuken Ohashi, *Nihon on Kaikyu Kosei* (The Composition of Japan's Classes), pp. 84–85.
NOTE: The labor force in 1950, 1960, and 1970 was 36.3 million, 44 million, and 52.8 million workers, respectively.

where the occupational categories only imperfectly fit the classes we have distinguished, represents the best effort at determining these proportions. In 1950 the large majority were in conservatively inclined categories. However, by 1960 a balance had been achieved and by 1970 the dominance of the progressively inclined categories was evident. These labor force figures need to be adjusted to take account of the housewife vote and the differential propensity of members in the indicated groups to vote with their majority. Still, they provide one way of illustrating the well-known political fact of the steady erosion of the social base of the conservative camp. The change in the relative size of conservative and progressive aligned classes is also reflected in the proportion who vote for the Liberal Democratic party and the number of candidates from this party who are elected to political office. Throughout the postwar period, while the Liberal Democratic party has maintained control of the national government, its majority has steadily waned (Thayer, 1976), and its control over many local governments, espe-

ern organizational sector—the professionals, white collar, gray collar, and blue collar of large- and medium-scale organizations. These aggregates, as seen in Table 3.3, tend to be progressively inclined whereas those in Ohashi's first three classes are conservatively inclined.

cially in urban areas, has become increasingly unstable. When the conservative party enjoyed a substantial majority, it was willing to take relatively inflexible positions on key policy issues and fight for their realization. However, as its strength declined, the conservative party showed less willingness to fight and more interest in moderation. These generalizations apply with particular force to educational policies. In the 1950s and early 1960s, there were frequent and violent clashes over educational issues. In the 1970s, there is a greater willingness to compromise. Beginning with a discussion of this conflict at a time when the Liberal Democratic party was at its strongest, the theme of its declining position will be incorporated into an overall assessment of the postwar educational struggle.

PRINCIPAL THEMES OF THE EDUCATIONAL STRUGGLE

The legal provisions for the old system of education enabled most policies to be determined by government officials without the need to seek the approval of the Diet or other bodies. In contrast, the Occupation provided the new educational system with a constitutional basis that required parliamentary debate and legislation of major reforms (Kobayashi, T., 1976). While this change was consistent with the Occupation's democratic ideology, it allowed dissenters a favorable opportunity to obstruct full implementation of several of the Occupation's intended reforms of the administration and organization of the educational system. In some instances, the intended reforms were formally launched but lacked the critical support of the ruling conservative party. Postwar political developments would determine their fate.

A critical new factor in the political scene was the emergence of Nikkyoso (the Japan Teachers' Union) following the conclusion of World War II to fight for improvements in the working conditions of teachers. The union developed a close association with the progressive camp and became the leading articulator of opposition to the conservative camp's educational policies. The major issues separating the two groups form the themes of the struggle that has characterized educational policy-making in postwar Japan.

Is the Teacher a Worker or a Professional?

Teachers formed unions in the immediate postwar period for a variety of reasons, but unquestionably the most common motivation was to exert pressure for an improvement in their economic status. While most of the teacher organizers believed that class struggle would become necessary to improve the status of teachers, the rank-and-file union members tended to prefer more peaceful tactics. The Occupation's new labor laws, although guaranteeing collective bargaining and the right to strike, supported the more re-strained approach. In 1947, General MacArthur ordered labor, in-cluding the various teachers' unions, to abandon its intention of carrying out a general strike. Subsequently, the Diet enacted legis-lation circumventing the channel for centralized collective bargain-ing by teachers' unions. These actions shocked many teachers and radicalized their perception of the process necessary for improving their economic status. Within a short period, the various independ-ent unions joined to form Nikkyoso. Within Nikkyoso, radical in-tellectuals affiliated with the Socialist and Communist parties achieved prominent positions in the central committee. The radical national leaders were determined to keep teachers and the educa-tional system in the forefront of the struggle for revolutionary change. These leaders articulated the orthodox hierarchical theory of class relations and declared that teachers belonged to the subor-dinate or working-class tier. Article 8 of the Nikkyoso Code of Ethics elaborated this position:

> Teachers are laborers whose workshops are the schools. Teachers, in the knowledge that labor is the foundation of every-thing in society, shall be proud of the fact that they themselves are laborers. At the present stage of history, the realization of a new society of mankind which respects fundamental human rights, not only in word but in deed as well, and which utilizes resources, technology, and science for the welfare of all men is possible only through the power of the working masses whose nucleus is the laboring class. Teachers shall be aware of their po-sition as laborers, shall live forcefully believing in the historical progress of man, and shall consider all stagnation and reaction as their enemies (Duke, 1973:226).

Defining teachers as workers has far-ranging implications (Makieda, 1975; Oki, 1975). For example, as workers teachers do not consider administrative superiors as colleagues, but rather as potential class enemies. Workers are suspicious of reforms to ex-pand vocational educational tracks because they fear that the aim is merely to serve the capitalist class's desire for cheap labor. Schools and classrooms become as acceptable a setting for conveying radical ideology as any other place. Another interesting implication is the union's position on working hours. Traditionally, the ideal teacher was a selfless person who stayed at school long after normal classroom duties were finished to play with children, provide extra lessons, attend teacher meetings, and so on. These traditional expectations carried over to the new system, but Nikkyoso insisted that teachers should not be expected to perform these activities unless they were paid for overtime just as an assembly-line worker is paid when he responds to extra demands.

Through the 1950s most rank-and-file teachers considered themselves workers, and a surprising number participated actively in the broader political struggles. However, by the late 1950s the intensity of these struggles was leading to much hardship, and many teachers began to doubt the wisdom of politically oriented activism. Gradually, a more moderate concept evolved of a teacher as "educational worker." The implication was that teachers need not feel obliged to participate in all of the struggles of the working class.

Many of the most facile articulators of the teacher as educational worker doctrine were members of the educational faculties of the new universities that train teachers. The strategic position of these intellectuals in the teacher training process was particularly upsetting to the conservative camp. Thus, since the early postwar period the conservatives attempted to develop a counterideology for the teacher role. Essentially, what emerged was the notion that teachers were professionals or specialists who performed a duty for the government. As professionals, teachers were expected to conform to the professional code of carrying out their duty to completion, regardless of the amount of time required. The conservatives rejected the radical assumption of class divisions and the logic of class struggle. The conservatives maintained that because the government was established through a democratic process it was neutral. Hence, teachers were to be expected to conform to the authority of the government rather than to view this authority as coming from their class enemy.

These differences in the conception of the teacher's role led to disputes over issues such as working hours, duties, pay, promotions, and discipline. In addition, the government made significant efforts to counterreform the new system of teacher training and promotions developed during the Occupation. One of the boldest steps on the part of the government was to close down Tokyo Education University, one of Japan's leading institutions of higher education but also one whose educational faculty had several of the nation's most radical intellectuals. The more moderate staff from this disbanded university found employment at the new Tsukuba National University (Cummings, 1974).

Should Education Be Neutral or Convey a World View?

The new constitution and educational laws explicitly advocated the neutrality of education, and both camps paid lip service to this ideal. Yet, the two camps remained firmly committed to distinctive world views and sought to use the educational process as a vehicle for propagating them. The progressive camp typically asserted that social classes, with their dominant–subordinate relations, constitute the fundamental principle of social organization; in that this mode of conceptualization was largely alien to Japan prior to World War II the progressives sought to teach this view through the schools. In the immediate postwar period, when school texts were neither standardized nor censored, leftist intellectuals composed many social studies texts that explicitly introduced their dialectical world view. Leftist-oriented teachers freely conveyed this world view in their lectures. Educational authorities, typically responsible to conservative local governments, were dismayed by these practices and tried to stop them by censoring or dismissing individual teachers. These punitive activities, in turn, led to stiff resistance from local units of Nikkyoso.

Perhaps the most famous incident of this kind was that which occurred in Ashigaoka, a middle-class suburb of Kyoto (Duke, 1973:120–122). A large proportion of this suburb's population was sympathetic to Nikkyoso and thus were not especially alarmed when the local teachers' union decided to introduce a special program of "peace education" in the schools. However, other parents became upset once the peace education program started, and on December 15, 1953, a delegation from the Ashigaoka Lower Secondary School issued a formal complaint. In their complaint, the parents charged that mathematics and science teachers, during regular class hours, argued against Japan's rearmament and the presence of U.S. military bases. Teachers were also charged with reading sections from the Japanese Communist party newspaper *Akahata* to students as well as teaching students to sing the "Internationale." In response to this complaint, the superintendent initially attempted to transfer the teachers said to be most responsible for the peace education program. However, when the teachers rejected the transfer, the superintendent dismissed them. But this action was opposed by the targeted teachers' colleagues as well as by a large group of sympathetic parents. Ultimately, the conflict was adjudicated, and the courts supported the superintendent's action, while the government prepared legislation that would restrict future occurrences of such overtly biased education.

One reason conservatives objected to the propagandistic activities of leftist teachers was they also wished to advance their world view of the Japanese people, unified in harmony, loving their country, respecting the emperor, and sacrificing through hard work for the realization of greater prosperity.[6] This view, which has obvious parallels with the imperial state ideology of the old system, served the interests of the modern organizational sector elites while at the same time it resonated with the emotions of more traditional rural Japan.

However, the conservatives were not in a favorable position for advancing their world view. Relatively few rank-and-file teachers identified with the conservative ideology, nor were the conservative-oriented teachers' associations very active. In lieu of an approach through the teachers, the conservatives opted for a focus on the curriculum and texts. Using their parliamentary majority, they brought about a situation in which the central Ministry of Education prepares a unified national curriculum (The Course of Study) and censors the texts developed by private firms to convert this curriculum into classroom materials. Furthermore, in 1958 the conservatives introduced a new moral education course into the curriculum reflecting many aspects of their world view. In 1965 they authorized the publication of a similarly slanted document titled "The Image of an Ideal Japanese," which they hoped would influence the educational goals of teachers. Conservative politicians, as well as the Ministry of Education that supervises the curriculum, vehemently denied any propagandistic intentions and insisted that their efforts were consistent with the principle of neutral education. Yet these claims were no more credible than those of their leftist opponents. Both sides believed that the educational process shapes

[6] These themes are most explicit in *Kitai-sareru Ningenzo*; for an abridged translation, see Duke (1967).

the values of youth, and both sides sought to bias that aspect of the educational process over which they had the greatest control.

Is the Primary Mission of Schools To Develop Skills or Rich Personalities?

The Fundamental Law of Education and other legal bases for the new educational system stressed the noncognitive and nonutilitarian goals of education: independence, individualism, self-actualization, friendship, peace. In general, these values were congenial to the higher educated and especially to the leftist intellectuals who identified with the humanistic side of Marxism. Thus, the progressive camp, from the beginning of the new system, urged these qualitative goals on the educational system.

Conservatives participated in the process of formulating these early ideals, but in subsequent years began to question their appropriateness for the Japanese situation. For example, they charged that the new youth became too enamored of freedom and independence and thus neglected responsibilities, and that youth emphasized rights while neglecting duties and the virtue of loyalty. Thus it was not long before conservative educators began to criticize the qualitative themes of the new education. Although the conservatives wanted the schools to teach values, they rather preferred greater emphasis on self-control, duty, responsibility, and loyalty. These preferences were reflected in their counterreforms of the curriculum, the introduction of the new moral education course, and the practice of censoring texts.

At the same time, the conservatives placed a much higher value on the utilitarian outcomes of education than did the progressives. Even before the departure of the Occupation, the conservatives questioned the wisdom of dismantling all the old-system higher technical colleges and the various secondary level vocational schools. In 1956 the influential Nikkeiren (Japan Federation of Employers' Associations) issued a report sharply criticizing the manpower implications of the new educational system. The gist of this report was that the educational system failed to place enough emphasis on science and technology and that it was not graduating a sufficient number of technicians and engineers. The conservative government was responsive to this argument. In 1958 the Ministry of Education revised the school curriculum to devote more time to science and mathematics and upgraded the contents of these subjects. In 1962 it established a new system of higher technical col-

leges, and a substantial proportion of its new programs for secondary schools and universities focused on the improvement of facilities for science and technology courses.

These reforms brought strong protests from progressives that
the government was neglecting the qualitative side of education
and was too responsive to the manpower demands of big business.
The progressives argued that the proper role of education should be
to develop whole people (*zenjin kyoiku*) and not to merely create
workers useful for the economy (*hito tsukuri*).[7]

Underlying the leftist critique is the assumption that schools, in
the time given them, can encourage only a finite amount of learning. To the extent that schools are required to teach an increased
volume of cognitive materials without corresponding increases in
the number of teachers or teaching hours, the qualitative aspects of
the curriculum suffer.[8] Teachers also fear that the increased emphasis on cognitive materials results in a widening dispersion in the actual achievement of pupils—teachers complain that, due to the excessive cognitive demands of the curriculum, too many pupils fail
to master the basics for their grade level and thus experience learning handicaps in subsequent years. Parents also feel their children
are forced to study too hard and worry their children may fall behind. The parents of new middle-class children are most worried
and hence most supportive of the progressive critics; yet, ironically,
these parents' children tend to perform relatively well in school.

[7] The translation provided in the text is connotative, not literal. Hayato Ikeda,
when prime minister, made a speech that clearly set out the conservative goal of
using the educational system to make workers for the economy. In this speech, he
used the phrase *hito tsukuri*. Since then, the left has often referred to Ikeda's phrase as
a way of summarizing the conservative camp's utilitarian thinking. *Zenjin kyoiku*
was used long before the postwar educational struggle to describe the educational
goal of creating "whole people." Most progressive educators feel comfortable in
using this phrase to describe their objectives. However, a minority feel *zenjin kyoiku*
has too much of a militaristic or nationalistic connotation, and hence avoid using it.
All progressives feel comfortable with the phrase *minshu kyoiku* (democratic education), but this is really a slogan and does not readily connote the concrete educational
goals of progressive teachers.

[8] A typical expression of these assumptions can be found in Umene (1975:12-27).
A well-written illustration of the negative human consequences of the excessive
cognitive emphasis is the ongoing series, Asahi Shinbunsha (1973a). The first three
volumes on primary schools published from 1973 to 1975 particularly are helpful.
Nikkyoso also maintains that a large proportion of students are unable to master the
cognitive demands of the curriculum; the results are reported in the Nikkyoso periodical *Kyoiku Hyoron*, 338 (July 1976:16-110). For a somewhat different interpretation of the available evidence, see Chapters Six to Eight below.

Should Education Be for All, or Must Education
Participate in the Process of
Social Selection?

A major thrust of the Occupation's educational reforms was to expand opportunities in the new educational system and to relieve educators of much of their traditional responsibility for social selection. "Education according to one's ability" was declared a right, and compulsory general education was extended from six to nine years. Other reforms such as the small district high school system, comprehensive and coeducational high schools, and expansion of the higher educational system were aimed at eroding the elitist selection tracks of the old system. Progressive educators identified with many of these changes. For example, several features of the Occupation's high school reforms were adopted as "basic principles for democratic education" by the Kyoto Prefecture teachers' union, and ever since it has insisted that these principles be followed in Kyoto, even as other prefectures reverted to more elitist and selective practices (Sasaki, 1976). On the other hand, the more pragmatic conservatives objected that the nation could not afford a larger system and that the new reforms failed to take account of the nation's manpower needs. Likewise, conservatives defended the old elitist educational concept on the grounds that the elite track, while open to all, cultivated vital leadership traits in those who experienced it. Thus, even before the Occupation's departure, conservative-dominated local governments began implementing counter-reforms.

Initially, the debate over education's role in selection focused on the high schools. How many places should be provided, should these be in a college preparatory course or in a terminal vocational technical course, and so forth? Subsequently, the debate shifted to lower levels. On several occasions over the postwar period, conservatives proposed that tracking be introduced in the primary schools and an elective system in middle and high schools so that the academically more able students would be able to concentrate on more difficult materials. Progressive educators persistently opposed these initiatives arguing that these different tracks might become a vehicle for the discriminatory treatment of students and, moreover, would promote elitist sentiments among the favored students. While the progressives tended to phrase their critique in class terms, there was an underlying political logic—the modern middle classes, which are key supporters of the progressive camp, are the very same classes that most wish to send their children to general education courses and that would feel most threatened if tracking were introduced.

In 1961 the Ministry of Education proposed to administer a nationwide student achievement test for several grade levels, and while the ministry's intentions were not clear, it appeared that one objective was to establish an information base for the eventual classification of students into ability-differentiated tracks. Leftist teachers across the nation united in opposing this test, and their efforts were so impressive that the ministry abandoned its original plan. The test was given, but the results had no effect on tracking.

Should the Central Government or the Teachers Control the Curriculum?

Perhaps the most fundamental objective of the Occupation's reforms was to take control away from the central educational bureaucracy and turn it over to parents and teachers. Thus, the Occupation compelled the central government to abandon such activities as censorship of textbooks and inspection of schools, and in place of centralized control urged the establishment of locally elected school boards. Initially, neither the conservatives nor the progressives were enthusiastic about this proposal, both fearing that they would lose the local elections. Also, it was doubtful whether local people had sufficient experience to vote wisely for school board members. However, upon the insistence of the Occupation, the legislation was ultimately passed with the provision that it be implemented gradually (Kawai, 1960). In the initial stage, elections were arranged for the boards to administer the schools of various urban districts. The results of these elections were surprising: Where the teachers' union was well organized, its members promoted several of their own candidates, and due to the high regard in which teachers were held by parents, these candidates often succeeded. Teachers union candidates were not deterred by the frequent charge that their participation on local boards might constitute a conflict of interest. At the same time, conservative politicians were energetic in promoting their own candidates. The result was that many boards came to be composed of members with sharply divergent political and educational convictions.

Local board members, being part-time, often failed to resolve their differences, and thus the new decision-making machinery could not always provide clear guidance to schools. Also there were many practical difficulties arising from the new system. With local boards making annual decisions on textbooks, publishers found it very difficult to estimate the volume of books that they should print to satisfy demand. These problems multiplied as the local board system was extended from the urban areas to all parts of the nation.

Progressive educators, pleased with the success that they often achieved in the local board elections, became enthusiastic about the change. They argued that the difficulties encountered were the price that had to be paid in order to build "democracy." However, conservatives became increasingly disenchanted with the local boards, and finally in 1956 used their majority in the Diet to repeal the earlier law authorizing local boards. In its stead, the conservatives created a new system where governors of prefectures and mayors of Japan's six large cities appointed boards to assume responsibility for the local areas under their control. The effect of this law was to reduce the potential number of local boards from over 5,000 to 52 and to shift the process of selection from an election to appointment. In that most prefectures and large city governments were at that time controlled by the conservative camp, this counterreform effectively reduced progressive influence in most local boards. The most important exception is Kyoto prefecture. Since 1950, when Ninagawa Tomizo, a former Kyoto University professor, became governor, the prefectural educational board and the educational office have been staffed predominantly with leftist educators. The Kyoto educational office always has insisted on carrying out its independent evaluation of educational policies and has often rejected directives of the central government. Kyoto's autonomous approach has served as an inspiring example for radical educators throughout the nation.

Following the change in the nature of local boards, conservative educators began to consider ways in which they could exert greater leverage over the activities of individual schools and teachers. Technically, school boards held the responsibility for appointing school principals, teachers, and other educational personnel as well as paying their salaries. The authority to appoint principals, particularly, enabled the local governments to exercise some influence inside the schools: providing a principal was responsive to the local school board, he could instruct the staff of his school concerning the wishes of the local board. However, in many cases principals found that teachers were not willing to conform to these instructions.

To understand their reluctance, it is necessary to consider the traditional structure of school administration. In this structure, the
principal was the only nonteaching member of the educational staff,
and thus to perform the various administrative tasks, responsibility
was shared by all of the educational staff. To achieve harmony
among staff members, weekly staff meetings were conducted to exchange opinions. In the old system, it was usually assumed that the
principal would have final authority over the decisions in these
meetings. But in the new system with its democratic ideology and
the presence of Nikkyoso that maintains the teachers' meeting
should be the decision-making organ, the principal's authority was
often challenged. In such cases, the principal might face the near
impossible task of trying to persuade a staff, the majority of whom
sympathized with Nikkyoso, to accept a policy advocated by a conservative local board or the central government.

In part because the administrative board load of schools steadily
increased, but also out of a feeling that principals could exert more
effective control if they had additional intraschool allies, the ministry periodically proposed an expansion in the administrative component of school staff. In 1963, in the face of considerable opposition, a new law was passed authorizing the creation of the position
of assistant principal, and in 1975 a ministerial order was issued authorizing the position of head teacher. Nikkyoso protested both of
these actions, stating that they would disrupt the harmony of
school staff meetings, that it would be more difficult for schools to
be managed through democratic procedures, and that an increase in
money for school personnel could be better spent by increasing
either the salaries of the school "working class"—the teachers—or
their number than by expanding the size of the "ruling administrative class." In the case of assistant principals, Nikkyoso's protest
was fruitless. But with the position of head teacher, the union's
campaign resulted in the indefinite suspension of the central government order by nearly half of the local school boards.

A related issue in the control controversy was the government's
effort to provide principals and local boards with greater control
over the procedures for pay increases and promotions. The personnel laws established at the beginning of the new system created a
situation where a teacher received job tenure as soon as he was
hired. Moreover, teachers' salaries were determined according to a
simple schedule with automatic annual increments but no recognition of performance. In thinking of ways to provide principals with

means to encourage greater teacher cooperation, conservative leaders settled on the idea of altering the system of inducements by requiring a trial period prior to tenure and introducing an "efficiency rating system." The trial period was never implemented, but the government's efforts between 1956 and 1958 to implement the rating scheme provoked the most protracted and violent educational struggle of the postwar period.

The Local Public Servant Law of 1950 included a provision for the rating of public servants by their supervisors. In the case of teachers, this provision was ignored until 1956 when the ministry suggested that Ehime prefecture, which was facing a huge financial deficit, use an efficiency rating system as a means for cutting down its school personnel expenditures. Although the Ehime prefectural government accepted the suggestion and transmitted it to the schools, most principals chose to ignore it.

Following changes in the prefectural administrative structure, the order was repeated. This time, the Ehime prefectural teachers' union, supported by the national headquarters of Nikkyoso, indicated its opposition, maintaining the proposed rating system was not appropriate for the occupation of teaching. In late 1956, in a mass negotiating meeting, prefectural officials agreed with teachers not to implement the rating scheme that year. Nevertheless, two months later, without consulting teachers, the prefectural government reactivated its plan to effect the rating scheme. Principals were ordered to complete rating forms for each teacher in the school. The local union was shocked and began to struggle "for the complete fulfillment of [its] goals." A strike headquarters was established in a tent outside the prefectural office and union leaders entered into daily discussions with prefectural officials. One school day, two thousand teachers took leave en masse.

Meanwhile, in June, 1957, the Ministry of Education under Nadao Hirokichi, a hawkish minister known for his desire to break the union, indicated its intention to implement the efficiency rating system throughout the nation. The central office of Nikkyoso interpreted this announcement as a significant challenge and quickly organized for resistance. Launching the attack, several hundred union members went to the Ministry of Education to protest the central plan with a sit-in; on this occasion, two of the top Nikkyoso officers were arrested. Teachers met throughout the nation in an effort to build a united front.

In this context, Ehime became a test case and some three

thousand teachers from other prefectures visited to provide support to the local union. By this time over half the principals had turned in their ratings; others either would not or could not turn in theirs because the teachers forcibly intervened. Finally, on December 15, in negotiations with central Nikkyoso, the Ehime local government officially agreed that no protestors would be punished and that a rating form would not be approved until it gained the acceptance of the teachers. This negotiation was understood to have national implications. Thus the struggle appeared to have concluded with a union victory.

But then, only five days later, the National Conference of Superintendents drafted a new rating form without consulting teachers and proposed its nationwide enforcement from April of 1958. The central leadership of Nikkyoso was outraged at this seeming duplicity and, declaring a state of emergency, adopted the policy of "absolute opposition by force." Chairman Takeshi Kobayashi stated:

> Our major concern is that the implementation of the rating plan will result in subservience to authority, characteristic of prewar Japan, thereby distorting education. Under the new system the local school board principal must evaluate the teacher's performance. In this role the principal will become merely a representative of the controlling powers, that is, the boards of education and the Ministry of Education. The resulting disastrous effect will be an emotional struggle between the principal, representing the entrenched power structure, and his teachers. The principal will then be able to coerce his teachers through the implementation of the rating system. In addition, teachers will lose their identity as educators responsible to their students and the country as a whole. Therefore we are resolutely committed to resisting all efforts to effect the Teacher's Efficiency-rating Plan which would sacrifice the students for the benefit of the ruling powers (Duke, 1973:141).

Over the next year and a half, despite factional conflicts within the central office of the union, this policy was carried out on a national scale. To begin the struggle, on April 23, thirty-five thousand Tokyo union teachers took a mass leave from school causing 80 percent of the schools to close temporarily. This practice was repeated in other prefectures on a staggered basis, and on September 15, 1958, a nationwide strike was attempted. Similar strikes were carried out on October 28, November 26, and December 10.

These strikes invited counterattacks from teachers who did not approve of the union's policy and especially from nonschool groups. The counterattacks became increasingly violent including this incident. On December 18, 1958, Nikkyoso Chairman Kobayashi attended a rally in Kochi prefecture and while he was making a speech in a local hall, a gang of local ruffians entered a back entrance, turned off the lights, and attacked Kobayashi and his audience. Kobayashi was hit on the shoulder by a *hibachi* and lost consciousness; apparently, the ruffians then kicked him in the face because when he awoke his face was badly cut and his front teeth were missing; he and fifteen other union members were hospitalized that day. Kobayashi charged that a local political boss, a prominent member of the conservative party, had hired the ruffians.

In addition to this physical coercion, many teachers faced disciplinary action for violating Article 37 of the Local Public Servant Law, which stated they could "not resort to strike, slowdown, or other acts of dispute against their employer." From 1956 to 1960, the period during which the efficiency rating struggle was conducted, authorities issued over 56,000 administrative punishments: 112 teachers were dismissed, 292 suspended, 1,018 demoted, 3,076 formally reprimanded, and 52,273 had their salaries reduced. In addition, 4,420 teachers were involved in criminal procedures (Duke, 1973:154).

The heavy arm of established authority and the extreme tactics advocated by union leaders led many teachers to question the wisdom of struggle. Indeed, large numbers of teachers resigned from the union: in Ehime prefecture, the focus of the struggle, the union lost the majority of its members. Nationally the union lost at least ten percent of its membership by 1959 and the union treasury was severely taxed. Without some resolution of the efficiency rating struggle, the union's future was dark.

Fortunately for Nikkyoso, at this point the central government was forced to shift its attention to another threat generated by the progressive camp, the struggle against the U.S.-Japan Treaty (*Ampo-toso*). Although local government officials were still prepared to pursue the efficiency rating system battle, the struggle against the treaty commanded the full attention of national government officials including the leaders of the Ministry of Education. Student groups at many universities were active opponents of government policy, and thus the atmosphere on the campuses was threatening.

Also, an important change took place within Nikkyoso. Fearing for the union's survival, a national convention of union delegates voted in February, 1959, to appoint the moderate Miyanohara Sadamitsu as the new secretary-general. Under Miyanohara's leadership, a face-saving formula was first worked out in Kanagawa prefecture: the conservative camp could implement the efficiency rating system but teachers would monitor the process. Each teacher would submit his "Record of Educational Activities" to his principal, who, in consultation with the teacher, would fill out the ratings for submission to the local board. Because of the teacher role, principals generally ended up giving uniformly favorable marks to all their staff. Variations of this innocuous teacher-monitored system were adopted throughout the nation. For example, in Iwate prefecture the local union developed a guidebook that all teachers and principals agreed to use in filling out the efficiency rating reports. In the section for comments on each teacher, principals were instructed by the guidebook to write "he is an extremely diligent person."

The compromise was timely. It is questionable whether the union could have survived if the conservatives had been in a position to persist in the battle. But if the conservatives had carried through to the end, the blow to teacher morale might have been irreparable. Subsequently, under the new moderate leadership, the union was able to restore its losses. Membership increased and the union's financial position improved.

THE OUTCOME OF THE EDUCATIONAL STRUGGLE

The struggle over the efficiency rating scheme was exceptional in terms of the violence and the short-run damage suffered by the union. But it was not unusual in terms of the outcome. As with many other educational issues, the conservative camp launched a drive for reform only to have their plan blocked by the progressive camp. Typically, the conservatives formulate a policy change, use their parliamentary majority to push the change through the Diet against vigorous opposition, and then begin the process of implementation. With the Liberal Democratic party's influence over the Ministry of Education and most local governments, the directives authorizing the new changes are successfully communicated down the administrative hierarchy. But once the directives reach the schools, teachers refuse to cooperate in their proper implementation (Thurston, 1973:262-266).

In order for teachers to resist authority in this way, they must hold strong views about proper educational policy, and these views were recently surveyed (Nagoshi, 1976; Kawakami, 1977; Ito, 1971; Takashima, 1976). These surveys differ in their samples and their phrasing of questions. Nevertheless, taken as a whole, they suggest a definite pattern. Concerning involvement in economic and especially political activities, there is significant variation in teacher attitudes. But concerning issues that are more closely related to school and classroom activities, the majority of today's teachers agree with the positions taken by Nikkyoso. Thus, on several of the school and classroom issues, teachers' attitudes clash with those of principals and the conservative-dominated educational bureaucracy.

Nagoshi's survey of 685 teachers and 14 school administrators in the Kansai area covers the widest range of issues. He reports that 83.7 percent of his teacher sample considered themselves educational workers (an additional 4.3 percent chose the extreme response of production-line worker) while only 11.6 percent viewed themselves as professionals. On the other hand, only one third placed themselves in the working class when allowed the alternatives of lower, working, middle, and upper class. Likewise only one third clearly stated their preference for one of the progressive political parties, while nearly half expressed no political preference. Only two fifths favor teachers strikes as a means for realizing union goals. Kawakami, who collected data from a somewhat older sample of teachers in Osaka (one part of the Kansai area), reports that nine of ten approve of the union's efforts to advance the economic status of teachers and to gain a voice in national bodies that formulate educational policy; however, only four of ten approve of the union's involvement in politics, and over one half express reservations about allowing teachers the right to strike.

Turning to the control of education, Nagoshi reports that slightly over half the teachers are dissatisfied with Japan's current educational policy (one of ten say that it is completely mistaken) and four of ten feel a strong enmity toward the Ministry of Education. When asked who should have the responsibility for determining the content of education, one half mention the government while three of ten point to the teachers. Both Nagoshi and Kawakami report that four of ten express strong reservations about relying on the government's course guidelines in their work.

Concerning internal school management, Kawakami reports that nearly six of ten teachers view the school staff meeting as the final decision-making body on school policies (the government's view is that principals have the responsibility for making decisions, and in Kawakami's survey nine of ten principals say that the staff meeting is only a deliberative body). Ito, in a survey of over 700 teachers from Kanagawa, Nagano, and Kagawa prefectures, reports that six of ten view the school principal as simply an administrator, while believing that they should have control over classroom activities (only three of ten school administrators agree with this). Eight of ten teachers think that the selection of texts, teaching materials, and methods should be their responsibility. Finally nine of ten believe that teachers should have full authority over the procedures for grading and promoting teachers. Reviewing these various findings, it appears that teachers strongly agree that they should have full control over school and classroom education.

If teachers want control over education, what do they plan to do with it? The majority—seven of ten in the Kawakami survey—believes that education changes society rather than that it is controlled by society. However, the surveys tell us little more than this. When directly asked whether they think education should be neutral, nine of ten teachers respond yes. Less than one of ten give a politicized response. Yet the teachers' union and pro-government activities are at odds with this response. Apparently, survey techniques are unable to elicit valid answers in this sensitive area; the only way to understand what teachers are trying to achieve is to watch them in their actual classrooms (see Chapter Five for a detailed account).

However, in anticipation it can be said that many teachers are attempting to realize a remarkably egalitarian style of education. They want all their pupils to master the curriculum, and at the same time the teachers strive to convey complementary egalitarian, participatory, and individualistic values. In addition, many teachers succeed in conveying these values, which are actually incompatible with the prevailing class system. Thus, as children are exposed to these values, one would expect them to question the authority of the established order.

The Persistence of the Union

The sustained resistance of the teachers' union with its strong roots in the individual schools accounts for the inconclusiveness of the conservatives' counterreforms. Throughout the postwar period, despite the difficulties encountered during the struggles, over two thirds of all teachers in primary and secondary schools were dues-paying members of the union. The urban prefectures, especially in the Kansai area, had high membership proportions, whereas those in rural prefectures, especially in Shikoku and Southwestern Japan, were relatively weak (Thurston, 1973:120-127). Likewise, the commitment of individual union members varied. Nevertheless, for each of the major struggles a sufficient number of teachers were available to create impressive strikes, walkouts, and other protest activities.

But how has the union been able to persist in mobilizing such a large proportion of teachers to oppose policies developed by Japan's government? After all, if the normal functions of a union are considered, Nikkyoso has little to offer. In 1948 it was effectively deprived of the right to bargain collectively when the new public service laws transferred the approved locus for collective bargaining from the central government to the local governments. Because the former rather than the latter determines the salary schedules and working conditions of teachers, Nikkyoso was deprived of a direct channel for promoting the economic interests of its members. Moreover, because local governments which appoint administrators, have been controlled by the conservative camp, the union has not been in a favorable position to help the careers of individual teachers. In most local areas a teacher who wished to become a school principal or an administrator in the local government knew that he should avoid a conspicuous role in the union.

There is no fully satisfactory explanation for the union's ability to neutralize these disincentives, but the following considerations appear to be significant:

Nikkyoso's expression of vanguard values. For various reasons, Japan's organizational sector middle and working classes have tended to oppose the policies of the nation's conservative political leaders. To some extent this opposition is rooted in their respective class interests: the leaders, while promoting economic development policies that have steadily improved the position of the modern middle and working classes, still have not willingly promoted a return to these classes that is proportionate to their contribution. For example, the government has been negligent in providing housing, roads, health services, and social security.

However, of even greater importance than these material conflicts are the differences in value preferences of the respective class groups. The organizational sector middle and working classes favor more humanistic self-actualizing values whereas the conservative leaders urge discipline, sacrifice, and tradition. Out of this cultural division has emerged a cultural politics. The modern classes feel compelled to oppose the conservative leadership as a matter of principle for the sake of a Japan consistent with their new values. These cultural differences constitute a fertile background for the union's struggle. In general, even when the union promotes policies that conflict with the interests of the modern classes, it stands for the values of these classes. Thus, the union enjoys a significant level of sympathetic support from the modern organizational sector classes. The national newspapers tend to publicize union activities. Many intellectuals approve of the union, and modern sector parents, while often disturbed by the union's militant struggle tactics, respect it.

Nikkyoso fills an ideological vacuum. Until World War II, the majority of teachers were recruited from agricultural homes and attended specialized normal schools strictly supervised by the central government. Many were firmly committed to traditional values and responsive to governmental authority. Following the war, due to the fear of being purged, the more extreme chauvinists of the older generation resigned from the teaching profession. Other teachers, deeply disturbed by the extent to which old-system education had served the war effort, were looking for a new educational philosophy. At this point, Nikkyoso formed and began promoting its new world view. Nikkyoso filled an obvious void and thus was immediately attractive to teachers.

The social origins of teachers. Moreover, as the educational system began to hire new teachers, conditions favored their acceptance of Nikkyoso. With the gradual displacement of the agricultural sector by the organizational sector, increasing proportions of new teachers came from modern homes.[9] As already noted, these homes tend to empathize with Nikkyoso.

Postwar teacher education. The postwar system of teacher education, to which increasing proportions of prospective teachers have

[9] Nagoshi's (1976:198) sample survey reports that most teachers think they come from upper middle-class (38.9 percent) and lower middle-class homes (39.5 percent). An additional 5.2 percent reported they were from upper-class homes and 15.7 percent from lower-class homes. Younger teachers were somewhat more likely to indicate humble social origins: 22.4 percent of the teachers in their twenties said that they came from lower-class homes compared with 15.7 percent, for the full sample.

been exposed, provides a significant contrast with its nationalistic forerunner. Although each school level provides the opportunity for Nikkyoso teachers to influence the values of youth, higher education is most noteworthy. In contrast with the former system, higher educational institutions today are no longer subject to direct government supervision. In general, they have a progressive atmosphere: the majority of Japan's professors vote for progressive political parties, and radical student groups can be found on nearly all campuses. Students who intend to become teachers follow one of two study plans. They enter either an educational faculty or a normal arts and science faculty where they receive supplemental instruction by educational specialists. Over the postwar period, educational faculties have become among the most radical in the entire educational system. Thus, the contemporary higher educational experience surely predisposes many prospective teachers towards Nikkyoso.

The struggles as socialization. In addition to the above formalized socialization experiences, each new struggle in which Nikkyoso engages provides a new opportunity for influencing the public. Nikkyoso's views are placed in the newspaper and on the television. Teachers discuss the issues. Special rallies are called where any interested teacher, union or nonunion, can hear both sides. In most of the postwar struggles, the conservative camp took the first step. But the conservative initiatives need not have evolved into struggles if Nikkyoso had not been prepared to fight back. A major consideration in Nikkyoso's decision to oppose a conservative initiative is the propaganda value of the prospective struggle. Would the issue capture the imagination of the rank and file? Would it add to union solidarity? In general, the union leadership is wise in choosing issues that contribute to membership solidarity.

Moderation. However, in the selection of issues, the above-mentioned efficiency rating system struggle constituted a major watershed. Up to that point, the central union leadership was strongly influenced by Communists, who urged union members to participate in many political conflicts that had little relation to education; moreover, the Communists were favorably disposed toward violent techniques. Due to the Communist influence, union members were urged toward extreme tactics that the government countered with stiff punishments. At the peak of the efficiency rating system struggle, it became apparent that a growing proportion of the membership no longer supported these tactics. At this critical juncture, a more moderate group captured the control of Nikkyoso.

The moderate leadership steered the union away from a militant political role and focused mainly on working conditions and educational quality. Also, responding to the emerging postbourgeoisie value trend in its membership, growing emphasis was placed on strictly educational issues—support for the expansion of opportunities for high school education and criticism of the censoring of textbooks and of the demanding curriculum. Moreover, Nikkyoso began to increase its program of teacher workshops in response to the growing interest of young teachers in pedagogical technique. By shifting away from political issues, Nikkyoso became more able to convince teachers it offered an important service that would otherwise not be available.

Maintaining the nation as a stage. Nikkyoso was formed because local teacher's unions felt a central secretariat would provide them with greater leverage in negotiating with the central government. When in 1948, the government wrote new public servant laws disallowing "central negotiations," Nikkyoso's *raison d'etre* seemed to be eliminated. However, local unions recognized that the central government was a principal financer of local school systems and hence that central representation was necessary. Thus they continued to back Nikkyoso. The central office provides many services that have contributed to the vitality of the teacher movement. The central office facilitates a more profound analysis of educational developments. When issues develop in one local area, it publicizes these in its bulletin so that all teachers can take interest. When a teacher movement weakens in a given area, specialists from nearby areas can be sent to diagnose the situation or lend support. The national stage provides a greater opportunity than would a number of localized settings.

Nikkyoso's central position in the progressive camp. As a final explanation for Nikkyoso's persistence, we should emphasize its central position in the progressive camp. Perhaps the most predictable support for Japan's leftist parties comes from the labor unions. The largest association of these unions is Sohyo, and the largest union in Sohyo is Nikkyoso (Evans, 1971). Although Nikkyoso, being a public employees' union of essentially white-collar workers, cannot match certain other unions in raw force, it has nevertheless accepted an important place in the labor movement and hence in the leftist camp. If anything, Nikkyoso's prominence has increased as was indicated by Sohyo's choosing Nikkyoso Chairman Makieda as its new head in 1975. In its various struggles, Nikkyoso has invariably received the moral support of other unions. Moreover, progressive politicians readily support Nikkyoso's cause in the Diet and before the mass media. On occasion, other unions have demonstrated their support of Nikkyoso through proposing joint strikes. Thus, Nikkyoso's central position in the progressive camp provides a significant meaning to those members who are committed to social change. They can think of their activities in the teachers' union as one component in a larger fabric of action destined to restructure Japanese society.

CONCLUSION

A number of recent studies have concluded that school systems in both advanced and developing societies are controlled by the government and the classes most closely aligned with it. In that the ruling classes are unlikely to favor egalitarian change, if these findings from other societies are also true of Japan, it is unlikely that Japanese schools can promote equality. Is there anything special about Japan?

In this chapter Japan's pattern of class structure was examined, and it was found that value commitments play an exceptionally important role in class alliances. While Japan's classes are linked through complicated processes of social exchange, they tend to be culturally divided. On the one side are those classes, now controlling the central government, who affirm more traditional and economically conservative values. On the other side are the intellectual and white- and blue-collar classes of the modern sector who affirm more modern and economically progressive values. Education is perceived by the two sides as critical to the advancement of their cultural proclivities. Thus, through the political process educational issues are a continuing focus for class conflict. Focusing on several of the themes, the discussion reviewed key developments in the postwar educational struggle revealing it to be a remarkably evenhanded battle. Neither the conservative nor the progressive forces have been able to claim decisive control of the educational system. Instead, each has achieved relative spheres of influence. The conservatives have greater impact on finance and curriculum whereas the progressives through Nikkyoso have greater influence on school and classroom activities. In fact, a situation obtains where teachers

Chapter Four

THE IMPORTANCE OF CLASS
AND FAMILY

An impressive body of research in advanced societies indicates that the social class into which a young person is born has a significant association with his achievements in school and later in society. Similarly a number of studies indicate a relation between class of origin and value acquisition (Kerckhoff, 1972:123-124; Banks, 1971:61 ff.). Some of the available research suggests similar associations in Japan, though the strength of the relations is often weaker.[1] The mainstream interpretation of these associations states:

1. An adult's social class can be identified best by the type of work performed by the head of the household to which he belongs. This work-role is the major source of the family's income, status, power, and social network.

2. The work-role leads family heads and the other adult family members to accept a wide range of class-specific norms. These class-specific norms include prescriptions for ideal family structure and appropriate child-rearing practices.

3. The families of different social classes tend to observe their class norms. Thus the families of the respective classes differ in their structure and child-rearing practices.

4. These class-specific differences in family structure and child-rearing practices have a differentiating impact on the cognitive skills and values of children from the earliest years of their development (the family-first assumption).

5. The contexts for the children of the respective classes differ in important ways. The educational resources available in their homes, the neighborhoods in which they play, the schools that they attend, and the way in which teachers respond to their efforts are all permeated by their class position. These differences in contextual features reinforce the more fundamental varieties of class-based child-rearing practices.

[1] For an illustration of the weaker relations between class and cognitive achievement in Japan, see Table 6.1.

6. Thus, children from the respective classes come to differ in their values, skills, and achievements. Although some children move out of their class of origin, the general tendency is for the class system to reproduce itself through these processes.

These propositions underlie the mainstream interpretation of the well-known empirical association between class and individual development. Individual investigators introduce their qualifications: for example, the operational measure for class, the extent to which class is said to determine family, and the extent to which reproduction is realized. Yet allowing for these qualifications, one discovers that conservatives and liberals are as firm in their adherence to these propositions as radicals.[2]

THE FAMILY-FIRST ASSUMPTION

Still, a minority objects to one or the other of these propositions. This chapter particularly is concerned with the validity of the family-first proposition (no. 4) and the proposition that families observe their class norms (no. 3). It was Ogburn (1955) who first questioned the family-first assumption in his well-known thesis that technological change was causing the family to lose its functions. Riesman (1953) also suggested the family's demise; in Riesman's opinion, contemporary other-directed youth are more susceptible to the influence of their peer group than to that of their parents.

There are other grounds for questioning the family primacy assumption. For example, Prewitt, in reviewing the first decade of political socialization literature, argues that the associations between "family" variables and specific developmental traits do not necessarily confirm the family primacy hypothesis. Prewitt focuses on the well-known example of the strong correlation between parental and child party identification. While the political socialization literature maintains that party identification and the associated political orientations are transmitted from parent to child in early childhood and are resistant to later influences, Prewitt asserts several anomalies: if the transmission occurs during early childhood,

[2] Though most American social scientists would object to having their research classified as "radical" or "liberal," it is possible through reviewing the assumptions, goals, and tone of different reports to classify them into these ideological categories. Even so, Bowles and Gintis (1976) adhere as firmly to the above list of propositions as do Blau and Duncan (1967).

then parent-young child correlations should be stronger than parent-older child correlations; but the opposite pattern prevails. In addition, whereas the family primacy argument implies that the political orientations should be stable during an individual's early years, they tend to fluctuate extensively. Only as young people mature do their political orientations stabilize. Other findings suggest that parent-child similarities in political orientations are not established in the early childhood years but rather at a later stage in the life cycle.

Prewitt goes on to observe that while the majority of children eventually assume political attitudes similar to those of their parents, some adopt very different postures. These deviants tend to belong to a social milieu that differs from that of their parents. "The child is not a product of family influence only, but of family influence as mediating and mediated by the social milieu to which the family belongs—its class status, its race, its religion, its region, its ethnicity, etc." (Prewitt 1975:109). Insofar as the child assumes an adult role in a milieu similar to his parents, their political orientations will be close. The similarities would materialize even if the parents did not specifically transmit political orientations, because aspects of the common milieu would serve as surrogate teachers. As a child's experience departs from that of his parents, his political orientation will tend to differ.

These considerations lead Prewitt to reject the widely accepted family primacy model for explaining the acquisition of political attitudes, and in its place he suggests a model that he describes as "feeling one's way into the real political world." According to the new model, life experience teaches. So long as lessons along a common theme repeat themselves over the course of maturation, individuals will learn them. Where inconsistencies appear, the individual will have to make choices; these choices are as likely to be affected by the expectation of the milieu toward which the individual thinks his life is heading as by that milieu from which he has come.

An analogous perspective has been proposed for the study of moral development. Maccoby (1968), in a review of the literature on the development of moral values, notes how most studies tend to adopt the family primacy assumption, but the evidence in its support is not unequivocal. In particular, she cites a study by Reiss where, for a number of moral orientations, the influence of family variables was negligible. Indeed, Reiss finds that subsequent experiences had a significantly stronger association with individual moral orientations. Based on this evidence, Reiss argues that the values "learned early in the family setting are not internalized in the sense of becoming self-maintaining" (cited in Maccoby, 1968:263). De-emphasizing the role of the family in the transmission of values, Reiss maintains that "values must be continually reinforced and maintained by inputs from the social setting in which an individual finds himself, and will change if these inputs change."

Reiss, as does Prewitt, believes that statistical evidence of associa-tion between family variables and value acquisition may reflect nothing more than that subjects conduct their affairs in milieux similar to those of their parents. Discontinuities in milieu are likely to result in value discontinuities. Reiss's approach, in that it makes frequent reference to reinforcing experiences, can be called a rein-forcement model.

Reproducing Class Cultures

Returning to the list of propositions it is desirable to examine whether families follow their class norms or whether class norms are distinct. Parsons (1964) in reaction to Ogburn's (1955) loss of function thesis has argued that the modern family is simply more specialized and its effective performance of its more limited func-tions is more important than ever. In this argument, Parsons strongly supports the family-first assumption. However, Parsons does not identify class-differentiated family norms. Rather he sees all families as conforming in greater or lesser degree to the contem-porary middle-class norm. Other Western social scientists have ad-vanced a similar position.

Figure 4.1 helps in focusing the target of the above objections to the mainstream interpretations. The vertical axis represents the divergent perspectives with respect to the family-first proposition and the horizontal axis represents the divergence concerning the persistence of class-differentiated family norms.

If it were necessary to rely on the common folklore concerning the Japanese family, there would be little need to express any inter-est in these objections to the mainstream propositions. Traditional-ly, Japanese society was rigidly stratified, and families were ex-pected to perform a major role in child development. Confucius, the great sage who profoundly influenced Japan's institutions, con-sidered the family to be the fundamental agent of socialization and

FIGURE 4.1   PERSPECTIVES ON CLASS AND FAMILY

		Class-differentiated Family Norms	
		Yes	No
Family is First	Yes	Mainstream	Parsons
	No	Ogburn	Postwar Japan

social control. In his *Greater Learning* there is the well-known adage: "Their family being regulated, their states were rightly governed. Their states being rightly governed, the Whole Kingdom was tranquil and happy" (cited in Dore, 1958:93). Also the available information indicates that there were significant class differences in personality development.

However, a number of leading Japanese social scientists question whether these generalizations hold for the postwar period. Sumiya, perhaps Japan's leading student of value transmission, says: "The Japanese family has completely surrendered its educative function to a single-minded value: getting children the best possible formal education so they can enter social life with the best possible academic background" (1967:130). Similarly, Fukutake, the dean of community studies in Japan, reports: "Today's parents lack self-confidence in child-rearing and they seem to be growing even less certain about what methods are best" (1967:130). These Japanese observers are raising the same objections to the mainstream propositions as the Western critics cited earlier. The remainder of this chapter will, through reviewing recent research, suggest that the two mainstream propositions do not fit the situation of postwar Japan.

CLASS AND FAMILY STRUCTURE THROUGH WORLD WAR II

Scholars who investigate Japanese families report a variety of family types, and through World War II they find a close relation between these types and the family's class position. Most of Japan's family types share a notion that they are a stem (*ie*) of a broad family tradition and thus they attempt to achieve continuity from one generation to the next by designating successive main family heads. Where a head is not available among the male blood kin, adoption may be resorted to. Or where there are several male siblings, one will be selected to continue the main line, and provided that family resources are sufficient, the others will be encouraged to set up branch families. Through these procedures, most *ie* groups perpetuate themselves over several generations (Nakane, 1967). Families honor their ancestors by visiting ancestral shrines and tombs. In this respect Japanese families differ from the nuclear family, which forms and dissolves with each generation, characteristic of much of the West.

Although the notion of *ie* provides a common thread, in other respects there has been much diversity of family structure, based in class and regional cultures. Referring to the Tokugawa period, Befu draws a simple contrast between the families of warriors and peasants. Whereas the samurai practiced exogamy, endogamy was common among the peasants; the prominent role of family heads and go-betweens in selecting marriage partners in the samurai classes contrasted with the reliance on youth-initiated trial marriages among the peasantry. Samurai households tended to include three generations and were subject to the authority of a powerful family head, whereas peasant families were more likely to be nuclear with shared decision making. The emotional tone in the peasant and warrior homes also differed. Filial piety and the family's welfare were stressed in the samurai household, and individual gratification was suppressed; peasant households were more carefree and hedonic. Within the peasant ranks, one finds additional variations. Whereas trial marriages and female-dominated households were common in humid Southwestern Japan, male domination was typical of the northeast (Befu, 1971:38 ff.). Apart from the samurai-peasant differences, the merchant and artisan classes had their distinctive variants as well (Nakano, T., 1964). In contrast with the warriors' asceticism, merchants, insofar as they had the means, engaged in a much more lavish life-style inviting nonkin to their tables and even supporting concubines. Artisans were carefree in their family life, frequently dissolving alliances and generally living for the moment.

The variation in the structures of families during the feudal period was extensive. The Meiji government, partly out of a feeling that the nonsamurai variants were a national embarrassment and partly out of a sense that the samurai family system was most conducive to its modernization efforts, initiated a campaign to "samuraize" the family units of all classes. An official family code was promulgated along the lines of the traditional samurai family and an intensive official propaganda campaign promoting the "Japanese family" was launched through the school curriculum and the media. There followed a gradual convergence toward the samurai form—at least as gauged by superficial indicators. For example, from the 1880s one finds a steady decline in divorce rates and the incidence of children born out of wedlock—events that were common outcomes of the peasant trial-marriage pattern and the urban artisan class's casual approach to sexual liaisons (Kawashima and Steiner, 1960).

It would be a mistake, however, to assume that these trends indicate the unqualified success of the "samuraization" process and the elimination of alternate family types. Certain of the converging trends are better understood as a function of other forces. For example, the demand for go-betweens increased, because, in the wake of rapid urbanization, many young people found that they lacked other means of finding mates. Extended families continued to prevail at least in part because young couples in urban areas found the cost of setting up new homes to be beyond their means. Moreover, careful studies of family organization over the course of the early modern period indicate the persistence of considerable variety in family organization and child-rearing practices that had a significant relation to class position.

It would seem that the samurai family ideal gained the widest acceptance in the rural areas and among the urban upper classes. However, even in these groups there were many exceptions. For example, in the more marginal farm enterprises, the wife necessarily assumed a prominent role in the farm work and in domestic decision making. Women also were prominent in many merchant homes due to their participation in the family business. In urban areas, which up through World War II still accommodated less than a half of the population, the nuclear family was more common, with the husband working in a salaried position and the wife staying home to take care of the children. Among these urban families, the new middle class, whose members often had a samurai background, tended to outwardly conform to the official ideology. In contrast, working-class families exhibited considerable diversity: some claimed a samurai heritage and, responsive to the official ideology, maintained a sober hierarchical structure, whereas others reflected the influence of their more carefree artisan and peasant heritages.

Up through World War II these respective urban subclasses tended to live in segregated areas of the new cities and to hold different child-rearing ideals. The new middle class and the upper strata of the traditional urban and rural classes sought to send their male offspring to the university and into the large bureaus of the modern sector, whereas the remaining classes exhibited less ambitious goals. The educational system and the other socialization agencies of this period tended to reinforce the reproduction of the class system (Smith, 1960; Sumiya, 1963:Chs. 3 and 4). As already noted, there was a decided tendency for class-related values and abilities to be transmitted across generations. Thus, despite the propagation of the official family system ideology, there may well have been as great a diversity of family forms in early modern Japan as in the feudal period.

FAMILY STRUCTURE SINCE THE WAR

Since World War II, a number of forces have operated to reduce the diversity in family forms or at least to push a growing proportion of families toward a modal nuclear conjugal form. In this modal form, role relations tend to be complementary and nonhierarchical. In most cases, no more than token respect is paid to the traditional ideals of *ie* continuity and obedience to family elders.

Among the forces promoting this new model family structure, perhaps the most important single development was the arrival of the U.S. Occupation with its extensive program of reform and reeducation. Certain of the Occupation reforms constituted a direct attack on the earlier class system. Many of the most prominent families watched their fortunes dwindle to a pittance; moreover, all but the inner circle of the imperial family were stripped of their hereditary aristocratic titles. These reforms, at least for a time, ended the life of wealth and leisure that had characterized the Japanese aristocratic family.

Family structure was yet another target of institutional reform. The Meiji government had imposed a particular legal structure for the family that invested tremendous power in the male household head and left the wife and all but the household heir virtually without rights. The father was to be the household's spokesman for all official matters such as property registration, voting, taxes, and so forth. Sons could not marry without their father's consent until the age of thirty (twenty-five for daughters). The wife had no rights to family property even when the family dissolved due to divorce or the husband's death. Rather, property passed on intact to the first son as heir to the family line. In addition, the wife did not even have the right to divorce her husband, whereas the husband could easily obtain a divorce. Among the grounds upon which he could sue were infidelity, failure of the wife to bear a son, and the wife's habit of talking too much.

The patriarchal pattern of relations between authoritarian husband-fathers and obedient wives and children was often used as a model for other role relations—between boss and employees, military officer and his subordinates, professor and his students. Occupation authorities felt the Japanese people moved so easily into hierarchical adult-role relations because that was what they had been familiar with since childhood. Viewing hierarchy as antithetical with democracy, they sought to eradicate the problem at its roots. A new family code was introduced that recognized the essential equality of all family members. Wives were given equal claim to family property and equal right to seek a divorce. The principles of the stem family and legal primogeniture were abandoned, and each new household was required to register as an independent unit. Children could enter into a marriage without parental consent from the age of twenty.

These legal changes set the stage for family change. At the same time, occupation authorities used all educational means at their disposal to familiarize young Japanese with these new ideals. They found that college students and army veterans returning from the battlefields were especially eager listeners. What followed was a shocking departure from the former arranged-marriage pattern. In 1947 it was reported that over 40 percent of all new marriages were formed by individuals who selected their mates on their own (Blood, 1967:8). However, many of these spontaneous marriages ended as quickly as they began, and others proved to be less satisfying than those formed through traditional procedures. Gradually an accommodation developed where young people sought at least the approval and often the intervention of their parents or other go-betweens. Thus, marriages came to be formed partly on love and partly on more traditional considerations such as parental judgments of personal compatibility, physical vitality, family status, and so forth. Although the relative weight of these traditional considerations tends to be somewhat greater in upper-class marriages (of both urban and rural areas), still, in far more cases than before the war, the partners to be married are allowed the final say on whether they wish to go through with it. Today, the parental role is more advisory and less interventionist (Yuzawa, 1973:60).

The rapid economic recovery with the accompanying shift from primary to secondary and tertiary industries has also promoted changes in family structure. Perhaps the most significant consequence of this growth is the rapid expansion of white-collar jobs in large urban corporations and government bureaus, to the point that these constitute one of the most common and certainly the most sought after work opportunity. As shown in Table 3.4, today roughly one of five members of the labor force is a white-collar employee. These jobs are often not as remunerative as other possibilities, nor do they provide the individual worker with as much freedom as might be enjoyed in, for example, a smaller enterprise or his own business. However, because of the lifetime employment system, most of these jobs offer security and the chance for a predictable income over the life cycle.

Especially since World War II white-collar employee working conditions have led to a new *sarariman* (salaried male employee) life-style. Employees typically take up work immediately upon the completion of at least a high school education; many attend a junior college or full university. In their early working years, they endure an ascetic bachelor's life while learning the company routine and putting away some of their income for later home building. Many young women are also in the employee sector, but in contrast with their male coworkers, most of the women employees expect to work for only a few short years after which they will become housewives. In the short employee phase of their life cycle, these women tend to use their income to purchase frills, such as nice clothes and overseas trips.

As the employees reach their middle to late twenties, they select mates and, after obtaining parental approval, become married and settle down in a humble urban dwelling. The great majority, especially among the females, prefer to set up separate households so they can escape the daily interference of in-laws. Surveys indicate that the members of this class, in part because they have been influenced by the new education, do not feel a strong sense of attachment to the traditional family norms including the need to preserve the *ie*'s continuity or to obey their parents. Thus most *sarariman* couples begin marriage in a small apartment, usually considerably distant from the husband's work place. By their late thirties these couples hope to save enough to move into homes of their own, though they increasingly settle for condominiums. However, given the scarce supply of satisfactory urban housing and their residual sense of filial piety, a minority move into the homes of either the wife's or husband's parents. In such cases, the wife usually shares housekeeping chores with the former madam of the house, though other arrangements are also common.

Vogel, in his detailed study of *sarariman* family life, says that once the marriage is consummated, the bride is likely to abandon outside involvements, including work, to concentrate on home duties. If all goes according to schedule, she will bear a child within a year or so. A second will follow soon after, and then child-bearing will cease, for the parents recognize that neither their home size nor family budget can accommodate another.

Almost from the beginning of the formation of this new family unit, a division of labor will emerge with the husband assuming the major responsibility for bringing in the income and the wife the responsibility for child-rearing. The respective priorities are neatly illustrated in Yawahiko Yuzawa's 1962 survey of ordinary Tokyo families. The wife's main concern is that her husband work hard, and the husband looks to his wife as a consoler and child-rearer (see Table 4.1).

According to Sumiya (1967), the wife's main concern in child-rearing is to facilitate the child's success in the schools. In contrast to the more traditional farm and merchant households, which can transfer the family business to their offspring, the new middle-class parents have little property or wealth to offer their children. Without the education that parents view as a passport to a *sarariman* job, their children would have difficulty in later life.

Sarariman families have a strikingly egalitarian role structure. An investigation of domestic decision making among Kobe nuclear families, found that shared decision making was characteristic of 86 percent of the sample. Of the 14 percent of the family units where one of the partners dominated, it was usually the wife who was the stronger (Morioka, 1967:57). In contrast, in a Detroit study by Woolfe, it was found that husbands dominated in 25 percent of the units and wives had the upper hand in 4 percent; shared decision making was less common than for Kobe. As Befu notes in summarizing trends of postwar family change in Japan:

TABLE 4.1
RECIPROCAL EXPECTATIONS OF SPOUSES FROM THEIR MARRIAGE

Husband's Desire of Wife	Strong Desire	Wife's Desire of Husband
	1.3	Hard working
Good conversational companion	1.4	Doesn't hit her
Zealous about children's education, loves children	1.5	Interesting talker
No boyfriends; keeps house neat	1.6	Loves children; understands home situation
Can manage family budget; considerate	1.7	Planner; zealous about children's education; does not gamble
Values in-laws; understands his work; looks nice	1.8	No girl friend; lets wife manage budget
Planner; looks after husband	1.9	Values family; allows wife to attend outside meetings
Understands the importance of his socializing Not too pushy; similar tastes in food	2.0-2.9	Social consciousness; easy to get along with; similar hobbies; similar tastes in food
Can bring in money	3.0+	Does not overdrink
	Weak Desire	

SOURCE: Adapted from Yawahiko Yuzawa, *Kazoku Mondai* (Problems of the Family), p. 81.

NOTE: Spouses were asked to indicate their relative valuation of a long list of traits using a four-point scale from very important (1) to not so important (4).

Criteria of differentrial status, such as age, generation, and sex, though by no means completely gone, are nevertheless far less important than before. As one expression of this, in many urban middle class families, the traditional kinship terms for father and mother, which connote respect and deference, are now replaced by the English loan words "papa" and "mama" (1971:55).

Some social scientists maintain that the family structure in which a child is reared serves as an important teacher for subsequent role learning; if so, it can be inferred that the egalitarian family structure provides children with important lessons in the egalitarian sentiment even prior to the stage when they enter school.

Thus far the *sarariman* family type has been linked with the particular occupational context of employment in modern organizations. However, a number of social forces have led to extensive imitation of the *sarariman* type by other occupational groups. This trend is especially notable in the case of those blue-collar workers who are fortunate enough to acquire jobs in large enterprises. These workers receive almost as much income as their white-collar co-workers (see Table 3.1), at least in the early stage of their working careers. As often as not, they share the same aspirations for their children's educational and occupational futures.

Even in groups where familial work-roles are not so obviously congenial, the *sarariman* type casts its shadow. As Vogel notes, "The way of life of the salary man dominates the mass media, the popular stories, the 'how to' books. The advertising and the standard package for the consumer are probably geared more to the level of the salary man than to any other group. The educational system is dominated by the spirit of the salary man" (1963:267).

Also the changing urban ecology has played a role. Small shopkeepers and industrialists once constituted a distinct class living in segregated areas of the city, and apart from their business activities associated largely with others of their class. One of the fascinating aspects of postwar Japanese growth has been the numerical persistence of their small and seemingly precarious enterprises, whereas in other advanced societies the independent businessman has rapidly declined toward extinction. However, the survival of small businesses in Japan has been accompanied by changes in their pattern of location. Except in the downtown districts, one no longer finds these enterprises and the homes of their family members clustered in the same area. Rather, most small shops are strewn throughout the metropolis where they can be accessible to a local clientele. The dispersion of these enterprises necessarily weakens the traditional community ties between small businessmen and forces the family members from the old middle-class units to come into extensive personal contact with those from other social backgrounds. Especially for the wives and children of small entrepreneurs, the *sarariman* family style is attractive—it offers them greater independence and more free time. Often today when young women discuss marriage to small-scale entrepreneurs, they seek guarantees against being pressed into entrepreneurial duties; the presence of in-laws under the same family roof might even become an issue. In the more stringent days of the past, small entrepreneurs would have experienced difficulty if they made such concessions to their wives, but these days many do well enough to hire part-time help; hence, they are more likely to accept the demands for independence they hear from family members. Indeed, growing numbers of families with small enterprises have succumbed to the temptations of the *sarariman* family style.[3] Several of the recent studies of urban family structure report surprisingly little that remains distinct about the family structure and goals of entrepreneurial families (Yuzawa, 1973:34 ff.). The only area where these studies consistently report a major difference is with respect to child-rearing goals: entrepreneurial families appear less concerned with the educational success of their children, presumably because they hope the children will succeed them in the family enterprise. At the same time, the entrepreneurial families tend to be generous in expenditures for their children's education.

Rural farm families have been more insulated from the influence of the new urban family ideals. As noted above, the samurai family ideal gained the widest acceptance in rural agricultural areas, and through World War II many rural families were able to conform with this ideal: family heads assumed a prominent role in the labor of the family agricultural enterprise and exercised extensive authority over other family members. First sons were raised to succeed their fathers, and the remaining children were encouraged either to consider setting up a branch agricultural enterprise or to prepare for an alternate career. Extended families were not uncommon, and much respect was paid to older family members and ancestors. However, with the postwar reforms and economic development, this traditional family form became less common.

The initial shock to rural society came from the Occupation land reforms, which equalized the amount of tillable soil that individual families could possess. Although prior to the reforms the inequality in land holdings was, by comparative standards, not especially great, it was nevertheless true that those families with the largest households were most likely to conform with the traditional family ideal. The large scale of their farm enterprises provided them with sufficient income to make it worthwhile for all family members to concentrate on agricultural work. Families with smaller holdings

---

[3] In Kyoto, where this research was conducted, although there are large clusters of small shops in the downtown areas, most of the shopowners now have homes in the suburbs. One downtown primary school that once had over six hundred pupils now has less than forty.

tended to diversify into other activities—food processing, small supply shops, and so on. Tenant households were notably unstable with members frequently abandoning agricultural labor for some other pursuit. To the extent members of these households combined other activities with agriculture, they found it difficult to maintain the traditional family ideal; inevitably, power in the family became more equally shared.

The land reforms and the economic growth in the urban economic sector exacerbated this tendency toward part-time farming. For an increasing proportion of rural households, farming failed to produce sufficient income to maintain an acceptable standard of living. Thus many household heads began to divide their energies between agriculture and some form of seasonal labor, such as construction, or to take up work in a nearby factory on at least a part-time basis. In many instances, the rural family head abandoned agricultural labor altogether, leaving the farming to elderly parents and wives. As in the past, this diversification of labor commitment compromised the traditional family ideal. In the absence of a strong family head for extended periods of time, the authority of the wife and her children increased.

Wives, especially, are not enthralled with the prospect of becoming full-time farmers while their husbands work in other pursuits. In many instances, they have urged their husbands to abandon the family farm. In recent years, young men who look ahead to taking over the family farm discover that it is difficult to find wives. Few of the girls in their communities are prepared to marry a farmer; rather, they cherish dreams of an easier life as the wife of a *sarariman*. These conditions have led for the first time in Japan's modern history to a perceptible decline in the number of rural households. As parents die, more and more of their children are giving up the family farm to take up urban employment—and in all probability to adopt an urban family style.

A somewhat different pattern of rural adaptation, discussed by Vogel, is the conversion of the traditional village economy composed of separate enterprises into a cooperative. Through pooling land and resources, farming can become more rational and productive. In these cases, individual cooperative members become employees and receive a salary just like urban company men; their bonus becomes their cut of the cooperative's annual profit. Because of improved productivity under this arrangement, there is a lessened need to press wives into work. Presumably, these cooperative economies enable the development of a family life-style in the countryside quite similar to the modal type found in the cities.

Thus far, this discussion of postwar trends in family structure has focused on the convergence toward a nuclear conjugal family where partners agree on a division of labor and where role relations are relatively egalitarian. This does not mean that all families can be characterized in this way, but clearly, the differences between classes are less marked than before the war. At the same time, it is likely that there is greater intraclass variation today. Contributing to this intraclass variation are a number of factors: the increased incidence of intergeneration mobility for males, the increased incidence of class heteronomous marriages, and the growing tendency for couples themselves to negotiate the type of marriage and family structure they personally prefer. Also as noted, many young entrepreneurial and farm families have evolved structures that are, from the point of view of their class position, deviant.

These trends of class convergence and intraclass diversity have important implications. First, they suggest that standard indicators of class background will be less useful predictors of individual development today than in the past, if for no other reason than that these indicators are less related to the actual bases of variation in family structure. Second, in view of the convergence towards a common type, it is meaningful to discuss general patterns of child-rearing rather than patterns characteristic of each respective class.

BASIC CHILD-REARING PATTERNS

Japanese families have always accorded considerable importance to the task of child-rearing. The traditional families discussed earlier achieved continuity in child-rearing practices through the frequent presence of grandparents in the homes where young people were raising children. Along with relaying conventional child-rearing practices to the young parents, the grandparents played an important direct role: where parents were too severe on young children, the grandparents would add a soft touch, perhaps providing a hurt child with some candy or telling an amusing story to relieve the strain. Moreover, in earlier days, child-rearing goals were relatively comprehensible—although the specific content varied by class, the general goal was the cultivation of virtue and diligence. Hereditary patterns of succession guaranteed social placement for offspring. However, with the advent of modernization and the trend toward reliance on the school system for social selection, ambitious and well-placed families who wished their children to maintain the family's status found it increasingly necessary to devote special attention to their children's academic achievements. This preoccupation with academic achievement filtered down to the middle class as modernization proceeded, but it is only since World War II that the majority of families has developed much concern about it. The growing proportion of the population concerned with academic achievement has created the arduous situation for young people and their parents known as "examination hell."

At the same time, modern families are confronting a context of rapid social change where traditional child-rearing formulas have less relevance; more and more often, they live in dwellings of their own, where their grandparents are not available for consultation. Postwar families often appear confused by this new situation and uncertain of how to bring up their children. Parents turn to a great variety of sources for advice—professional advice, books and magazines on child-rearing, television programs, and the suggestions of friends and relatives. The result is that some mothers breast-feed, whereas others rely on bottles; some use store-bought foods, others prepare their own; some wean early, others late. Although most parents muddle through, the typical couple lacks a clear set of principles for child-rearing. Finally, there are no clear class differences in child-rearing practices. Just as in the case of family structure, personal preference appears to be the major cause of the variation in child-rearing practices that researchers have observed.

Although personal preference does result in considerable variation in actual child-rearing practices, Befu suggests it is possible to discern several salient "patterns of child-rearing which hold generally for most Japanese" (1971:151), and that contrast with patterns observed elsewhere as in the United States. In particular, he identifies the following:

A quiet soothing infancy. In comparison with American mothers, Japanese mothers tend to talk less to their babies and more generally to avoid actions and demonstrations of affection that might result in stimulation. Rather than swing or rapidly move their babies, the Japanese mothers prefer to rock them quietly. On the other hand, Japanese mothers tend to spend more time in close physical proximity so as to provide their babies with a sense of emotional security. In contrast, American babies are left alone much more. As early as three to four months after birth, perceptible differences can be found in the babies. American babies tend to be more active and vocally expressive.

Avoiding separation. Befu suggests that the continuous physical presence of the Japanese mother lays the groundwork for the baby's strong emotional dependence on the mother. In fact, in the early months the mother will choose to sleep in the same room as the baby even if this separates her from the husband.[4] As the baby matures, the mother tries to foster this close relation through minimizing the periods when she is separated from her baby. Thus, the mother rarely leaves home without her baby, and she would not consider going out for an evening and leaving the child to a baby-sitter.

Reliance on demand-feeding. Further contributing to the dependent relation is the tendency of Japanese mothers to feed their babies when the baby begins to cry and demand food, rather than to stick to some kind of predetermined schedule. In Befu's view, scheduling and refusing to respond except at the appointed hour helps to teach babies that they are separate and independent from their mothers. In contrast, on-demand feeding "tends to create the opposite effect, not only eliminating opportunities for developing emotional independence, but creating further opportunities for reinforcing emotional dependence on the mother."

Minimizing punishment. Consistent with their responsiveness to the baby's feeding demands, Japanese mothers generally show much greater reluctance to rebuke babies regardless of their behavior. Befu (1971:156-157) cites several studies that report the "Japanese child-rearing pattern of not going head-on against a child, not directly saying 'no,' but instead inducing the child to behave properly." This inducement normally consists of reasoning, and if that does not work, of begging or pleading; as a last resort, the mother might offer the child some sweets. In contrast, Befu suggests that the American mother is more likely to stand firm with her child and to resort to threats and spankings when the child fails to comply.

In another context, Fukutake (1974:43) suggests that the soft approach of the Japanese parent is a relatively new development. He says that prewar parents and especially the father tended to be much more authoritarian, relying on the grandparents to develop a softer,

---

[4] One study (Caudill and Plath, 1966) of family sleeping arrangements finds no differences by class in Japan despite significant class differences in bedroom to family member ratios.

more overtly affectionate and cajoling relation with child. With the decline of the extended family, Fukutake says that fathers and mothers have abandoned their traditional role in place of a more affectionate approach. Although Fukutake regrets this trend, as he feels it is the source of certain postwar problems in child-rearing, he nevertheless would agree with Befu (1971:155) that "Japanese parents, especially the mother, tend to be much less authoritarian vis-à-vis children than American parents."

The tolerance of Japanese parents is especially notable with respect to at-home behavior. Although a mother might ask her child to go to bed, rarely are fixed bedtimes enforced—at least until the child begins school. Mothers are concerned about the nutritional intake of their children, but do not fuss too much if vegetables and meat are skipped or if the child eats too many sweets. At home, in the early years, the main concern is to foster a cooperative atmosphere. However, once the family moves into a public setting, parents become highly conscious of their child's deportment and frequently exhort the child to avoid disturbing others or hurting their feelings. In the subways, shoes are taken off so as not to dirty the seats. When with grandparents or relatives, children are expected to show their best behavior, at least at first. And when with friends, the stress is on getting along and sharing toys without fights. In these extrafamilial settings, parents are more explicit about the type of behavior they expect from their children. The greater strictness in public settings does not stem from parental concern to convey moral lessons, for in this area they lack confidence. Rather, their strictness is related to a concern for others and for avoiding embarrassment to the family. Also, as Befu suggests, persuasion rather than punishment is the typical means of control.

SOME POSSIBLE IMPLICATIONS OF THESE MODAL CHILD-REARING PRACTICES

In that the above tendencies appear to be typical of all social groups, there follow certain implications for personality development. But two caveats must be stressed. First, as already pointed out, there is enough variation in all of these practices to dispose young Japanese along a great variety of routes of personality development. Second, although there are different opinions on this issue, experiences that occur in the family are no more likely to determine personality than those that occur in other settings. These family experiences will

have personality consequences only to the extent they are reinforced by subsequent experience. Thus, a national character approach that assumes these child-rearing practices have a determinant effect on the "Japanese mind" would be unsound.

Given these qualifications, the tendencies that the modal practices
encourage can be examined. One implication Befu draws from
these practices, especially the stress on dependency training, is that
Japanese children are more likely to associate positive affect with
their parents, especially their mother, than are American children.
In the strong maternal attachment, we can see the prototype of the
Japanese tendency to feel strong positive affect toward the small intimate group of friends, coworkers, neighbors, and so forth.
American child-rearing is not likely to foster as positive an affect in
children to their family, or to lay the emotional groundwork for
strong positive orientations to the small groups in which the individual will find himself. The relatively strong affect of the Japanese
child to his family group makes the process of entering new groups
more difficult. For example, when a Japanese child visits the home
of his friend, his mother often goes with him. And for the first days
of kindergarten, the mother is expected to accompany her child for
the full morning; the routine continues until the child ceases burst-
ing into tears the moment his mother disappears from sight. However, once the transfer of affect is achieved, the Japanese child is
likely to develop a strong attachment to the new group—be it
playmates, schoolmates, or whatever. He comes to depend on his
new group for security and affection just as he once did on the family.[5]

Moreover, it can be surmised that contemporary Japanese children, because they experience a relatively egalitarian family experience, are prone to expect egalitarian relations in other social situations. Important in this proposition is the implication that the
dispositions of today's children are different. In the past, family relations in Japan tended to be much more authoritarian. This provided for some analysts an explanation for the apparent tendency of
the Japanese people to accept authority. Whereas today few would
accept this "family writ large" argument,[6] it is easy to appreciate

[5] The dependence theme is most fully developed in Takeo Doi (1973). Also see
Yoshiaki Yamamura (1971). For a critical analysis, see Hiroshi Wagatsuma (1977).

[6] Massey's (1976:158) finding that youths who report they are raised in families
with strong fathers are more rebellious is the opposite of what would be predicted
by the "family writ large" hypothesis.

how a more egalitarian family atmosphere might lead young children to expect more egalitarian relations in other contexts. Thus in interaction with friends, each child would expect to have an equal chance to talk or to play with toys—and would be upset when a playmate attempted to dominate. Similarly, in kindergarten or school they would prefer a setting that allowed considerable participation over one where they might be ignored, excluded, or merely talked down to.

This summary of patterns has also noted how Japanese mothers tend to spend less time talking to their children than do American mothers. Underlying the Japanese parent's, especially the mother's, relative lack of verbal exchanges may be a sense of inadequacy and doubt concerning what should be said. In the area of moral education, as Fukutake (1974:44) observes, Japanese parents are hesitant to instruct their children. Rather than firmly tell their children what is right or wrong, parents will reason, cajole, bribe, and if these strategies fail, submit to their children's wishes. Parents are reluctant to shape their children's morality, for they are uncertain what orientations will be appropriate later on. Also, to oppose the child is to threaten the harmony of the parent-child relationship. Figuratively speaking, parents leave a moral blank check for other institutions to fill out.[7]

From Kindergarten to Adolescence

As indicated in the next chapter, the primary school is a critical experience for most Japanese children. Whereas in their formative years, they are home centered, once children enter the primary school they become school centered. Not only do children begin to spend the majority of their waking hours at school, but they also begin to view the school and educational achievement as one of their major purposes and sources of satisfaction. Teachers come to compete with parents as objects of admiration. Also, children begin to form friendships with classmates who live outside their immediate neighborhoods.

The tendency to become school centered has always been characteristic of the minority of school children who were destined for further schooling beyond the primary level. But today all youth

---

[7] Caudill and Weinstein (1969) report that Japanese mothers spend less time talking to their children than do American mothers. Similarly, for a sample of Aichi first graders, Honna (1975:207) reports the lack of association between social class and the way mothers communicate with their children.

expect to go on to complete at least middle school, and most expect to go beyond that. Under these new conditions, the primary school experience becomes meaningful for the entire cohort. The next four chapters will consider what actually goes on in Japanese schools and what consequences this has for the personalities of young people. There, the way the school experience gradually draws young people away from their families will also be examined. With every year in the child's life, this tendency becomes more profound so that by the middle school years the family's influence is sharply reduced.

Since World War II, stimulated by such studies as Riesman's *Lonely Crowd* and Whyte's *Street Corner Society*, American sociologists have become more conscious of peer contacts and their influence on youth's attitudes. Indeed, some have gone so far as to declare the emergence of a new stage, the "youth" stage, in the American life cycle, where physically and intellectually mature young people search for their identity and their niche in the adult work system. Implicit in this conception is the notion that much that children learn in their family and early school years is subjected to a reevaluation. Insofar as there is such a thing as the emergence of an independent youth stage, it is necessary to modify the traditional family imprint perspectives on socialization.

Studies of Japanese society have been slow to recognize the importance of the youth stage, and have rather stressed the centrality in adolescent life of the family circle. For example, Stoetzel (1955:169) reports that "both youth and girls give family relationships first place more often than any other kind of activity." Similarly, according to Vogel (1963:114 ff.), adolescents spend more time with their families than with their peers, most do not have particular peers whom they consider close friends. Possibly the family emphasis was justified in earlier periods, at least for certain social classes. At the same time, in considering these earlier periods, one would be remiss to ignore the important role that youth groups played in many village societies—helping young people select their mates or facilitating the military's mobilization for war.

Whatever the past situation, it is clear that most of today's youths, both in city and country, experience a distinct youth stage parallel to that in Western societies. As young people move into middle school, they are exposed to an extensive array of largely school-based extracurricular activities. In our own study of several Kyoto middle schools, it was found that 80 percent of all first- and second-year middle schoolers participated in these activities, and over half participated on a daily basis. The clubs organized along remarkably democratic lines and clearly reinforced many of the norms for group interaction, instilled during the primary school experience. They encouraged participation, expressiveness, and cooperation, and deemphasized competition. Most clubs included members of both sexes on a more or less equal basis. In the athletic clubs such as tennis, a single girl would never be pitted against a boy, but mixed doubles were not uncommon. Students viewed these activities as the most rewarding part of their school experience, and indeed of their lives. Thus they often showed up on Saturdays and Sundays for extra sessions and they selected many of their friends from among fellow clubmates.

Adolescent Independence in the High Schools

Grusen in a recent study of a cross section of Osaka high school students finds that they have a somewhat lower level of participation in school club activities than that reported above for middle schoolers; this is understandable, for high school students are much closer to the day when they take college entrance exams and, being tied to the grind of exam preparation studies, have less time for play. Even so, she reports that the high school students find other occasions for association—homeroom, movies or other cultural events, *juku*, and so forth. These young people clearly spend a much greater proportion of their extra-study time with friends than with family members. Indeed, one study reports that high schoolers spend an average of only 2.4 minutes a day talking with their mothers (Sorifu, 1969). High schoolers prefer to discuss their future plans and their personal problems with close friends rather than with parents or siblings. In fact, 81.6 percent report that they would confide things to close friends that they would not normally tell their parents (Grusen, 1971:132).

Young people report serious difficulties in communicating with their parents—and sometimes outright conflict. In instances where there are differences, a majority of youths feel they have the right to stick to their guns. In response to one question, only 20 percent stated they felt a duty to agree with their parents. Grusen notes that youths complain of their parents' lack of knowledge and "common sense": "There is no use discussing many issues with my parents because they are not equipped to discuss intelligently with me." "My parents are incapable of giving me any sensible advice because

they lack the education which I have." "I am embarrassed to ask
my parents serious questions because they have no understanding
of what is going on in the world" (1971:26).

With this low opinion of their parents' wisdom, it is not surprising to find that youths do a lot of thinking on their own and in consultation with friends. Indeed, their independent thinking extends
to making decisions on some of the most crucial developments of
their lives—including selecting their college majors and occupations. Nine of ten who are planning to go to college say they have
chosen their own major "based on my interest." Most deny direct
parental influence, pointing out only that they have tried to keep
within the bounds of what their families would consider respectable. Similarly, over three fourths say they will make their own decision about what kind of work to pursue (Grusen, 1971:156). These
findings on adolescent self-reliance have been corroborated by
other recent studies, most notably, a series of white papers on
youth prepared by the prime minister's office. The 1969 edition
(Sorifu, 1970) summarized a national survey indicating that "a
majority of adolescents either solve problems by themselves or seek
advice from friends and very few of them seek assistance from parents." Another survey (Sorifu, 1970) emphasized the important role
of the media in providing young people with the information to
make decisions.

Regrettably, one question bypassed in both the Grusen and the
prime minister's office's studies was the differential role of class in
shaping youth-parent relations. One might expect that upper- and
middle-class parents have a greater potential for communicating
with their children thanks to their superior education. On the other
hand, the elitist values of these parents and their tendency to persuade their children to compete in school might tend to frustrate
parent-child interaction.

Rebellion against Parents

Clearly, young people in Japan decrease their reliance on parental
advice and guidance as they proceed into adolescence. Yet at the
same time, youths still turn to the home as a place for support and
emotional fortification. The tendency among young people toward
increasing self-reliance generates parental concern and anxiety, but
surprisingly little conflict. As noted above, contemporary Japanese
parents exhibit considerable tolerance toward their children. Parents seem to feel that being young in today's world is difficult, an

experience they are unable to fully understand; thus, their children are looked to for suggestions and leadership. Also, for many mothers their children are their central life interests. To damage relations with their children is to undermine a major source of their personal gratification.

The traditional family was able to command the allegiance of children by presenting the prospect of an eventual transfer of family property and connections; as young people could not envision superior opportunities, this was enough to induce attitudes of respect and appreciation. In the modern meritocratic society, however, the typical urban family has little it can offer and the occupational alternatives for youths to choose from are much more diverse and less related to parental sponsorship. The practical ties that bind are weaker, and the likelihood of provoking youthful rebellion is greater.

Furthermore, in a small nuclear family without grandparents or numerous children, the emotional cost of alienating a child is much greater. Thus, today's parents often adopt a position that appears to minimize the possibilities for conflict. They impose a minimum of rules on their children and are lax even in the enforcement of these. For example, as Grusen's (1971:112) study reveals, the only rule imposed by a majority of parents concerned the time adolescents should come home. But even here, young men reported their parents rarely commented when they failed to return by the designated time. Krauss's (1974) report on student radicals shows they rarely felt that their parents attempted to change their political convictions. Mothers, particularly, according to this study avoided interjecting moral and political issues into the relation, preferring merely to maintain a close emotional tie. Even when the radicals took up activities that their parents strongly opposed, the parents usually remained loyal. One father continued sending his son a monthly stipend for school expenses even though he knew the son had ignored his wishes and dropped out for full-time political activity.

Some Western psychologists have argued that rebellion against parents is a crucial stage in the maturation of young people; without the interjection of their parents, it is difficult for young people to take up a serious committed role in the adult world. From this point of view, the minimizing of parent-child conflict poses a special problem for Japan, and leads to a unique solution. Because the Japanese family feels it cannot afford the cost of internal conflict, it displaces the latent hostility outward toward other institutions affecting the lives of youths. Political institutions become one of the foci of pent-up youthful libido. But the main symbol is the exam system. This system is viewed with complex emotions of awe and resentment, of fear and humor. It appears as a stern orderer of the lives of young people in the same way that fathers or mothers appear to many American youths. Indeed, according to this interpretation (Kiefer, 1970), much of the intense emotion surrounding Japan's examination system derives from that system's symbolic role in fostering the break between youth and adulthood—that the exams lead to success for some and failure for others is somewhat incidental. This interpretation suggests important functions for the examination system in the Japanese scheme of growing up that would be displaced to the extent that social reformers succeeded in ameliorating the evils of the exam system. Among other consequences, the harmony of the modern family might be threatened.

CONCLUSION

This chapter has reviewed major changes in the Japanese family that bear on the larger argument. Whereas there once were several class-related family types, class links have gradually weakened so that today the vast majority of families approximate the conjugal nuclear type. The structure of this family is much less hierarchical than was the idealized traditional family. Some would argue that this shift in family structure is an important causal element in the broader postwar trend toward egalitarian socialization.

Although contemporary families practice a great diversity of child-rearing practices, again there seems to be little relation between class position and the particular practices of a given family. The mother's education is the only class variable that helps to explain observed variations, but even this seems a weak predictor relative to personal taste. It is possible to make several generalizations about modal patterns that bear on the overall argument:

1. The modern family allows remarkably egalitarian patterns of interaction between family members.

2. Child-rearing practices are oriented to establishing close emotional bonds between family members, but they seem to be extremely permissive with respect to actual behavior. By and large, the family looks to outside institutions for guidance concerning

normative standards and for the actual inculcation of these standards in the children.

3. Finally parents encourage their children to develop a positive attitude toward school.

These practices facilitate a relatively smooth transition from home to school for young people. Furthermore, they serve to motivate children to accept what is taught at school with an open mind, thereby enhancing the school's potential effect. As will be seen, young people quickly become involved in school and in their own adolescent society—so much so that by the time they become teenagers, this becomes their major source for guidance and support. The family recedes into the background as a direct influence on their lives. Nevertheless, most adolescents continue to maintain warm emotional ties to their families, drawing emotional support as they pass through the stressful experience of preparing for adulthood.

Chapter Five

EGALITARIAN EDUCATION

Japan has always believed that schools should develop "whole people" rather than some narrow aspect of individual potential, and since the Meiji restoration, Japanese primary schools have been assigned the most important role in this process, that of transmitting a common culture and of motivating youth for their subsequent years in the school system.[1]

Over the course of Japanese history, the primary school's interpretation of the common culture has varied. In the early stages of modernization, much stress was placed on the hierarchical aspect of social relations. During the years leading up to World War II, nationalistic themes were promoted. And since World War II, humanistic and egalitarian themes have been stressed. In each of these periods, the school's emphasis was actually somewhat at variance with the real trends of the adult society. Up to World War II, the leadership of the nationalistic government was responsible for this deviation. Since World War II, the government's influence has been reduced in certain areas, whereas that of the teachers, led by their ideological union, has substantially increased. This chapter will be concerned with the postwar primary school, and the manner in which it conveys the common culture.

In the discussion of the old system it was found that the elementary school received all the nation's youth and exposed them to a common curriculum, but it did not give them an equal education. For example, some schools, by virtue of their location in backward prefectures or isolated areas, were poorly equipped and staffed. Moreover, within given schools teachers tended to favor certain children, especially bright students and those from higher status families.

But over the postwar period this situation has changed. Today's facilities and treatments appear remarkably equal. There are several reasons for the change: (1) The Occupation reforms and the new

[1] I wish to express my appreciation at the beginning of this chapter to the many teachers and students in Kyoto, Kagawa-ken, and elsewhere who cooperated to make the field work reported here such a memorable and communicable experience.

laws institutionalized egalitarian educational values. (2) Public policy has promoted equality of facilities.[2] (3) Selfish parents have always demanded that schools devote special attention to their child. With the rise of competition on exams most parents have become selfish. Teachers have found that the easiest solution is simply to treat all children equally. (4) The extension of compulsory education through the ninth grade has enabled teachers to practice equal education at least through the primary school. As students have a chance to accelerate later, most primary school teachers do not feel upset that their equal education holds the bright students back. They feel little strain in devoting more than equal attention to the slow students, who need it most. (5) Teachers draw support in their efforts to practice egalitarian education from the Japan Teachers' Union. The union is committed to a socialist conception of a more equal society, upholding a peaceful world order. Teachers are constantly reminded of these themes in union newsletters and meetings. Especially in recent years, this union has shown much interest in the actual process of education. The union has chosen as its special educational goal helping every child not only to perform (*dekiru*) but also to understand (*wakaru*) the tasks that are presented in the curriculum (Makieda, 1975; Umene, 1972). The union's educational ideal is not unlike that emphasized in the ideas of mastery learning, as we will illustrate in Chapter Six.

Schools teach many lessons. Some of the school's and teacher's lessons are intentional, but many are not. Some are found in the formal curriculum, some in what has come to be known as the hidden or latent curriculum—lessons that are learned through the

---

[2] As background for this chapter, it should be noted that the Japanese people trust their public primary schools. Over 99 percent of all Japanese children of primary school age who are physically and mentally able attend a public school; this compares with 87 percent in the United States.

Not only do Japanese children go to public elementary schools, but, with few exceptions, they go to nearby schools, where, thanks to the socioeconomic heterogeneity of Japanese neighborhoods, they study and play with children of diverse social backgrounds. As Sumiya observes, "During the unprecedented postwar housing shortage, people from both classes were forced to live side by side in similar areas, thus breaking the prewar pattern of segregation and erasing significant differences in consumption patterns" (1967:121). Soon after the Meiji restoration the tradition of separate schools for samurai and commoners was abandoned. Since that time, the resistance to separate schools for different groups has strengthened—at least at the primary level. Today, even the handicapped (except for extreme cases) attend schools alongside normal children, and insofar as possible, are expected to join in the same activities.

structure of schools, the rhythms students are put through, the manner in which they are rewarded, the example teachers set.

Those who are involved in schools are unlikely to be able to provide an especially revealing account of these lessons—in part, because they are so busy with the formal curriculum. Nor can one find any accounts of these lessons in the literature. In that there is such a scarcity of information on what schools teach, I decided to go to school myself. In late 1975, for a few weeks I visited schools in the Chicago area to freshen my childhood memories of school life, and then I went to Kyoto, Japan, where I spent the better part of a year visiting schools and talking to people about them.

Needless to say, the expression of my desire to visit schools caused considerable confusion. At first I simply visited a couple of schools with a statement in Japanese about my interest in education and social change and my desire to visit several schools to conduct intensive fieldwork.

While principals could recognize the value of what I planned to do, they were concerned with the disturbance it might create in the classrooms. Teachers were wary for the same reasons, and some were suspicious of my ideological position. There were several refusals, and as it worked out, personal connections to a school proved to be the key to entry. The first school I was allowed to visit and observe was one that several of my Japanese relatives attended. One of my nieces was a student in the first class I observed. Roughly half the teachers in this school agreed to let me watch their classes; the teachers, taking into account my desire to see a representative spectrum of courses, decided on my schedule. Usually I spent six to eight days over a period of three weeks in a single classroom; after the observation period, I chatted with the teachers for from one to three hours. Following the initial observation period, several teachers invited me to come back for checkups, and I gratefully accepted.

Gradually, I overcame the fears of the members of this school, and they spoke about their "new student" to friends. Within three months, I was welcomed to several schools in the local area and received many chances to check out the generality of my initial observations. Later I traveled to other prefectures for short periods of observation.

These visits to various settings helped me to appreciate the diversity in Japanese education—and in Chapters Three and Eight, I discuss some aspects of the diversity in greater detail. One key aspect is the extent to which the teachers of a school are unionized. Where they are, the egalitarian educational themes are paramount; in Kyoto unionization is virtually universal, so my concentration of fieldwork there leads to a certain degree of bias. However, my visits to other areas of Japan left me with the strong impression that the regional deviations are not significant until the middle school, whereas there is a common pattern at the primary school level.[3] The following is my effort to summarize that pattern based on my experience at the first school. Where its practices proved exceptional, I have adjusted it. Occasionally, comparisons are made with "American schools" by which is meant a small group of urban schools I observed in Chicago prior to my departure or those that were the subject of specific studies that I reference. Given the decentralized patterns of control and finance in the United States, I am much less willing to attempt generalizations about the American school than I am about a modal Japanese school.

PRIMARY SCHOOL EDUCATION

The Opening Ceremony of the Primary School

In traditional Japan, growing up was signified by such events as boys or girls day or youths day. However, with the increasing importance of the school system, a child's progress through life has come to be marked by his status in the school system. School is a common experience for Japanese youth, even more so than for Americans. Textbooks, facilities, and school events are remarkably uniform throughout Japan. Also, in contrast with the United States, one can accurately determine a youth's age from his school year. Entering first grade, primary students are all six years old as of April first of the year when they begin school. The Japanese school does not fail to accelerate the grade level of any of its students so six years later, when these students begin middle school,

---

[3] The assumption here that the differences at the primary school level are not that great across areas is reinforced not only by investigations in other places but also by communication with Thomas Rohlen, who worked in Kobe, and Professor Hashiya, who worked in rural areas of Nara prefecture. It is further corroborated by the three volume account of the observations of a team of Asahi Shinbun reporters who made frequent visits to schools largely in the Tokyo area; their account is reported in *Ima Gakko de.*

they will be twelve years old, and then fifteen when they begin high school.[4]

Stages in school (and stages in growth) are celebrated by elaborate ceremonies, at least by American standards. On the first official day of school, each new first grader comes to school dressed in his best clothes along with his mother or father. While the parents go to the assembly hall, the children line up in their new classrooms, and at the call they solemnly march in to take seats before their parents. The principal introduces the students' teachers and delivers a short speech on the ideals of the school.

At the school I attended the principal's speech was brief but moving; he told the children that they now would become members of a larger family, where they would have an opportunity to make many new friends. They would need to cooperate as this new family was much larger than that at their home. If they were confused or did not understand things, they should feel free to ask anyone in the school for help because all belonged to the family. However, before they sought help they should always try to solve the problem by themselves. The principal told the story of Thomas Edison, the famous inventor, who said that achievement was 99 percent perspiration and 1 percent inspiration. He also mentioned the comment of Japan's Nobel Prize winner, Yukawa Hideki, that success in any endeavor comes through continuous repetitive practice until one masters every detail. So, the principal asked his new charges to work hard to understand what they were exposed to in the school and to seek help only after they had exhausted all other possibilities. Finally, he told them to be careful of the traffic when coming to school.

Turning to the parents, the principal asked that they trust the school and the teachers, for these people were professionals with deep experience. School, he stressed, aimed at developing not only the minds but also the spirit and the body. He said that parents were too worried about the academic achievement of their children. They should not feel that their child's future was going to be de-

[4] There are few repeaters and an even smaller number of dropouts in the Japanese system, as well as an unknown percentage called *ochi-kubori*, who are promoted with their age-mates even though they have not mastered the material of the previous grade-level. This latter group is discussed at the end of this chapter. As for dropouts, it is enough to observe that one is unlikely to find twenty-four-year-old primary school students, as are said to be not uncommon in the United States, according to Office of Education surveys.

termined by what happened in a single day or even a year of school. He entreated the parents to relax and help their children enjoy this new stage in life. To complete the ceremony a group of second graders stood before the newcomers to chant a hearty welcome and to extend the hand of friendship.

Following the assembly, each child went to his new classroom, and as the parents stood around the back, the teacher explained the procedures he intended to follow. As did the principal, he tried to reassure the parents. He told them that he loved children, especially first and second graders, and that he already had several years of teaching experience (only rarely is a new teacher assigned the diffi-cult task of handling first graders). He explained his concern to de-velop not only the minds of these children but also their hearts and bodies. He emphasized that the classroom is different from the home, and that some might experience problems. But he entreated the parents to be tolerant and to trust in him. He urged parents to come to him for discussion of their child's adjustment, but always in these discussions to keep in mind that their child was not the only member of the class. Rather each parent's child was one among forty. Then the teacher turned to the students and called out their names, and for the first time each student stood up to say pre-sent. Some forms announcing school procedures were handed out, which the children were asked to take home to their parents. And the first day of school came to an end.

Establishing Order

One of the first problems the Japanese school attacks is that of creat-ing order in the classrooms. In certain obvious respects, this prob-lem is more pressing in Japan than in the United States. The typical Japanese primary school has between forty and forty-five students per teacher in every class at every grade level; moreover, there are no extra assistant teachers or specialist teachers to assist in over-crowded classes. Without a high level of student compliance, this system would rapidly fall into chaos. In contrast, American class sizes tend to be much smaller, particularly at the first and second grade levels. In addition, the teachers at these grade levels are likely to have assistants. In a sense, the American teacher can substitute attention for order.

Order in the Japanese classroom includes greeting the teacher each morning, standing beside one's desk when speaking, listening to others and the teacher in silence, and cooperating in group activities. Even those teachers who personally adopt an informal style try hard to establish this order, for these "soft" teachers recognize their style is somewhat exceptional, and they feel a responsibility to impress in the children's minds a picture of proper classroom behavior that will last them through their school days.

Because a full day of school can be exhausting for the newcomers, the school schedule is planned to ease them slowly into the routine. For the first several weeks, the students come to school for only three to four periods a day, and return to their homes for lunch. After this initiation period, the days are extended to from four to five periods. Most of the four-period days end with school lunches eaten together in the classroom; on the two five-period days of each week the first graders stay for one more period after lunch—often music or some other favorite, which easily catches their attention.

Within the framework of this relatively undemanding schedule, the teacher works to establish order. One typical strategy is to announce certain basic rules, such as the arrangement of desks, and to keep checking to see whether students comply. Still another is to establish a hectic pace of activity in the classroom composed largely of things that the students want to do—opening texts, reciting, performing exercises, singing songs. Thus, the students are left with little time to become disorderly. A teacher adopting this strategy might spend an unusual amount of time preparing colorful displays to put on the blackboard or might try to teach through gamelike devices, often prepared by the students. Classroom order is also developed by having students cooperate in groups that prepare contributions for the rest of the class.

One of the most impressive strategies to establish order was demonstrated by a veteran teacher who particularly enjoyed the first and second grades. This teacher told the students that they had to use all of their senses when they worked in the classrooms: their fingers, their tongues, their eyes, and their ears. The teacher often pointed to her own eye, ear, tongue, or hands as a way of asking students to turn on one of their senses; especially, she stressed the need for students to open their ears and listen when she pointed to her ears. In turn when it was the student's turn to present, this teacher focused her eyes and ears on him. This teacher was remarkable in her ability to keep her side of the promise; she would seem to lend her total attention to the student presenters and always managed to express some gesture of appreciation, whether through a twinkle in her eyes or a brief comment (although the actions seemed natural they were part of a complex system of rewards she had developed over the years). The students were apparently impressed by the sincerity of their teacher for within only a few weeks a sort of classroom culture had developed where one was really a bad person if he failed to cooperate when the teacher pointed at her forehead. The students became so accustomed to lending their attention when the teacher spoke that by the end of the first year she rarely needed to point to her forehead.

In most Japanese primary schools, the six grades are split into a lower pair (*tegakunen*), a middle pair (*chugakunen*), and an upper pair (*kogakunen*). Insofar as possible, students are kept together in the same homeroom through the full span of each two-year period. Moreover, they usually keep the same teacher. Thus, the woman mentioned above took her class into the second year, and by the end of that period the students were the perfect picture of concentration. Whatever the activity turned to, the students were practically totally involved. The teacher had to devote no more than 10 percent of her time to maintaining order. Benjamin Bloom has commented that this high level of concentration and discipline is a key ingredient in the successes of Japanese education. According to Bloom, if the average Japanese classroom were given a score of 20 percent in terms of time devoted to keeping order, the typical score in an American classroom would be close to 60 percent. Indeed, studies of American classrooms, especially those in the urban centers, indicate that many teachers spend more time ordering than teaching.[5] The Japanese school attacks the problem of order right from the beginning, impressing on students the importance of paying attention to their teacher and their fellow class members. Once this pattern is implanted, periodic reminders, such as the greeting prior to starting each class, are sufficient to remind students of the need to apply themselves. As a result, beyond the second grade a far greater proportion of each school hour is available for the teachers to address their educational program than in the United States.

[5] The figures presented in the text were suggested by Benjamin Bloom in personal conversation. There are a number of studies of American primary school classrooms, and these indicate that control-oriented interaction can range from as low as 10 percent to as high as 75 percent of all teacher interaction in American primary school classrooms. See Dunkin and Biddle (1974:esp. pp. 134-175) for a summary of some of this research; see also Gump (1971). Although it is difficult to make precise cross-national comparisons with respect to this statistic, one could expect the frequency of control interaction to be at least twice as high in the United States.

Preparing to Present Oneself

One of the most difficult tasks of formal education is to get started. By the time children enter the primary school, most have had some experience in an educational institution. For example, in 1974, 75 percent of all Japanese five-year-olds attended a kindergarten or nursery school (Sorifu, 1975). Although much of their preschool education is focused on play activities, a surprising proportion of these children can write the alphabet (the *kana*), read simple passages from story books, and perform other intellectual activities that they will elaborate over the next years. However, although the children may have these skills, they tend to look on them as games, much like their blocks or dolls. They do not appreciate the significance of these skills and certainly are not anxious to demonstrate them before a group of strangers in the classroom.

One of the first goals of the primary school and of the teacher is to get the children to overcome this fear of formal presentations. In the first year of a Japanese primary school, probably no other objective receives as much attention as this. From the first day of school the teacher asks the students to answer when he calls their names. But in this request the teacher really asks for more; he explains that the room is large and he wants all the students to know each other so it would be best if they stood beside their desks to answer and spoke in a loud voice. Later in the term, the teacher insists that students stand up when they speak, regardless of the type of presentation they are asked to make. Most students respond readily to this routine, but a few present problems. Some of the more rebellious refuse to stand or intentionally slouch; the teacher may rebuke these students before the class or make some joke about how weak they are; as many of the slouchers tend to be the class jocks, their self-image straightens their posture. Students who will not stand properly are required to repeat the procedure of standing and responding two or three times until they manage a passable presentation. Another group of students have small voices, or simply are afraid to speak, and as these students tend to be quiet and sensitive, the teacher approaches them very carefully. One teacher proposed to "lend her voice" to a quiet student in an effort to convince the little girl that the other students were interested in what her small voice had to say. In another class, the teacher asked the classmates to clap when a quiet girl finally spoke loud enough for all to hear. In these examples, the teacher leans heavily on the classroom group to draw out the problem students.

In many of the early classroom activities, the teacher tries to obtain full participation. For example, in a reading lesson the teacher might provide the sentence model and then ask eight students of a given row to repeat after her. Then the next model and the next row. In this way, the teacher can get all the students to speak at least once during a forty-five-minute period.

In the early fall, the school has a skit day (*Gakugeikai*), in which each class, from the first grade through the sixth, performs before the visiting parents (attendance is close to 100 percent). Although all the classes devote considerable energy to preparing their performances, the first grade devotes the most. A skit is chosen where all can participate—for example, in one Nativity scene skit the script was split into five two-minute acts with a different set of students playing the lead roles of Mary and Joseph in each act. Of all the grades, the first graders put in the most time practicing—possibly as much as one fourth of each day the last two weeks before the presentation. Also, they spend the most time on costumes. The effort is worthwhile, for their performance tends to be the best, with well-enunciated lines and a smooth rotation throughout the scenes. Within a few short months, most of the first graders have overcome their fear of public presentations.

The Centrality of the School

Although students are eased into the school system, it soon becomes their major activity. This is the case even more in Japan than in the United States. In almost every respect, Japan seems to take an extra step towards enhancing the centrality of the school.

The Japanese school is required to hold classes for at least 240 days each year or roughly 6 days a week for forty weeks. Even though the school year is much longer in Japan, attendance rates are much higher. Parents believe their children should go to school, no matter what. Rarely do parents plan a family trip when school is in session, and the tendency for most fathers to work a six-day week discourages long family weekends at the beach or other diversions. The major excuse for absence from school is sickness, yet many children with severe colds and other maladies refuse to stay home. The face masks and runny noses speak for themselves. At the schools I visited, which averaged in size from four hundred to nine hundred students, from five to ten students would be absent on a given day—about 1 percent. The absentee rate in American primary schools is at least three times as high.

The school year in Japan runs from April to March; rather than a long summer vacation as in the United States, there are several smaller breaks—two weeks between school years, a "golden" week after the first month of school, one and a half months of summer vacation, a week in October, and then two weeks for the New Year's festival. This series of short breaks provides children with relief, but never gives them a long enough span of time to completely forget their status as students. Even during the summer break, students may have assignments, and some go on excursions planned by their school club.

As the Japanese population and economy have grown, land, especially in the cities, has become quite scarce. Thus in many communities the school grounds are the only space available for children to play. Hence, even during the summer many children come to their schools to play with their friends. During the school year, they linger after school until the grounds are closed. In a more spacious America, children are more likely to find play space near their homes—a local little league ball park, a wooded area, or an armory.

Traditionally, in Japan the public school was the only place available in a community for holding community sports days, assembling for local festivals, and listening to speeches by politicians or famous men of letters. Partly for this reason, the school was considered a very important institution, and parents vied to gain positions on the school parent-teacher association board.[6] To a degree, especially in the cities, the broader community functions of the school have declined. Nevertheless, most parents still esteem the school and its activities.

Invariably, all families who have children in school pay their dues to the parent-teacher association and attend the appropriate functions. The monthly observation day is one such function; on this day parents are invited to come and watch their child's class for an hour or two; of mothers with children in the lower grades (despite the other obligations they have such as part-time jobs or housework), easily 70 percent attend each month. The high level of par-

---

[6] Theodore Brameld (1968:108) indicates that parent-teacher association positions are still avidly sought after in rural areas. John Singleton (1967:60 ff.) also comments on the centrality of the school in *Nichu* (1967:60 ff). He notes that the post of chairman of the parent-teacher association often serves as the springboard for a political career.

ticipation stems from the parents' desire to see their children adjust comfortably to the school routine.

The parents expect a lot from the schools. Increasingly parents recognize the critical role of cognitive achievement in determining educational success and hence (so they assume) occupational success. As will be seen later, the anxieties of Japanese parents for the cognitive achievement of their children easily outdistances that of American parents. But the Japanese parents expect even more. They seem especially positive about the school's extensive program aimed at developing the noncognitive aspects of personality—for example, ambition, social attitudes, and moral orientations. One of the reasons for the reinstitution in 1959 of a formal course in moral education was the sense that the schools were falling down in this regard. Of course, at times there are protests about the specific content of moral education promoted in the schools, but few parents dispute the important role the school plays in this area of personal development. In contrast, American parents seem to believe this broader education should take place in the homes, the community, and the church.

Moral Education

Formal schooling in morals has a long history in Japan. Some would say that Tokugawa education consisted of little else. The founders of the modern educational system included this course in the curriculum, originally borrowing texts from France. However, it was not long before native texts were developed, many of which were quite inspiring. Unfortunately this course was misused by the military during the wartime period to indoctrinate youth, and hence, as it acquired a bad reputation, it was originally eliminated from the postwar curriculum. However, against the strong objections of many progressive intellectuals, who feared a revival of narrow indoctrination, the course was revived in 1959.

Given this background, I expected the worst when I went to my first moral education class: dull Confucian texts sermonizing on the need for patriotism or greater filial piety. Much to my surprise, the class had no text. Rather, at the bell, one of the students turned on the television at the front of the classroom and for the next fifteen minutes we watched a short drama. Afterwards, the teacher and the students joined in a discussion to try to identify the moral lessons contained in the drama. From week to week the content varied, but never did I see programs concerned with political themes. Rather they emphasized fundamental matters such as the value of life, the foolishness of fighting, the importance of friendship, the problems of old people. Actually, no drama conveyed a specific message. The lesson was developed through the subsequent dialogue of the teacher and the students. In a drama where a child failed to respect a parent, the teacher could have directed the discussion toward the traditional theme of filial piety. Instead, in the class I watched the teacher steered the discussion toward the more general value of respect for the dignity of others. The format allowed considerable flexibility.

I quickly overcame my bias against moral education and looked forward to each week's new drama. From the rapt attention the kids paid to these programs, I could tell that I was not alone. These classes by themselves probably achieved very little. However, the lessons they presented were reinforced by other school activities, providing a dimension of education that is not found in the American primary school.

The School Routine as Moral Education

The great pains the teacher takes to establish order in the classroom have already been noted; most teachers try to explain to the students that proper classroom behavior is a way of showing respect for fellow students. Also, by relying on groups, the teacher tries to get the students to appreciate the worth of their fellows.

Monday morning of each school week begins with the *chorei*, a simple ceremony in which all the students line up on the school grounds to listen to various announcements from student government officers, club leaders, and teachers. After these are completed the principal stands and makes a small speech, which usually has a moral element in it. One memorable speech reflected on the importance of "things," both inanimate, such as the school grounds and equipment, and animate, such as the animals kept by one of the student clubs; above all, the principal emphasized the importance of human life and concluded by asking the students to look out for their own lives and those of their fellow students, to be careful of the traffic, to not extend themselves when they caught colds, and so forth. When a disciplinary problem such as untoward name calling, emerges among a group of students, the principal might speak in an oblique way about the delicacy of human feelings. At the end of the quarter, as the students prepare for vacation, the principal usually urges them to try to think of one special thing to do each day that will help their parents. These little speeches are delivered in good humor and rarely last for more than five minutes. Most students appear to forget the specifics of these speeches by the lunch period. However, the spirit of the principal's words do seem to stick with them.

Each day's routine also includes several events with definite moral messages. The most impressive of these is the noonday lunch period. Partly for economic reasons, most primary schools do not have a separate lunchroom; rather, the children eat in their respective classrooms with the teachers. Cooks prepare the basic ingredients (usually a porridge, a condiment, a bottle of milk, and two slices of bread) and around noon divide these into trays intended for each class. At 12:15, following the bell for the fourth period, a group of students from each class puts on white aprons and masks, walks to the kitchen, and collects its class's portion. Each group then carries its class's portion back to the classroom and serves each student. When all is prepared, the students sing a little song of thanks and begin their lunch. After lunch, the entire class cooperates in putting away the dishes. Then, after the rest of the class leaves to play on the school grounds, the lunch-period group takes out a set of brooms and rags and proceeds to clean the classroom. Over the course of a month, every student serves on a lunch-period group.

This lunch routine contains several moral messages: no work, not even the dirty work of cleaning, is too low for a student; all should share equally in common tasks; the maintenance of the school is everyone's responsibility. To underline these messages, on certain days each year the entire school body from the youngest student to the principal put on their dirty clothes and spend a couple of hours in a comprehensive cleaning of the school building and grounds.

The schools actually depend on the students and teachers, for they have no budget to employ personnel especially for cleaning. Although in the opinion of some, teachers and students shouldn't perform such dirty tasks, it is likely that the educational merits and the economies far outweigh whatever liabilities there might be. American schools, with their more lavish cafeteria facilities and their special personnel for cleaning, forego an important educational experience.

Student government provides another vehicle for moral education. Each semester, the fourth to sixth graders meet to hear speeches from candidates and then select the officers for a student self-government association, which performs an impressive array of services. Student government helps in the planning of school events such as sports day and cultural day; it sponsors various clubs, such as the animal club, which maintains a small collection of animals on the school grounds, the gardening club, which plants flowers, several sports clubs, which among other things help to keep the grounds in good condition, and the radio club, which operates the school public address system, making most of the announcements and providing a daily lunchtime musical program. Teacher advisers supervise these student activities, but insofar as possible they stay in the background and let students learn on their own to make decisions and assume responsibility.

School events also provide occasions for moral education in the broadest sense. At a minimum, each year every class takes a day trip to some well-known place they might not otherwise go to, such as a shrine or a botanical garden. The sixth graders take an overnight trip. The major aim of these trips is to promote fellowship and memorable common experiences. At the same time, little lessons, such as the need to keep in line, to throw trash away, and to give seats on public buses to old people, are not neglected. The annual sports day and cultural day provide occasions for classmates to work as a team. In sum, virtually every aspect of the school routine is permeated with the manifest objective of getting something done and the latent objective of developing student character.

Handling Problems

Perhaps because so much energy is devoted to moral education, most Japanese primary schools experience very few serious problems with their students. The attendance rates are high, and virtually all absences are involuntary. One sees very few fights, and most that do occur are broken up almost immediately by classmates. Cliques and heckling are rare.

In the school I visited most intensively, there was only one serious problem throughout the year, and it was interesting to watch how this was handled. The incident began during the morning roll call when the boy in charge called a girl by her (unappreciated) nickname of "pig." The girl was offended and refused to answer so the boy raised his voice and yelled the word several times. There was snickering, but the girl still refused to answer. Later that morning during a break several children gathered around the girl and chanted, "Pig, pig, pig . . ." Deeply hurt (or as Japanese would say, "having lost her face"), she ran away from the group. For the remainder of the school day she did not speak a word; that afternoon she went home and would refuse to return for over a week. The teacher in charge of the class had not been present during the periods when the girl was insulted, so she did not appreciate what had happened.

Later that day the girl's mother called to ask what had gone on. Immediately the principal began a quiet investigation in cooperation with the teacher. By that evening, parts of the story were known, and the principal visited the child's home to apologize to her parents. The next day, and on each successive day until the problem was solved, special teachers' meetings were held with all present to seek a solution. On three occasions the principal or the girl's homeroom teacher went to the girl's home and talked with her. The final resolution involved a visit by the entire class to the girl's home, where apologies were offered along with a request that the insulted girl forgive her friends. Two days later she returned to school, and two weeks later the involved teacher read a final report to the regular teachers' meeting and then apologized for having caused the school so much trouble. This process involved a tremendous amount of consultation and patience. Yet throughout, no one was blamed or reprimanded, and no one received a bad mark on his record. The goal was restitution rather than punishment, and it succeeded. The school went on as before, and all were a little wiser for their trouble.

The Curriculum

The Japanese teacher is harnessed to a demanding curriculum decided by the central government.[7] At the primary level, this curriculum covers three different areas—moral education, special

---

[7] Some idea of the detail of this prescription can be gleaned from a reading of the Ministry of Education's *Course of Study for Elementary Schools in Japan*. The English language translation runs to 228 pages; as a random example, four full pages are devoted to describing the contents of third grade sports education. In the section on gymnastics, ten new warm-up exercises are recommended as a preliminary for teaching elementary skills on the horizontal bar, the vaulting horse, and the tumbling mat. Although the introduction to the course says that a "school may organize a curriculum not following the order of teaching prescribed," it is difficult to find a public school with the courage; after all, they are all heavily subsidized by the central government. On the other hand, experimentation is quite common in private schools and those "laboratory schools" affiliated with national universities.

events (such as ceremonies, excursions and athletic meetings, and classroom guidance on health, safety, and so forth), and regular subjects. The first two are treated in greater detail elsewhere. Here the regular curriculum will be considered. This consists of eight subjects: Japanese language and literature, social studies, mathematics, science, music, arts and handicrafts, homemaking, and physical education.

Although, as in other advanced nations, the subject receiving the largest amount of time is language and literature, in view of the reported complexity of Japanese, it is of some interest to find that the Japanese primary school spends a smaller proportion of its total educational time on language (Ministry of Education, 1971:49). On the other hand, the Japanese primary school spends relatively more time on music, fine arts, and physical education—subjects that children, especially young ones, tend to enjoy the most. Although comparisons in other areas are more difficult, it appears that the Japanese primary school spends a greater proportion of its classroom time on arithmetic than most American primary schools do, and a somewhat smaller proportion on social studies; also, it treats science as a separate subject from the first grade, whereas American primary schools tend to integrate science with other subjects.

However, these dry statistics do not really convey the complexity of the Japanese curriculum, nor the demands it makes on the teacher. Whereas in America some of the subjects such as physical education and music tend to be strictly for fun and with no real curriculum, that is certainly not the case in Japan. Even for physical education the teacher gives a lecture before the students parade out onto the grounds. The curriculum goes through a systematic program from the first through the sixth grade designed to develop motor skills in a sequence related to scientific research on physical development. Toss ball, dodge ball, and a number of other related games are introduced in primary school, but basketball is postponed until the first year of middle school.

Of all the courses in the Japanese primary school, music was to me the most impressive. The vast majority of schools have special rooms for music equipped with pianos, organs, accordions, xylophones, and several standard percussion instruments. From the first grade, students begin to practice the recorder, and by the second grade they are familiar with a longer wind instrument similar to a simple clarinet. Also, they begin to read music. From the third grade, those who know something about the piano (in urban areas, as many as 80 percent of the girls take lessons) try the organs, and gradually they share their skills with the others. At this stage, the students are sometimes split into several groups to play different scores of music. By the time they are fourth graders, they have sufficient diversity in their music reading and playing skills so that they can produce an orchestral sound. And although the quality varies from class to class according to the skill of the teacher, some sixth grade classes produce a very impressive sound. Moreover, most students at this level are able to switch readily between at least three different instruments. The first time I saw this level of achievement I could not believe my eyes; but after the fifth primary school I had to recognize that it was widespread. Although the members of the orchestras and bands in American primary schools achieve this level, most of the remaining students are musically illiterate. Comparisons in art are nearly as dramatic.

These achievements are all the more impressive in that they are nurtured by the ordinary homeroom teachers, who have responsibility not only for these subjects but also for all the other subjects of the curriculum. The typical primary school has no specialists; each teacher is expected to be able to teach the full curriculum, and most do. One who feels especially weak in a certain area might exchange his responsibility in, say, music for another teacher's responsibility in science for example; but such arrangements are private and relatively exceptional. Seventy percent of the primary school teachers teach the full array of regular subjects. Although it is a strain to cover so many subjects, the teachers seem to enjoy it, and moreover, they think it their responsibility as conveyors of the doctrine of education of the whole person to be as close as possible to this ideal.

The Texts for Social Studies

Educational innovation places increasing stress on audiovisual techniques and learning through experience. Nevertheless, texts remain the principal vehicles for education both in Japan and the United States, and so a modest effort was made to become acquainted with them.[8]

One is immediately struck by the friendlier feel of the Japanese

[8] I read all the social science texts used in the Kyoto city system as this area is closest to my own academic specialty of sociology; also its cognitive content has the most direct bearing on the study. I also inspected texts in other areas, especially science.

texts. Usually, they have a face the size of a large pocketbook with some humorous picture on the cover; at the primary level they are no more than a centimeter thick. The cover is made of paper, giving an appearance closer to that of a comic book than to that of a real book as American schools seem to prefer. Partly, this difference stems from the practice in Japan of giving free texts to the students (which they can keep after the year is over), in contrast to the text-loaning system adopted by most American schools. Also, the Japanese prefer light texts, as the schoolchildren take most of their texts home each day rather than leave them in their desks.

Although it is easy to comment on these external differences, the analysis of what is found inside the texts is much more complicated. To do a proper job, one almost has to perform an autopsy of every page of every subject, obviously beyond the scope of this report. Instead, this discussion will be limited to mentioning a few impressions relevant to the theme of egalitarian education of the whole person. For this purpose, the social studies texts are the most interesting.

Texts in Japan are written on the basis of a course guideline developed by the Ministry of Education, and, moreover, have to be approved by ministry-appointed examiners. In that the ministry is responsible to a conservative regime and its examiners are reputed to censor progressive themes (as in the case of Ienaga Saburo's high school text on Japanese history), I expected that these texts would present a distinctly conservative picture of society. To my surprise, the texts if anything were predominantly progressive in tone. Although they celebrated work, it was primarily the ordinary work of the common people that they highlighted. And the texts were critical of the ravages of recent heavy industrialization.

The first-year social studies text dwells on places that are part of the immediate experience of students—their schools, their homes, and their neighborhoods. The chapter on the school introduces the students to the various people involved with the school, placing special emphasis on the important contributions of the building and grounds personnel and the cooks. On the other hand, no mention is made of the principal. The section on homes begins with a picture of the various tasks performed by the members of a gray-collar family, and then portrays variations in homes centered around other work. All the homes illustrated in the text have parents working in blue- or gray-collar occupations, and the text seems intent on emphasizing the contribution children are expected to make to family life. In a later section the text lists the various people who come to the home, the milkman, the mailman, the oilman, and so forth, and stresses how family life depends on these services.

The second-year text picks up on the work theme by introducing people who work in the market from which the food for the family's meals come, and then goes beyond to discuss the lives of farmers and fishermen. Finally the text turns to bus and train drivers and public servants, including firemen and policemen. As in the first-year text, the descriptions are limited to working- and lower-middle-class occupations. The third-year text shifts the focus toward geography and ecology. On the very first page is a picture of Fuji City, lying at the foot of Mt. Fuji, Japan's premier symbol of naturalism. The picture features a factory belting clouds of smoke into a hazy sky and pumping out a white scum that floats on top of the harbor water. Underneath is a caption that notes how the city is troubled now by pollution. The text begins with several lessons on map reading and in the process gives the students a picture of imaginary "Green City." Gradually it turns to the types of facilities located in the city and the problems that develop: lack of water, an inadequate sewerage system, garbage, pollution, automobile accidents, and fires. Finally, the text reviews the process of city government and notes how citizens can participate. The fourth-year text builds on many of the above themes, but fans out to introduce children to ever-wider areas of Japan, stressing the varying lifestyles of the people—especially farmers, fishermen, and sailors—and the transportation that facilitates movement between the different areas.

The fifth-year text focuses on technology and the productive processes of various industries, while the sixth-year text begins the formal study of Japanese history, stressing the interrelations of Japan and the world. It concludes with a discussion of the atomic bomb that fell on Hiroshima and the importance of peace, and then notes some activities of the United Nations.

All in all, these texts present a remarkably open-minded, even progressive, picture of Japanese society.[9] Their strongest theme is

[9] According to Huthwaite (1974:119-120), "McClelland found that the most common themes in Japanese primary school textbooks were kindness and obligation. In a study of the trends in postwar moral education in Japan as reflected in the new textbooks . . . Fujishiro concluded that there was a de-emphasis on nationalism, a pronounced growth of concern for social and individual morality, and a shift from blind loyalty and obedience to an understanding of rules and responsibilities in a

the diversity of work performed by the Japanese people. Rather than picture some occupations as more worthy than others, the texts stress the interrelatedness of all occupations. Clearly, the hidden agenda is to cultivate a climate of mutual respect between students from diverse social backgrounds that will carry over into their adult lives. Many of Japan's social problems are openly recognized, as is the importance of the democratic governmental process in providing solutions.

Teachers report that these texts are among the favorites, especially of upper grade boys. The themes they cover tend to draw out many of the children who seem restrained in arithmetic or language. The texts carefully avoid references to Japan's minority groups, and naturally they do not portray minority-group people in low-status social roles, as often appears to be the case in American texts. However, teachers are quick to note other deficiencies—for example, the picture of the typical family in the first grade text clearly places the mother in the home. But the texts are so flexible in their tone that a teacher could correct this image by asking students to imagine what life might be like in another home where the mother worked. Indeed, especially through the early years the texts seem designed more for promoting discussion than transmitting information. Thus, the social studies texts enable the students to reflect on their own social situation.

Conventional Teaching

Japanese schools throughout the nation are remarkably similar in design. The buildings, whether wooden or ferroconcrete, consist of halls on one side from which doors open into rectangular classrooms. At the front of each classroom is a blackboard and often a raised platform from which the teachers are expected to teach. On the side opposite the door are windows, and along the back side are a bulletin board and cubbyholes for each student. Desks and chairs

---

democratic society." Huthwaite, in her own thematic analysis of 20 children's books selected from a stratified sample of 500 concluded that the most common values found in folk literature were courage, cleverness, loyalty and cultural pride. The most common values found in realistic fiction were cooperation, kindness, independence, honesty and love of nature. Hierarchical loyalty was evident in the folk literature, but it was virtually absent in fantasy and realistic literature. Indeed, "none of the sample books of realistic fiction recommended loyalty to a superior, allegiance or blind loyalty. Authority was questioned and even defied on occasion" (1974:126). Huthwaite concludes that hierarchical relations are much less frequently stressed in contemporary texts than cooperative horizontal relations.

are usually arranged in six straight rows (alternately girl-boy) of six to seven seats facing the front. One rarely sees a classroom that departs from this arrangement—with for example, extra rooms for individualized instruction or with a pie-shaped design so that students find it easier to look at each other.

The classrooms are designed for conventional teaching, and by and large, that is what *seems* to take place. The basic pattern of teaching involves lectures, directions, and questions from the teacher to the students with relatively little interaction initiated by the students. At any given time, all of the students concentrate on the same subject matter and rarely is classroom time set aside for independent study or individualized instruction.

Each school day is divided into a series of periods of equal length with breaks in between—at the primary level these are normally five minutes, though between the second and third periods there is a 20-minute play time and 75 minutes are set aside for lunch. Usually the teacher starts a new lesson at the beginning of each new period: even if the children enjoy the reading they begin in period one, it is put away to take up math in period two.

Many Japanese teachers, especially those with classes in the early primary grades, express doubts about the conventional teaching approach, but explain that they have to use it in order to cover what is in their view an excessive amount of material. They express interest in the supposedly freer teaching methods of the United States and in innovations such as the open classroom that they see and read about in the mass media. Especially, they are envious of the smaller classroom size in American schools, and feel they might be able to try different methods if they enjoyed these favorable conditions.[10]

Despite the apologies and claims to the contrary, one discovers that most Japanese teachers do make significant departures from the traditional approach. For example, they devote a significant effort to maximizing student participation. As noted earlier, the stress on participation begins almost from the first day of school with the aim of building up the self-confidence of students. Depending on

[10] It was found that most Japanese teachers had an impressive knowledge of educational reforms in other places (both national and international), thanks to fequent local, area-wide, and national weekend research meetings, weekly in-school pedagogy workshops, and Sunday morning television series by both public and commercial networks on themes such as "Education Around the World" and "Our Schools."

the subject matter, a teacher may get from ten members to the whole class to make a presentation during a given period. Most teachers carefully control the procedure for selecting students so that no individual is called more or less often than the others. One procedure is to go down the rows; another is to go by the alphabet; a third is to ask the student who completes a presentation to select the next person, and so on. One teacher, a true master at achieving full participation, attempted to get every student to make at least one presentation every hour; during one 45-minute mathematics class she elicited 82 different acts of student participation. Most of these involved students advancing to the front board to solve a problem. Although this teacher maintained a calm face as if there were nothing unusual about the level of participation she achieved, to the outside observer, at least, the pace was dizzying. In this environment, it seemed perfectly appropriate for the teacher to periodically interrupt each frenzied day with sprees of simple exercises. These relieve the muscular tension that seems to develop in the necks and shoulders of the students.

Another departure from traditional methods is the extensive reliance on subgroups, both for education and for other school tasks. Indeed, the subgroup structure is often so complex that one wonders how the children can keep up with it. For normal classwork, the teacher usually splits the class into groups of four or six children sitting in adjacent seats. For special assignments, such as a science experiment or putting together a collage, these basic groups work together. Sometimes the teacher even asks the class to break up into these groups to discuss a problem, such as the cause of pollution in the rivers or the lack of a sewerage system in certain areas of their city; a representative of the group (the person usually rotates from day to day) then provides a group report. A different set of groups is formed to alternate in managing the weekly student activities class. Still another set of groups is formed to assume responsibility for the various class chores, such as keeping the blackboards clear, preparing exhibits for the bulletin boards, and so on. And yet another set is created for the physical education period. As can be seen, the organization of a class is surprisingly complicated.

The most frequently used groups are those mentioned first above. These basic groups, which do something together at least twice a day, are kept intact for about two months and then the members are reshuffled. The teachers explain that they form these groups and rely on them largely to promote a friendly and cooperative feeling among the students (*nakayoshi*). Teachers put a lot of thought into the composition of their groups. In general, they try to create balanced groups composed of people with diverse abilities, and they encourage the students to help each other. Sometimes when students work on their arithmetic, the teacher asks the fast members of a group to coach the slow ones. Indeed, one teacher clearly planned her arithmetic and language class assignments so that the quick students would be done in fifteen minutes; then after checking their work she would send them off to help others. She consciously employed "a learn it then teach it" approach, because she felt it promoted comradeship among the students. In another class, a male student was socially immature for his age, so the teacher put him in a group with three exceptionally tolerant girls, who seemingly took it as their mission to bring the boy around; when he would not stand up for a class presentation, they would push him up, and when he struggled with an answer they would supply him with tips. Under no circumstances do the teachers consciously form groups stratified by ability as is the practice in growing numbers of American schools. Although the teachers recognize differences in ability among their students, they feel it is their responsibility as public school teachers in a democratic society to try to bring all the students up to a common level; rather than promote the bright students at the expense of the slow, they seek to channel the energies of the bright into pulling their slower fellows up. Groups are conceived of as educational vehicles in the broadest sense rather than as mere instruments for rationalizing cognitive education.

When the teachers shift to the group method, they often ask the students to rearrange their desks so that those of each group of four come together. Other seating arrangements are also employed. For example, in the student activities class desks are often rearranged in a semicircle to face a central table behind which the week's discussion leaders are seated. Occasionally this same arrangement is used when the class discusses a problem in social studies. On rainy days when the students cannot go outside for physical education, they push all the desks to the back and play games in the classroom. These departures from normal seating arrangements are perhaps not as frequent as one finds in the typical American school; on the other hand, the desks of a Japanese classroom are never nailed to the floor as Silberman (1970) says sometimes happens in the United States.

Japanese teachers also utilize unconventional teaching aids such as slide projectors, special drawings and graphs, mimeographed sets of arithmetic problems they prepared at home, and so on. However, various factors prevent them from using these devices as much as they seem to want to, or as much as seems to be the practice in American schools. Commercial companies have not made the same advances with these devices in Japan as in the United States, and even when appropriate devices are available their cost is often beyond the reach of school budgets. So if a Japanese teacher wishes to use one of these devices, he often finds he has to prepare it at home. The heavy teaching schedule does not leave large amounts of time for this.

As can be seen, Japanese teachers often depart from the framework of conventional teaching, but restraints of class size, the demands of the curriculum, and the time and money they have available for preparation keep them from straying very far. Japanese teachers seem interested in more innovation; on the other hand, one is impressed with their confidence in their present styles. Those teachers especially who have been at it for five years or more exude a sense that they know exactly what they are doing when they go into the classroom, and seem able to adjust readily to the unexpected developments of each school day.

In contrast, American teachers are much more prone to try unconventional teaching approaches: the teachers' colleges in the United States constantly generate new ideas, which they share with the future teachers who study there. Also America's educational administrators, who take a much stronger role in school administration than their Japanese counterparts, seem much inclined to experimentation.[11] Thus some American schools are lively centers of innovation: bells are ignored; teaching aids are heavily relied on; specialists are employed in areas such as remedial reading and science laboratories; and, individualized instructional devices are utilized. Although these new approaches offer great promise, especially in the hands of the teachers who fully understand them, most American teachers apply these mechanically at best. Many in the

---

[11] This cross-national observation is speculative; however, one cannot help but be impressed, as one reads the American school literature, with the extent to which the principals view the local school boards as their major reference group; in many cases, principals use talk of proposed "innovation" as a gimmick for impressing the school board with their leadership qualities. For one case study, see Vidich and Bensman (1968).

American teaching profession feel uncertain and uneasy about the effectiveness of the innovations they find themselves using (Lortie, 1975: Chs. 5 and 6). The Japanese teacher, through sticking closely to the tried and proved conventional pattern, rarely suffers in this way. As in other areas of life, perhaps confidence in one's ability rather than the particular approach used is the most important ingredient.

ENCOURAGING AND EVALUATING STUDENTS

American schools assume that individuals have different abilities. This accounts for their advocacy of many of the recent educational innovations noted above. Yet, despite claims to the contrary by their promoters, these innovations actually seem to accelerate differences in student performance.

Japanese teachers are less ready to concede that there are inherent differences in ability, or even that the environments from which students come have indelible effects. Far more than their American counterparts, they assume that children are equal in endowment and that differences in performance stem from lack of effort on the part of the students. They further reason that inadequate effort stems from inadequate teaching.

Most Japanese primary schools administer I.Q. tests to their students soon after entrance and record the scores on the student's school record. But these scores are kept in the school office, where even the teachers rarely go. The schools also seek reports from the parents on their financial status, the study space available for children, and so on. Teachers turn to this material when they become worried about the performance of an individual, but otherwise they ignore it.

Essentially, the teachers do not believe the tests and background information record what they should know in order to go about their work. They believe that excessive attention to this data could lead them to discriminate against students who score low but have hidden potential. Also they fear that the release of this information to outsiders, whether as individual scores or as averages for the school, could lead to social discrimination against the graduates of their school. Especially in recent years, Japanese schools have resisted the attempts by outsiders to perform the traditional school achievement studies, which measure various personality traits and study their relation to school performance. Even if I had wished to show, with hard data, that the Japanese school develops the whole person (and not merely the cognitive area), I would not have been able to find a school where I could administer the appropriate tests—at least not in the Kyoto area.[12]

As an observer sitting in a primary school classroom, especially up to the fourth grade, one can tell after a couple of days that two or three students are not performing up to the average level, and another handful are way ahead of the rest. Most teachers try consciously to ignore these differences and to bring all into classroom activities. The very slow students often pose problems, but teachers sometimes find areas where these students do well—for example, in art or physical education—and make a special effort to call on them during these periods. In other classes the teachers might steer the easier problems to these students. Although there are these subtle departures from equal treatment, it is doubtful if the members of the class are aware of them. The teachers work hard to give the impression to each student that he can and should pull an equal load. Apart from presentations before the class, the teachers assign various problems to do either at home or in class. Each teacher has his red pencil, and seems to take great delight in splashing every student's page with a sea of check marks. In the in-class exercises, the teachers allow the brighter students to supply the answers to the slow students before descending with the red pencil. Thus everyone seems to win in the academic competition.

This approach seems to motivate students. Even if a student is unable to perform at the class level, he gradually develops the feeling that he should be able to. Thus by the sixth grade, it is really quite difficult to spot the weak students; somehow they develop techniques to cover up their inabilities—on tests, though they might not answer all the questions, they turn the answers in promptly so as not to appear slow. Prior to class, they might write the *kana* beside the difficult Chinese characters to prevent stumbling during the reading period. Thus the prevailing assumption of equality is self-fulfilling.

The relatively narrow range in academic achievement among Japanese students is possibly attributable to the assumption of

[12] The resistance to testing gained momentum after the early sixties when the Ministry of Education attempted to introduce a national achievement test for the purpose of evaluating school and teacher performance. Resistance is especially strong in the Kansai area where I located my study, and more generally wherever the teachers' union is firmly entrenched.

equality of endowment. If one were to listen to the critics of Japanese education, one might conclude that teachers also assume that their students are equal in performance. For example, one professor at Kyoto University (Katsuda, 1974:16) claimed that all the children in his daughter's class were given a grade of three (average) in music, whereas the professor protested that surely at least in this area differential performance was easy to detect. Actually these critics exaggerate, for at least in my experience I never found a school that granted equal grades.

In the schools observed for this study, the teachers' meetings decide on the principles they will use in grading. In most cases, the teachers agree that the readers of each class will be graded on a five-point scale relative to the other members of their class. Roughly 5 percent will be given the top grade (5), 15 percent the better than average grade (4), 60 percent the average grade (3), 15 percent the lower than average grade (2), and 5 percent the lowest grade (1). This distribution has a fat middle category; some schools put only 50 or even 40 percent here; some go above 60 percent; but all preserve some latitude to recognize exceptionally good and poor performances. Tests, often prepared by the manufacturers of the texts used by the school, are administered to the students, and the test results along with class performance become the basis for assigning students a grade in each regular subject. Taking a careful look at the grade distribution, one sees that all teachers keep close to the above standard, even the softest teachers give their quota of 1's and 2's. And despite the desire on the part of teachers to find strong points in all their students, some report cards consist of only 1's and 2's.

After handing out the grades, the teacher tells the class that most have done a good job, but ʿhe wants each student to do better next time, to try to get more 4's and 5's on their card. Especially those who received 1's and 2's are asked to try harder. Later, on a prearranged consultation day the teacher spends ten minutes with each parent talking about the performance of his child and especially about those aspects not noted in the official report card—behavior in the classroom, ability to get along with others, health, language, and so on.

At this stage of official performance evaluation, the Japanese primary school appears to do at least as explicit a job as its American counterpart. However, one senses that in Japan the process generates much more strain on the teachers. At one school, the teachers had been conducting research on grading for the past several years. Some of the teachers wished to move from a class-based absolute performance criteria to an individual-based criteria—how much each child had developed relative to his level at the previous report period. Also, the teachers wished to simplify the number of grades to two or three levels from the existing five as well as to broaden the categories evaluated in each subject. Rather than give a single grade for literature, they wanted to include separate evaluations for reading, speaking, writing, knowledge of literature, and so on, so that parents could have a clearer sense of their children's weak and strong points. Also, they felt the report card should include comments on nonacademic performance. Actually, the records teachers prepare for the school office contain information of this kind. And in some areas of Japan, notably Kyoto prefecture outside the main city, these newer methods for preparing report cards are being practiced. Rather than dwell on each student's academic standing compared to his peers, the new report cards stress total development relative to each individual's past.

Graduation

At the end of the primary school, a graduation ceremony is held, in which students are given a degree and asked to hold up the good name of the school. Traditionally, the school chose a valedictorian to deliver a speech on behalf of the graduating class, but out of deference to equality this practice was discontinued about twenty years ago. Instead, the members of the graduating class chant a beautiful song of nostalgia celebrating their struggles to learn, the gratitude they feel toward their teachers and parents, the fun they had on the school athletic days and the class trips, and their sense of anticipation about their next life stage as middle schoolers.

MIDDLE SCHOOL EDUCATION

The Middle School's Opening Ceremony

The very same students observed in the last year of primary school took their seats in the middle school auditorium one month later wearing uniforms to mark their new status.[13] The principal wel-

---

[13] Western observers often see in school uniforms some lingering sign of identification with an earlier militaristic and authoritarian era. Indeed, it was for this reason that the American Occupation removed the formal requirement that schoolchildren

comed them and expressed his hope that they would work and make the best of the new experience. He explained the opportunities that were before them—to study, to participate in the clubs, to take responsibility for the management of the school—and then in a very serious tone he said that the students were likely to follow one of three routes: some would devote themselves wholeheartedly to all the school activities right from the beginning and thereby build a strong foundation for life, some would devote themselves to the extracurriculum and then in their final year break open the books to prepare for the high school exams, and a final group would merely coast through, wasting their new opportunity. The principal said it was up to each student to choose his path; now as middle schoolers they would have to take greater responsibility for their own development. The speech was much sterner than that delivered by the primary school principal six years earlier, and it signaled to students that they were now entering a new and more critical stage in their educational career.

The Middle School as a Transitional Period

Given the neat age-graded character of Japanese education, most students enter middle school in their twelfth year. Over the next three years until they graduate from the middle school, these students experience major developments in their mental and social constitution and especially in their physique that bring them closer to adulthood. During these years most middle schoolers will achieve puberty; many will experience a rapid spurt of growth that will bring them close to the maximum height they will achieve by adulthood. Also these youths will become more independent and anxious to do things on their own, less receptive to authority.

The formal education that occurs in the middle school is more difficult and more explicitly cognitive oriented than that found in the primary school, though less difficult than that found in the high schools and universities. Although teachers are still concerned with

---

wear uniforms. To the Occupation's surprise, parents' associations at many schools, especially at the middle school level, decided of their own will to have children wear uniforms. Their reasons were: (1) children of this age level grew so fast that it was cheaper to clothe them in standardized uniforms than in commercial clothing; (2) as all uniforms looked alike, status competition based on stylish clothing could be avoided, and thus no child need be embarrassed by his inability to buy the latest; (3) finally, many parents, thinking of their own school days, wanted to have their children wear uniforms for nostalgic reasons.

developing whole persons, there are not as many opportunities for achieving this through the formal educational process.

The Middle School's Selection Function

In the American system, places in public high school are generally guaranteed to all those students who wish to go. Moreover, in most American school systems, the high school an individual attends is determined by his place of residence. For these reasons, most American junior high students (the equivalent of Japan's middle schoolers) do not have a very strong sense that their achievements during junior high school will affect their lives.

In contrast, in Japan places in public schools are guaranteed only through the middle school. Today most students (over 90 percent) go on for some kind of further education—but the opportunities these different institutions lead to are quite diverse. The big choices in high schools are between public and private schools (which tend to be more expensive), and between ordinary (academic) courses that prepare students for higher education and vocational courses. In 1975, 31 percent of all the high school places were in the private sector and 60 percent were in ordinary high schools.

Today's youth tend to want to go to a good academic high school so that they can improve their chances to get into a good university. Several of the most effective high schools in preparing students for universities are in the private sector. These "famous schools" select a relatively small proportion of the total high school cohort (perhaps 2 percent), based largely on their performance on competitive academic entrance examinations. Most middle school students cannot hope to meet the entrance standards of these schools, and even if they could, often times their parents would not be able to afford the tuition. Thus the typical college oriented student aspires to get into a good public high school or, failing that, into one of the less-noted private ordinary high schools. (Some are relatively inexpensive.)

Public high schools also use entrance exams, but often these account for only one half of the total score used in deciding admissions. The other half of the score is based on grades during the third year of middle school. In Kyoto, the high school entrance exams cover all of the subjects that students have studied during their middle school days (that is, not only what might be considered the core subjects of Japanese language, social studies, mathematics, and science but also the softer subjects of music, fine arts, health and physical education, and industrial arts or homemaking). Similarly, the formula for determining grade performance takes account of all subjects, with weights assigned according to the number of hours studied each week. The Kyoto educational officials explain that they believe each of the subjects is in the curriculum to develop a different aspect of their students. To insure that students do not neglect specific areas this comprehensive evaluative system provides the greatest incentive. Public high schools in many of the other prefectures, however, test only the core subjects.

The Cognitive Function in Middle School Education

Regardless of the system used or the type of school a student aspires to, what he has learned by the end of his middle school days is going to play a crucial role. What the ordinary student learns is in part determined by what he is exposed to—or at least this seems to be widely believed in Japan. This belief leads to a much stronger sense of purposefulness in the middle school classroom. One indication is the plain decor of the school—few flowers on the grounds, virtually no decorations in the rooms, and of course the sobering uniforms worn by the students.

Teaching in the middle schools is also more purposeful. Except for the smallest middle schools, each teacher specializes in a given subject, and he appears over the course of a day in several classrooms to teach his specialty. The style of teaching is far more cognitively oriented than in the primary school. Teachers lecture more and are relatively less likely to turn over time to subgroups in the class. Although the teachers call on students, they do not show nearly as strong a concern with achieving full participation. Indeed, in the classes that I attended, teachers actually seemed to bias their calls for student presentations to those who were the strongest performers. In part, this was to impress me. But when I asked the teachers, they also explained that this was more efficient from an educational point of view. Moreover, they indicated that they were more concerned with the development of the best students than with those who did not try. This last explanation, of course, reflected their belief that performance was essentially a function of effort.

Student behavior in the middle school classrooms generally reflects the seriousness of their teachers. Most students prepare their lessons and seem concerned about grades. During the exam period at the end of each trimester, they really buckle down, putting in four to six hours of home study each day. In general, they show the appropriate respect to the teacher: each class starts with a greeting, and students stand when called upon. There is, of course, some cutting up, especially in the afternoon and in courses the students do not get very excited about—English and homemaking, for example. But these rarely appear to be systematic efforts to disrupt; rather, they seem natural expressions of humor aimed at relieving tension.

The texts in middle school are stocked with many more facts and figures than those of the primary school, and I found those I read to be pretty dull. They reinforced my general impression that the middle school took learning, or rather the ingestion of material, very seriously. However, the teachers I met insisted that I did not have the full picture. A math teacher said he tried to get students to see the beauty of mathematical proofs and the possibilities for creativity in this subject. A literature teacher said he enjoyed trying to convey to students the wonders of great literature—the complexity of plots, the resurgence of themes, the sublety of symbols. Indeed, most teachers expressed lofty goals for their teaching, goals of teaching, through the curriculum, the feelings and behavior appropriate in the real world; but they also had to admit that these were difficult to achieve given the pace of the curriculum.

Evaluation in the middle school is more explicitly tied to achievement than in the primary school. Toward the end of each semester, exams are administered to all the students in all their subjects. However, in contrast with the primary school, the exams for each subject of each grade are usually prepared by all the teachers who have these classes. Moreover, the marking is performed jointly by all these teachers. As a result, a student's mark in a given course represents his performance relative to all of the students at his grade level in the school, and not merely relative to those in his immediate homeroom. Also the schools occasionally administer city-wide exams to size up the school's performance relative to other middle schools in the city and to help students understand their level of performance relative to a wider group.

Compared to the sobriety of the Japanese middle school classroom, the American scene is closer to a carnival. Classrooms are often disrupted, and teachers struggle to get through what is a much less demanding curriculum. In America, this is considered a period of adolescence in which youths should not be pushed too hard.

The Homeroom

Although the picture presented here is of purposeful formal education, the middle school has its lighter side, and this serves to round
out or humanize the total experience. One part of this more human
side is the tight-knit homeroom. Each year, the entering students
are divided into several homeroom classes of about 40 students
each. These students are assigned to a specific homeroom, in which
they will spend most of their educational time. Also, they are assigned a homeroom teacher, who meets with them as a class once a
week and who is available for private conferences whenever individual students wish this. As in the primary school, the members of
the homeroom assume the responsibility for cleaning their classroom. It is also the basic unit from which representatives are elected
to the student government.

Several intramural events are scheduled each year under the aus-
pices of the student government association to promote a group
feeling among the students. In the spring, boys of each homeroom
compete in intramural baseball, and girls compete in softball. In the
fall there is an athletic meet. And in the winter, the homerooms face
off in soccer and basketball. Also, a school culture day is held each
fall, and the members of each class prepare an exhibit of some kind
in their classroom as well as present a skit or musical performance
in the school auditorium. These activities occur with surprising
frequency throughout the year, and most homerooms try to do
well in them. In the process, the students get to know each other in
a more informal way. At the end of a year, many homerooms hold
private parties with their teachers at a tea house, where they
reminisce about the fun they have had together. Sometimes a
homeroom class becomes so close that its members form an alumni
club (*dosokai*) and make a pact to meet later on.

Student Clubs

Japanese middle schools have a large number of school clubs for activities such as tennis, basketball, soccer, music, art, and history,
and virtually every middle schooler belongs to one.

First-year students join these clubs simply by expressing an interest and participating regularly in the club's activities; if the student's ability is low (in tennis, for example, to which most middle
schoolers have had no prior exposure) the older club members provide instruction. The idea behind the club is to promote fellowship

and an opportunity for personal development; the clubs of a given school may play that of another, but this is usually in fun, and all members are allowed to compete, from the most skilled to the newcomers. These clubs receive small subsidies from the parent-teacher association to purchase necessary equipment.

Most clubs meet every afternoon after school for about an hour and a half and on Saturdays they might meet longer. At these times every inch of the school grounds seems to be employed. On a single tennis court six girls might be popping tennis balls back and forth at each other. Then after ten minutes they would rotate with a platoon of boys. And then back to the girls. In the meantime advanced players would give tips to newcomers, while others would find a corner to practice volleying. Nearby vigorous basketball and volleyball games would be going on.[14]

Student Government

One other vehicle for the education of the whole person is the student government association. As in the primary school, this association assumes responsibility for a surprising diversity of functions, and without it the school would truly be crippled. In addition to those activities mentioned for the primary school, the middle school association manages the various club activities, arranges the school events, selects and purchases books for the school library as well as provides the librarians, and develops and administers the regulations on student behavior (for example, uniform styles and length of hair).

Each homeroom class elects representatives to sit in the association. Also, twice each year, association officers are selected following a week of campaigning, which sometimes gets quite spirited

---

[14] Watching these sports clubs, one wonders why more of the energy of American junior high students, especially the girls, could not be channeled into such activities. Coleman (1961) has observed how the athletic teams of American schools become the focal point of adolescent society, and in his view this leads to a misdirection of youthful energy. He argues this occurs because the teams of American schools are promoted by school officials as a symbol of school pride. Coleman laments the fact that the championing of athletics diverts attention from studying, which in his opinion is what students ought to be immersed in; why, he asks, should the "brains" become a minority group? Japanese schools de-emphasize interschool competition, especially in athletics. Thus, sports does not become so professionalized, and most students join in the club system. The widely recognized importance of the exam system, on the other hand, prevents discrimination against "brains." A more equal balance is achieved between study and sports.

with long soapbox speeches and testimonials during the lunch break and in the special preelection assembly. These campaigns and assemblies, as well as the assemblies ending each "regime's" term of service, are also important as a means of channeling student complaints to the school administration. (The principal and most teachers attend these assemblies.) At one assembly, a female representative complained that the girls' bathroom stalls needed locks, for, in her words, it was very embarrassing for two girls to face each other "cheek to cheek." Naturally, this expression provoked a lot of laughter, but a week later locks were on the stalls. In this same assembly, another girl stood up and made a moving speech about discrimination; she touched on the discrimination of big people against smaller people, of older students against new students, and of teachers against students; possibly, this girl was addressing herself in as subtle a way as she could to the broader problem of class and outcaste discrimination, which has in recent years begun to trouble some of Japan's schools.

At the end of these assemblies, the principal stands up and comments on the proceedings; invariably one of his comments is that the students have not been very attentive to the speeches of their fellow students. This he points out shows a lack of maturity and respect. In response to the students' requests, the principal promises to do what is in his power, and also makes clear what is impossible. In this way, understanding between students and staff are enhanced. And presumably, the students develop a slightly better understanding of the nature of power and of politics.

Graduation

Although the middle school has these more human aspects, only the first- and second-year students take full advantage of them. From the first days of April third-year students concentrate on preparing for the high school entrance exams they will write ten months later. Many quit their clubs or reduce their attendance. Others retire from responsible roles in the student government associations so that they can have more time to study. At least one third of the students begin going to exam preparation schools in the late afternoon or evening, and perhaps a sixth receive special guidance from a private tutor once or twice a week at their home. After ten months of this regime, the students sit for the exams that decide their high school, and then in mid-March they attend their middle school graduation ceremony.

In some respects, this ceremony marks the most critical transition of their lives. Despite the pressures of study, these youth enjoyed much free time for horseplay and developing rich friendships during their middle school days. Those who secure entrance to an ordinary high school will have to abandon much of this fun in order to make a credible preparation for the university entrance exams. A minority of the middle school graduates will enter the labor force where, from the age of 15, they will be tied to a demanding daily routine. The graduation ceremony observed for this study ending the middle school was appropriately solemn. There was not even a single occasion of unruliness among the students. The school principal wished the students well and handed out the certificates. The head of the parent-teacher association also offered his good wishes. Finally the valedictorian of the graduating class—symbolizing the school's belief that some had made better use of their middle school days than others—gave a short speech, partly nostalgic and partly philosophical, but above all full of complicated words and phrases to symbolize the intellectual achievements of his class. The students then marched out of the assembly and through the school gate as their parents and the younger students clapped in rhythm. Thirty years ago, this scene would have meant the students were marching off to war. In a sense, things have not changed, for the next stage in the lives of most is what in Japan is known as the "examination hell."

THE HIGH SCHOOL EXPERIENCE

In looking beyond the middle school, perhaps the most important consideration is the particular high school a student manages to get into. Up to this point, most students have studied the uniform curriculum of public middle schools. Depending on the high school they enter, they will be exposed to either an academic or a vocational curriculum, a fast-paced exam-oriented educational style or a more extensive general education; they will either dedicate themselves to the rigors of exam preparation or they will have time for clubs and fun. High school marks the low point in the life cycle of many Japanese youth. They have to work harder and think deeper than before. And there are few human compensations. Still it is a place of growth and change: Of special importance for the discussion here, high school is the period in which youths solidify their identification with their peers and take bold steps to move away from familial and other adult institutional influences. In Chapters Seven and Eight, we will examine this development.

PARENTAL PARTICIPATION

Parents constitute an important background for the activities of Japanese schools, especially through the middle school level. It is surprising how much interaction goes on between parents and the school, and how hard the school works to try to explain what it is doing. The objective in the school's communication effort seems to be to win parents over to the school's way, or at least to establish a basis of empathy on which a reasonable discussion of differences becomes possible.

The parent-teacher association is the formal organization for coordinating parental participation. In the schools studied, at least one parent of each student belonged. From each homeroom, three mothers (sometimes a father) were chosen to participate in the council of the association, and the most active among these were made officers. The council met rarely, but the officers frequently telephoned council members or sent out notices. On the other hand, the officers met almost weekly with the school principal and thus had abundant opportunity to learn about the school as well as to convey parental concerns.

One of the major concerns of parents is to see how their children adapt to school, so the schools have a monthly participation day. On this day, parents are invited to watch their child's class for a couple of hours. Afterwards there is often a special lecture for the visiting parents on a topic such as family education, safety, or nutrition. With only a few exceptions, mothers represent their families on these days; in the primary schools usually at least two out of every three mothers are present. On special occasions, such as sport's day or report card day (teachers not only give out written report cards but also are expected to meet with all interested parents on a given day to discuss each student's performance), participation is close to 100 percent. These occasions provide parents with the opportunity to speak more bluntly to the teachers, and many do not hesitate. They complain that their child does not understand certain lessons, that there is not enough homework assigned, that they do not think their child has a very good seat in the classroom, and so on; and of course they ask about the grades. Teachers quickly become accustomed to these complaints and develop strategies of response. At the same time, the exchanges are human and serve to remind teachers of how much the parents look to them for effective education.

In addition, to facilitate communication most teachers send out periodic notices of class activities, requesting, for example, that students wear dirty clothes for a special painting day or good walking shoes for a nature excursion. Also, many schools, especially those of the middle school level or above, publish a monthly newspaper (financed by the parent-teacher association) in which teachers and the principal explain what the school is trying to accomplish.

Although parents are encouraged to participate and have channels that enable them to influence their school, they have no power. They cannot bring about the resignation of a teacher or principal nor force a reassignment. Decisions of this nature are the province of the teachers, the principal, and the local school board. Thus, despite the conspicuous presence of parents and the extent to which they participate in school life, the schools are in most important respects autonomous from parental influence.

THE DEMOCRATIC MANAGEMENT OF SCHOOLS

Through watching the ways their schools are run, students gain impressions about the appropriate management of other institutions. Although there is little question that what goes on in Japanese schools is ultimately the responsibility of local school boards and the principal, it is remarkable the extent to which the schools manage to obscure this fact. As we have seen, students perform a great variety of managerial tasks: they call roll, clear classrooms and buildings, serve their own lunches, run the intercom system, develop and enforce codes of conduct, plan and manage sports day, and take virtually total responsibility for the diverse program of school clubs. This is not accidental. Japanese educators believe that this student participation in school constitutes important training for later citizen participation in society.

It is also of considerable interest to find that teachers participate extensively in the government of their schools—much more so than one finds in the United States. As one principal remarked, "How can teachers develop whole-men if they, in their own affairs, fail to practice democracy." But of course, the explanation for teacher power is more complex.

Chapter Three discussed how the teachers' union has become an extremely powerful force in postwar Japanese education. In many prefectures the union organization is so strong that local governments cannot proceed in educational policy without first achieving the understanding of union leaders. This stand off between the union and the government casts its shadow on the management of individual schools. Especially in areas where the union is strong, such as Kyoto, principals find it imperative to develop a cooperative rather than an authoritative relation vis-à-vis their teaching staff.

Decisions on the budget, the various schedules, teacher and student class assignments, and a multitude of other matters are all made by the teachers' meeting. This meeting convenes for about five minutes every morning and for an hour or so one afternoon per week, and it is chaired on a rotating basis by each teacher. The principal and the assistant principal are treated as ordinary members in these meetings. The assistant principal's special contribution is to make announcements about matters in which he, as full-time administrator, is especially well informed—for example, repairs of the building and grounds, the content of the daily lunches, and other operational matters. The principal is often called on to give his opinions on questions of student guidance, discussions with parents, and other educational areas, out of deference to his lengthy experience. However, it is not unusual to see other teachers dispute the principal's assertions, and sometimes the teachers' meeting even rejects the recommendation of the two administrative officers. The principal can request that individual teachers do various things, but I found no area where he could give an order; thus even when I asked for the chance to observe schools, the principal stressed he was in favor but the final decision rested with the teachers' meeting.

Concerning conduct within the classroom, the principal has virtually no role. Teachers are selected by the local school board rather than by the principal, and once appointed, they have tenure. According to the regulations, teachers are supposed to submit daily and weekly teaching plans to the principal for his inspection. But those teachers who submit plans (about half) usually do this after, rather than before, they cover the indicated material. Principals are free to visit the classrooms of teachers and frequently do so, but in a year of observation, there never occurred an instance where a principal directly rebuked a teacher. Whenever a principal had misgivings, he would try to express these in an indirect manner—with a philosophical comment at a teachers' meeting or at one of the biweekly research meetings. Also, most schools conduct periodic demonstration classes, in which all the teachers and the principal visit the class of a specific teacher; the discussions following these sessions enable the principal to make his point if no one else makes it for him. In other areas of Japan where the teachers' union is not so strong, principals are more forthright and assert greater authority than in Kyoto. Nevertheless, even in the most conservative areas, teachers are allowed considerable freedom in their classrooms and an impressive degree of influence in broader administrative decisions.[15]

At the end of each calendar year, most Japanese work organizations have some kind of party to "forget the old year" (*Bonenkai*). I had attended a number of these in the past, but none was as memorable as that of the Kyoto primary school where I first launched my fieldwork. Arriving at the party, I along with all the other attendants drew a straw to determine where to sit—would it be with the principal, the prettiest teacher, or might it be the janitor? All the nonstudent members of the school were invited without distinction. In watching the way this school had managed its daily affairs, I had increasingly come to the conclusion that the principle of hierarchical authority was virtually absent. Rather, each member, from principal to cook to teacher, was a specialist in his particular function, having special say on matters pertaining to his specialty and equal say on matters affecting the entire school. The end of the year party reflected this everyday reality. Although I drew a seat at the principal's table, he was soon moving about the room sharing his cup with all the personnel. Likewise, most of the other participants were standing about pretending to be merry and making fun of each other. Songs were half-sung, and drunken dancing feigned. After it was all over, however, traditional Japan returned. The men retired to the assistant principal's favorite bar. And after two hours of drinking, he, as the most important member of our small group, picked up the tab.

CONCLUSION

I have tried to provide the reader with an account of the Japanese educational process as I witnessed it. I had an objective in mind, to

[15] The democratic pattern of management of Japanese schools provides an interesting contrast to America's more bureaucratic style. For a discussion of the evolution of the American system, see Katz (1971).

discover egalitarian themes. Perhaps the objectives closed my eyes to other phenomena of great significance. Regardless, I think I saw enough to reach a few conclusions that are difficult to dispute:

1. Education occupies a much more central place in the lives of Japanese than American youth. Japanese children believe their performance has great personal consequences; they go to school more hours out of each year; they have fewer alternate ways to spend their time. Moreover, their parents encourage them to work hard in school. It might be said that the Japanese student's relation to his school approaches that of a patient or criminal to a total institution. When individuals like total institutions, these individuals are likely to be positively affected by the institution's treatments. Japanese children like their schools.

2. The Japanese schools aim to develop an egalitarian, whole person, as can be learned through talking to principals, teachers, and parent-teacher association officials—or by watching what goes on. Teachers attempt to draw out the full potential of their students rather than focus narrowly on cognitive achievement. And they make a conscious effort to reach the whole class.

3. As the Japanese student progresses through his educational career the emphasis on egalitarian, whole person education declines, relative to other emphases. But these later years are normally considered to be less crucial for primary socialization. This stress on the egalitarian, whole person is so strong in the early years of schooling and the Japanese student's relation to his school is so involving that it is certain it has an enduring impact. The next chapters will identify the nature of this impact and its consequences for society.

Chapter Six

COGNITIVE EQUALITY

How often does one hear an American inner-city school described as a zoo or a jungle. Veteran teachers expect the worst from their students and readily resort to punitive measures to maintain control over their classrooms. These teachers show surprise when a "poor" student answers correctly but are unmoved when a "good" student does the same. Racial labels also shape interaction. Silberman in _Crisis in the Classrooms_ (1970:92) reports the following incident from a sixth-grade racially mixed classroom: "A black girl calls out the answer to a question the teacher had asked of the entire class. 'Don't you call out,' the teacher responds. 'You sit where I put you and be quiet.' A few minutes later, when a blond-haired, blue-eyed girl calls out an answer to another question, the teacher responds, 'Very good, Annette; that's good thinking.' " A shocking proportion of the graduates of our urban schools lack even a minimal command of the basic skills of reading, writing, and arithmetic. School disorder, presumptions about the innate ability of individual students, favoritism, and low achievement do not characterize all of America's schools. Yet they are sufficiently common to attract the attention of a number of the critics of today's schools.

I found little evidence of these tendencies in my observation of Japanese schools. Japanese teachers maintained orderly classrooms. They equally distributed rewards of praise and recognition, and they worked as best they could to help all the students complete the curriculum. As I was thinking about these differences in classroom behavior, I came upon the theory of "mastery learning." This theory presents a framework for analyzing the process of learning that seems particularly appropriate for highlighting several of the distinctive features of Japanese education. Particularly, the theory helps to explain why Japanese schoolchildren do so well in mastering their curriculum. Hence, in this chapter I would like to recast several of my observations within this framework.

THE THEORY OF MASTERY LEARNING

The most lucid exposition of mastery learning is found in Benjamin Bloom's _Human Characteristics and School Learning_. In the preface,

Bloom states the central thesis of mastery learning: "Most students can learn what the schools have to teach—if the problem is approached sensitively and systematically" (1976:21). To anyone who has studied processes of transformation in a factory or an office, this proposition does not seem especially controversial. Factories have techniques for fully transforming their raw materials into products of uniformly high quality. Properly managed offices complete most of their forms. Why is it that only the schools are slipshod in their transformative goal of conveying the full curriculum to their students? The theory, through focusing on the major variables affecting school learning that are pictured in Figure 6.1, attempts to answer this question.

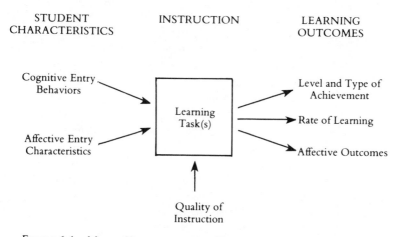

| STUDENT CHARACTERISTICS | INSTRUCTION | LEARNING OUTCOMES |

Cognitive Entry Behaviors

Affective Entry Characteristics

Learning Task(s)

Level and Type of Achievement

Rate of Learning

Affective Outcomes

Quality of Instruction

FIGURE 6.1 MAJOR VARIABLES IN THE THEORY OF MASTERY LEARNING

Instruction

The theory of mastery learning does not advocate a special curriculum, but it does have some definite implications for the organization of the curriculum. Bloom observes that it is difficult to learn if the learning objectives are not clear. Thus, he proposes a curriculum broken down into simple learning tasks.

The basic principles of instruction conducive to mastery learning are straightforward: (1) create a purposeful instructional atmosphere where frivolous distractions are minimized; (2) explain to students the tasks they will be expected to master; (3) encourage students to participate in the process of learning; (4) reward students for their achievements; (5) continuously check on the progress of students by relying on institutionalized feedback procedures; when students fail to master particular tasks provide some means (the teacher, a teacher's aid, student coaches, external tutors, or parents) for remedial learning. The theory, however, does not view these as sufficient to guarantee the expected outcomes. The techniques have to be combined with attention to the entry characteristics of learners.

Entry Characteristics

Mastery learning theory makes two simple but revolutionary assumptions about entry characteristics. First, it assumes that each learner has a personal learning history that has elevated him to a certain level of motivation and learning. It assumes that further individual development must proceed from this level—attempts to reach ahead of an individual's achievement level will be inefficient at best; more likely they will be fruitless. This assumption has different implications for individual and group learning situations. In the case of the individual, the instruction can merely be adjusted to the individual's level. In the case of the group, the instruction must be suitable for students at different entry levels. A number of different responses are possible here: individual instruction can be attempted; students can be broken into groups of different levels for separate programs; or all can be kept in a common group. Given the circumstances of a typical school, only the latter is really feasible. Hence, the most effective instruction first raises all students to a common level of achievement and then moves them through progressively advanced levels together. Behind this recommendation is the second major assumption of mastery learning: modifications are possible in the entry characteristics of individuals. Bloom suggests that it may take some time to bring those students who begin with inferior entry characteristics up to the common level, and that during this period the better-prepared students may not learn much. However, once the slow students are brought up to the common level they will be able to learn further material at virtually the same rate as their classmates.

Bloom noted how conventional teaching starts with a group of students who differ in their base level of cognitive behaviors. Due to differences in this entry characteristic, students differ in their level and rate of learning: those with higher entry learning levels progress at a faster rate, whereas the poorly prepared are soon hopelessly behind and cease to learn anything other than frustration. One consequence of different entry characteristics is a distribution of learning for a particular task that closely matches the distribution of entry behavior. A second consequence is a reduced motivation for learning among the slower students. In a large number of independently conceived studies, it is typically found that entry level explains roughly half the variation in learning of a given task. The cognitive inequality that emerges from normal educational conditions can largely be explained by the unequal entry characteristics.

Graphically, the conventional scenario can be pictured as follows (Figure 6.2). After learning task one, the students will have an average level of t_0 on some standardized test and a bell-shaped distribution of scores around that mean which have a standard deviation of $t_0{}'$. After learning task two, the mean goes up to $t_0 + x$ and the standard deviation becomes larger. After task three, these tendencies are further accentuated.

In contrast with the conventional approach, Bloom proposes a scenario in which cognitive entry characteristics are equal. Under these conditions, perhaps half the students will learn the task and half fail. However, if following the initial instruction, each student's progress is reviewed and those who do not understand are given special tutoring, then all can learn the task. To the extent all learn the initial task, they will again be equal when they approach the next task, and so on. The end result will be that all students master all of the material, and no cognitive inequality results. Entry

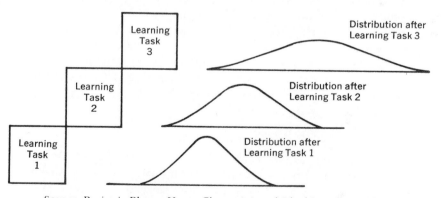

SOURCE: Benjamin Bloom, *Human Characteristics and School Learning*, p. 35.

FIGURE 6.2 THEORETICAL ACHIEVEMENT DISTRIBUTIONS IN WHICH INADEQUATE LEARNING IS NOT CORRECTED AT THE END OF EACH LEARNING TASK

characteristics will fail to predict cognitive achievement, because at
no stage will there be variation. In the studies in which mastery
learning was employed and individual mastery of each task in the
overall sequence was checked, these ideal outcomes were approxi-
mated. The relation between entry characteristics and cognitive
achievement is roughly half of what it would be with normal techniques; cognitive inequality is significantly reduced.

A more realistic scenario begins with an entering group at grade
one whose distribution of scores on a standardized test resembles
the bottom graph of Figure 6.2. However, with the application of
mastery learning techniques, a growing proportion of this class
gradually achieves mastery over the cognitive material. Thus, as
pictured in Figure 6.3, their distribution of scores gradually bunch
toward the mean with some skewing toward the positive side.

Individual "affective characteristics" are known to have an important bearing on success in conventional learning situations.
Drawing on data from the recent International Association for the
Evaluation of Educational Achievement (IEA) surveys of scholastic
achievement, Bloom shows how a student's liking for a subject is
strongly correlated with his progress in that subject. Moreover, a
student's affect toward schooling in general also is associated with
achievement. Finally, under normal teaching circumstances, an individual's "academic self-concept" is strongly associated with academic achievement, especially after the early years of primary education. Conversely, the level of an individual's motivation tends to
be influenced by performance in school: Those who do well in
school relative to their peers like learning whereas those who do
poorly develop negative attitudes. Under normal teaching circumstances this vicious circle cannot be broken. However, in several
cases where mastery learning techniques were used, there was a virtual absence of negative feelings toward learning. This was due to
mastery learning's emphasis on having all students master each task
and provision of obvious rewards for success.

Mastery Learning in Japan

Mastery learning as such has not been introduced in Japan. On the
other hand, traditional Japanese educational philosophy shares
many precepts with mastery learning. Japanese educators have
never paid much attention to the innate abilities of learners. They
have tended to assume that anybody can learn a task given a determined effort. Mind over matter is an assumption of Japanese
learning in settings as diverse as the modern classroom and the tra-

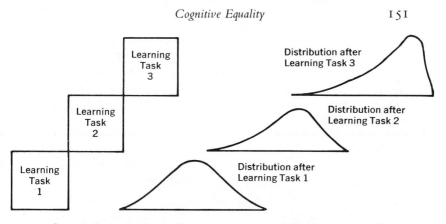

SOURCE: Benjamin Bloom, *Human Characteristics and School Learning*, p. 36.

FIGURE 6.3 THEORETICAL ACHIEVEMENT DISTRIBUTIONS IN WHICH INADEQUATE LEARNING OF THE PREVIOUS LEARNING TASKS HAS BEEN CORRECTED

ditional *dojo*, where *kendo, judo*, and other martial arts are taught. Japan's high opinion of effort is complemented by a relative disinterest in heredity: Japanese scholars, who are such vigorous translators of American fad books, have shown almost no interest in the currently popular American books that examine the heredity—intelligence—school achievement link.

It is no accident that Japan's nineteenth-century educators, after reviewing various foreign theories of pedagogy, expressed their greatest interest in the ideas of Pestalozzi and Herbart, two thinkers whom Bloom credits with laying the intellectual foundations of mastery learning theory. In the postwar period, Japan's educators have expressed strong interest in Dewey and in the Russian pedagogist, Markarenko—both of whom emphasized educational goals similar to mastery learning.[1]

Age-grading, the cultural norm of linking specific events in the cycle of social maturation with stages in biological growth, has a strong influence on Japanese social structure. When the modern school was organized, the official regulations specified the age when children should attend school. It gradually became understood that the schools should graduate their charges within the prescribed number of years, regardless of the level of each individual's

[1] See Passin (1965) for a discussion of some of the ideas affecting the early stages in the formulation of modern Japan's educational philosophy. Also see Mombusho (1972). For the postwar see Kobayashi, V. (1964).

achievement; failing a student or otherwise delaying his progress became socially unacceptable. Schools that failed students developed bad reputations, and students that were failed by their schools bore a stigma. To avoid these outcomes and, at the same time, to protect a reputation for quality education, schools came under increasing pressure to carry out a program of education that would reach all of their students.

These several external constraints, then, help us to understand why Japanese schools might be concerned with achieving the types of outcomes expected of mastery learning. However, they do not guarantee an identical set of techniques. What, then, can we say, based on our fieldwork, about the similarities and differences between mastery learning and Japanese schooling.

1. *Entry characteristics*. Clearly one of the most impressive characteristics of Japanese schooling is the care with which students are eased into the school routine. New students are treated to a series of ceremonies—beginning with a health checkup and some preliminary interviews, then an entrance ceremony, and finally a classroom welcoming ceremony—in order to facilitate their adjustment to school. Moreover, during the first ten days of school, new students attend no more than two to three hours each day so as to ease their transition from home to school. After the initial period, first year students eat lunch at school two days a week and return home on the remaining days. Only after they reach the third grade are they considered strong enough to do schoolwork every afternoon.

During the initial month of the first grade, relatively little attention is devoted to academic matters. The major goal is to get students interested in school and their classmates. Teachers rely extensively on games, art work, singing and other playlike activities to develop a cheerful classroom atmosphere. At the school where this fieldwork was done, it was found that much of the time of first graders is spent practicing a skit for the school arts day (*gakugeikai*). During this initial frivolous period, teachers attempt to bring the poorly prepared students (in, for example, the ability to write letters and numbers) up to the level of the rest.

Although these procedures to level differences in entry characteristics are impressive, one should remember that variations among students in entry characteristics may not be as great as in other advanced societies. The Japanese people are racially homogeneous, and today most enjoy a reasonable standard of living. Relatively few Japanese children come from broken homes or from isolated rural areas. Well over three fourths of all children attend at least one year of kindergarten before starting the first grade. The combination of the relatively undifferentiated cohort of students and the standard initiation to the schooling program results in favorable entry characteristics for learning.

2. *Creating a purposeful learning environment.* Classroom atmosphere is the first topic in Bloom's discussion of the quality of instruction. Much of the research on conventional classrooms indicates that teachers devote an extraordinarily high percentage of their time to managing students at the expense of time that might be devoted to managing their learning. Disorder in the classroom stands in the way of academic progress. Every minute devoted to the establishment of order is a minute lost from instruction. If, as some studies of American classrooms indicate, 40 percent of instructional time is devoted to order, the loss is enormous. It is further likely that the slow students, who require detailed instruction to master a task, suffer disproportionately from this time loss.

In Japanese classrooms, which typically have 40 students and a single teacher, the problem of maintaining order is vigorously attacked from the first day of school. As a result, by the end of the first year of primary school no more than 20 percent of classroom time (closer to 10 percent in the classrooms of experienced teachers) is devoted to managing students. The classroom, during the time of instruction, becomes a remarkably orderly and purposeful environment for learning.

3. *Participation and reinforcement.* Another feature of the Japanese classroom is the extraordinary level of individual participation—especially in the early primary years. As noted above, most teachers have the goal of eliciting at least one act of participation from each student each hour. In the most extreme case witnessed, during a single 45-minute period of a sixth grade arithmetic class, there were 84 individual verbal presentations before the class; each student spoke up at least twice during this single period. More typically, a teacher gets through about two thirds of the class in a single period; in the next period, the teacher picks up with the next student in line.

Teachers vary their strategies for eliciting participation, but generally they try to manage it in a way that does not embarrass those who participate. Whether through relying on a prescribed sequence for calling on students or through managing the difficulty of the questions tossed out, teachers generally try to give individual students a reasonable opportunity for successful participation. The goal seems to be to encourage participation with the promise that each act will be rewarded and thus to build up each participant's "academic self-concept."

Teachers are also generous in the rewards they hand out for written assignments and in-class projects. Their red pencil generously fills each student's notebook with circles for correct work.

As an additional method for enhancing participation, Japanese teachers break their classrooms up into several small groups, each with from four to six students. Frequently during each school day, the teachers turn assignments over to the groups, so each member can solve his problem and then check the results with other members. Sometimes the groups are given a problem for which they are asked to reach a collective solution. These procedures enable all of the members of the class to be involved simultaneously in intellectual work. What seems most important is that each group is assigned the identical problem—or a problem of comparable difficulty. In establishing these groups, the Japanese teacher attempts to balance each group's composition with individuals of varied ability. Teachers are resolutely opposed to tracking—that is, the establishment of separate groups for individuals with different levels of ability. They recognize that the establishment of tracking serves to aggravate inequalities in individual achievement and thereby make it difficult to carry out an orderly program of instruction for the entire class.

4. *Feedback and tutoring*. Of course, the large number of students in each classroom in Japan places severe restraints on the frequency with which teachers can check the work of students and provide appropriate rewards or remedial instruction. Every strategy observed had its advantages and weaknesses.

Perhaps the most commonly used technique was for the teacher to deliver a short talk on a new idea and then assign a set of problems at the beginning of the period. As soon as a student completed the assignment, he raced to the front of the classroom and stood in line beside the teacher's desk to have the work reviewed. When this procedure was used, teachers often asked the quickest students to help those who seemed slow. In this way, the procedure included both a teaching and tutorial mechanism. The main drawback in this approach was that a classroom tended to break down into a state of near bedlam toward the end of the period with loud conversations, some running, and other rowdiness. Glued to her desk in order to correct the problems, the teacher usually found it impossible to control the class.

In a second strategy students stayed at their desks, and the teacher walked around the classroom. This technique was more successful in maintaining order, but it reduced the number of student exercises the teacher could review. On the other hand, it provided the teacher with the opportunity to directly approach those students who were most likely to be in need of help. Through checking with the students, the teacher could readily determine the extent to which the lesson was understood by all.

Two other approaches are resorted to, though somewhat less frequently by teachers: correcting student exercises at home in the evening and holding special remedial classes after school for slow students. Traditionally, Japanese teachers were known for the extraordinary extent to which they took on those extra activities. But today's teachers are more restrained; their expressed excuse for avoiding these extra duties is that they would be working more hours than they are paid for. However, other considerations are also important. Compared with thirty years ago, actual classroom time has increased by 10 percent, and the amount of material to be covered in a year has increased even more. To provide quality instruction, teachers feel they need to set aside more time for preparation. To find this time, many cut back on the traditional tutorial and feedback activities. In this respect, then, the Japanese school has actually departed somewhat from the mastery learning ideal. The procedures for systematic feedback and remedial instruction are possibly inferior to those of the past.

5. *The demanding curriculum.* Although Japanese teachers develop their own teaching routines, they must work with a fixed curriculum. The Ministry of Education has developed an official course of instruction, which it uses to evaluate and approve texts for classroom use. Local governments have the option to choose from among these texts, and to do so, they seek the advice of their teachers. Unfortunately, many teachers find all the available texts to be poorly organized and overly demanding. In their view the responsibility lies with the central government. Twice during the postwar period the central government revised the course of study, and each time it increased the amount of material that young people have to learn. Teachers complain that the curriculum by 1958 already was too demanding. With the second increase in 1968, even more students are destined to be left behind. Their criticisms are based on their classroom experiences in which they find that many students cannot grasp essentials in the time allowed teachers to convey them and still complete the text.

Some teachers also question the organization of the course of study, in particular its underlying theory of instruction. These teachers favor a curriculum organized around learning tasks arranged in logical sequence. They ask, for example, why the character for forest (*hayashi* 林) composed of two tree ideographs should be taught before the basic character for tree (*ki* 木). And they ask what sense it makes to start on division before complex multiplication when the latter skills are basic to the former. Teachers report numerous flaws of this nature in the course of study, which becomes the guide for the creation of individual texts.[2]

In recent years, teachers have established their own working groups to develop new principles for the organization of the curriculum. One of the best-known groups, located in an isolated section of Kyoto prefecture, has taken the first step toward a plan of organization similar to that which mastery learning prescribes.[3]

A major concern of this group is to develop some new way of assigning grades to individual students. They feel it is unfair to grade students on their absolute level of performance, for this discriminates against the students who start out at a lower level. Through identifying learning units, the researchers feel they will be in a better position to identify each student's starting point. Then they can measure individual progress relative to this starting point, and use relative progress as a basis for grades. The resemblance of this experimental work to mastery learning's emphasis on individual mastery of clearly defined learning tasks is obvious. Although the research described here is in its infancy, it has caught the imagination of a large number of teachers across Japan. Clearly, this experimental work reflects a sentiment among teachers to approach the curriculum in a new way, not unlike mastery learning. However, this sentiment has not yet been translated into practice on a very wide scale.

6. *Conventional methods after the primary school.* We should emphasize that the generalizations we have developed apply mainly to

[2] The theme of an overdemanding curriculum has been characteristic of the progressive teachers' union throughout the postwar period. Along with Makieda (1975), see the official union position compiled by Umene (1972). In contrast, some conservative critics argue that different curriculums should be developed for children at different ability levels.

[3] The information on this project was supplied by members of the Kyoto Prefecture teachers' union.

the primary school. Our observations of the middle school suggest that teachers gradually shift away from mastery learning principles. Although all students attend middle schools and study a common course, they receive their instruction from specialists in each subject. Compared to the primary school teachers, the middle school teachers seem most concerned with covering all the material in the texts during classroom hours. They believe they will be held responsible if any material not covered is subsequently tested for in high school. Due to the emphasis on the text, middle school teachers show less interest in how much individual students master. Students are advised to seek help at home in mastering the material not learned in school. Despite this admonition, one could expect incomplete mastery and, hence, declining learning rates among many middle school students.

7. *The broader context of learning.* The theory of mastery learning does not take up several aspects of the broader context of learning that may have some bearing on cognitive equality—at least if the concern is with the distribution of cognitive scores for social units larger than classrooms. In that most of the available data is based on national rather than classroom samples, several ways in which the broader context affects cognitive equality should be noted.

a. A single nationwide educational standard. If students are taught different materials, they are unlikely to know the same things and thus perform equivalently on tests of cognitive achievement. In some of the advanced societies, a decentralized system of school control and a reliance on the unregulated free market for the development and sale of school texts results in a wide variation in the cognitive materials to which students are exposed. These conditions clearly apply in the United States. In contrast, as already indicated, the texts used throughout Japan are prepared so as to convey the learning tasks prescribed by the Ministry of Education's official course of study. As a result, children are exposed to virtually identical cognitive material regardless of the school attended. The uniform educational standard continues through the ninth grade with only modest tolerance for adjustments to special local circumstances. It is not until the high school level that students began to choose between different courses and lectures, and even at this level their options are constrained within national guidelines.[4]

---

[4] The text refers to the situation through 1979. Changes in the official course of study to have effect from 1980 will allow modest variation from the middle school level.

b. Equal educational facilities. Recent empirical research indicates that, at least in the advanced societies, the quality of school buildings, educational technology, and other facilities has a modest influence on student achievement when compared with variables such as family background and teacher quality. However, these studies suggest that facilities do make some difference, especially for slow learners who are not easily motivated by conventional cues. In Japan, facilities are also regulated by a national standard. Today, because of the central government's policy of equalizing local educational expenditures, expenditures per student vary no more than 55 percent between the most affluent and the least affluent prefectures (and much of this variation can be explained by differences in the cost of living). Within most prefectures, differences in per-student expenditures for schools with a common objective are also quite small. The central government has developed special programs to cover the extra costs of education in such outlying areas as island and mountain districts. These include salary incentive schemes to attract qualified teachers. Also, the central government provides special subsidies for those schools located in the special neighborhoods where Japan's outcastes (*burakumin*) are concentrated. As a result of measures such as these, there is little variation in the quality of facilities between schools and regions. The recent IEA (International Education Association) study of science achievement reported that in Japan, due to lack of variation, the several measures of school facilities had no relation to science achievement (Comber and Keeves, 1973).

c. Training and experience of teachers. Despite the aptitude of an individual for teaching, teachers still require time and experience to reach their maximum levels of effectiveness. In Japan, as elsewhere, new teachers are continually being recruited, and older ones are retiring, so that at any given time there are large numbers of teachers who are not performing at their peak. However, in contrast with certain other advanced societies, teaching in Japan is a respected occupation that provides a decent income. Moreover, Japanese teachers, along with most other workers of the modern sector, enjoy permanent employment; once hired, they are unlikely to be relieved from their duties except under the most extraordinary circumstances, such as moral turpitude. Even if a local area experiences severe depopulation, the local government will take steps to find jobs for unneeded teachers in a nearby area.

Due to these relatively favorable employment conditions, the

Japanese school systems recruit qualified people. According to the recent IEA survey of science achievement, 95 percent of the Japanese middle school teachers in charge of science courses had a university education, the highest percentage among the eighteen countries participating in the survey. Ninety percent of the teachers were male, second only to India with 91 percent. Even including women, for whom the tendency is to continue teaching during marriage and child-rearing, most teachers look on their jobs as lifetime careers. Thus, in the IEA survey, only 11 percent of the Japanese teachers were twenty-seven years or younger; in other advanced societies, the proportion of young and hence presumably inexperienced teachers tended to be higher: 28 percent for the United States, 16 percent for Scotland, 23 percent for Hungary, 32 percent for England, and 50 percent for Australia. Finally, the survey provided some indication that Japanese teachers approach their work in a more professional way: 74 percent reported that they belonged to some kind of teacher membership association in which they discussed teaching procedures with colleagues. In no other society was such a large proportion of teachers involved in these associations (Cummings, 1977).

JAPAN'S EQUAL EDUCATIONAL OUTCOMES

This selective review of Japan's educational system has identified many features that resemble those advocated in the theory of mastery learning: a concern with simplifying learning tasks, an effort to smooth out differences in the entry characteristics of students, the implementation of procedures to insure a purposeful classroom atmosphere, the maximization of individual participation in the classroom, and the generous allocation of rewards to students. In addition, Japanese teachers who are, comparatively speaking, well qualified and experienced are confident in the learning potential of all students. They are not impressed by the scientific evidence that suggests school achievement is genetically determined. Instead, they believe anyone can learn if he tries and is appropriately guided.

The several features of Japanese egalitarian education listed above lead one to expect cognitive and motivational outcomes for Japanese school graduates that resemble those predicted by mastery learning: a high average level of cognitive achievement with little variation around the mean, and a high level of motivation for further learning. The IEA study of science achievement provides strong confir-

mation of this expectation. The top half of Figure 6.4 provides a
graphic comparison of the performance of Japanese eleven year olds
and eleven year olds in eleven other advanced nations on the science
achievement test administered by the International Educational Association. The Japanese mean is far above that for other advanced
societies; and the coefficient of variation, which indicates degree of
dispersion, is considerably smaller. Moreover, the Japanese score
high on a standardized measure of motivation to learn. The bottom
half of Figure 6.4 provides a graphic comparison for fourteen year
olds. Again the Japanese mean is far above the average for children

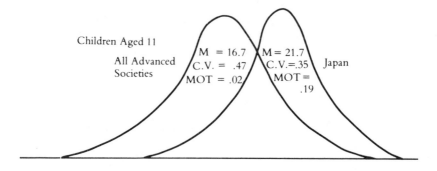

KEY: M = mean scores on the respective tests; C.V. = coefficient of variation on tests; MOT = average
standard score (average of all students in IEA survey is 0) on a scale that indicates attitude to school.
SOURCE: See Appendix to Chapter Six.

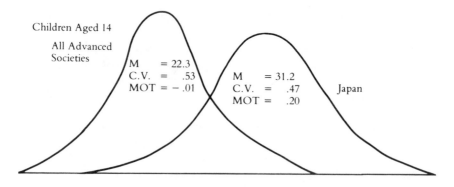

FIGURE 6.4   A COMPARISON OF THE PERFORMANCE OF JAPANESE
SCHOOL CHILDREN AND THE CHILDREN OF ALL
HIGHLY ADVANCED SOCIETIES ON THE INTERNATIONAL
TEST OF SCIENCE ACHIEVEMENT

in advanced societies, and the coefficient of variation is somewhat smaller. As with the younger group, Japanese youths score high on the standardized measure of motivation to learn. Much the same pattern of findings was reported in the international study of math achievement conducted in the early sixties. A more detailed report of the available comparative evidence, presented in the appendix to this chapter, provides an even clearer indication of the distinctiveness of the Japanese school's cognitive outcomes. In no other society are the schools able to promote such a large proportion of their pupils to the high level of mastery found in Japan.

A Thesis on Japan's Cognitive Inequality

Thus far, attention has been directed to explaining Japan's cognitive equality, the exceptional average level and the modest dispersion around this mean on internationally administered tests. This cognitive equality is especially notable at the primary level, but even at the middle school level Japan compares favorably to the other advanced societies. Still, all Japanese young people do not perform equally on these tests. It is the differences in performance that are more salient from the local point of view.

What explains the differences in the cognitive achievements of Japanese young people? A mechanical answer would point to the same variables that are known to be important in other advanced societies: favorable home circumstances including educated parents, books in the home, small family size, and a special room for study; the opportunity to go to a superior school, where the facilities are outstanding and the teachers highly qualified; and the individual's interest in learning. Most of these factors can be shown to have some relation to the differential performances of Japanese young people on cognitive achievement tests, and in that sense are important (Comber and Keeves, 1973:257). However, they do not take into account the special aspects of the Japanese situation.

Among these variables, those concerning home circumstances deserve more careful consideration. As indicated in Chapter Four, there is relatively little variation in Japan in those aspects of home circumstances that are likely to have a direct effect on the cognitive development of young people. There are few outstanding class differences in family structure or child-rearing practices, and compared to the other advanced societies, Japanese families have less variation in level of parental education and number of children and several other variables. These considerations lead to the expectation that home is relatively less influential on preschool development in Japan. In fact, several studies report low correlations between indicators of conditions in the home and the achievement of Japanese children in the early years (see Chapter Four).

However, as Japanese young people advance in their school careers, variables of home circumstance become more predictive of differential performance. Nakano (1974), following Bernstein's hypothesis of class-differentiated linguistic capabilities, investigated the language behavior of several small samples of fifth graders. She found little difference in the language patterns that students of different classes selected for their conversational behavior. On the other hand, when writing essays, children from new middle-class families tended to organize their thoughts with a more complicated logic and to express their thoughts with a more complicated sentence structure. Underlying these differences, she suggests, is class variation in basic intellectual ability, rather than the qualitative difference in linguistic codes found by Bernstein in the United Kingdom. The Japanese data from the IEA study also show a significant class effect for fifth graders and for eighth graders. Other studies show significant class effects for high schoolers (Ushiogi et al., 1972; Kokuritsu Kyoiku Kenkyusho, 1966–1968; Central Council for Education, 1972:129 ff.). Somehow, between the first and fifth grades, families begin to differentially affect the cognitive development of their children.[5]

Over these early school years, it is doubtful that differential material circumstances are the main explanatory factor. Children obtain their texts and most of the other materials they need from school. For the type and amount of homework assigned primary students, it is unlikely that an individual study room, encyclopedia,

---

[5] In a recent survey of nineteen studies of school achievement in developing countries, Simmons and Alexander (1978:348) find that class effects generally are weak, but among children going to school tend to be stronger in the lower grades. In Japan, with respect to cognitive achievement the pattern is opposite to that reported by Simmons—that is, class effects are stronger in the higher grades. One reason surely is that the variations in class background of students in many developing countries quickly narrow after about the fourth grade as children without economic resources drop out. In contrast, in Japan virtually all youths continue through high school. Although class effects on cognitive achievement appear to increase with grade level in Japan, class effects on motivation and value transmission possibly decrease (see Chapter Seven). Families, by and large, do not use their private resources for special programs in these noncognitive areas, whereas the schools that all children attend emphasize these areas.

or other favorable circumstances in the home would have much bearing on individual growth. The major differentiating factor in these early years is probably the quality of instructional aid that children receive at home, as they review each day's lessons.

In the discussion of the primary school's egalitarian education, two key problems were identified: the curriculum includes too much, and the instruction lacks systematic methods for feedback and remedial instruction. In the early years, when the curriculum is not demanding, these problems are not so serious. Beginning in grade four, however, they become more important. Those children who neither learn the lesson at school nor receive help at home are destined to fall behind. On the average, primary school students report spending seven hours each week on homework and review; interestingly, the poorer students spend relatively more time at home study (Comber and Keeves, 1973:250). Thus, normal progress may depend not so much on the time spent in review but rather on the efficiency with which that time is used. By the latter years of the primary school, a well-educated mother who is concerned with her child's school performance proves an indispensable aid in the daily study routine. As such mothers are most common in middle- and upper-class families, it is not surprising that class background begins to have a stronger relation to cognitive achievement.

However, as young people move beyond the primary school level, the curriculum becomes so difficult that most mothers find they are no longer able to provide direct assistance to their children. As the mothers' abilities become strained, many begin to send their children to special *juku*, where guidance is provided by professional teachers. In some cases, families hire a special tutor to provide instruction at home. Needless to say, the higher a family's class position, the more it is likely to be able to spend on these instructional aids. Thus, in Japan, after the early years of primary school, class position becomes a factor in cognitive achievement.

Still, it should be noted that class has a somewhat weaker association in Japan than in several other advanced societies. Compared with class variables, motivation variables have a stronger association with cognitive achievement in Japan (see Table 6.1). In that upper- and middle-class parents show a greater interest in the school performance of their children,[6] one might think that motiva-

---

[6] In their recent study of school children Fukaya and Fukaya (1975:144) report that in the most zealous families the parents are college educated, the father is a profes-

TABLE 6.1

PEARSON PRODUCT MOMENT CORRELATIONS OF SCIENCE ACHIEVEMENT SCORES WITH STATUS
VARIABLES AND MOTIVATION VARIABLES FOR SEVERAL ADVANCED SOCIETIES

	Japan	England	Federal Republic of Germany	Nether-lands	Scotland	Sweden	United States
Fifth grade primary school students							
Status variables							
Father's occupation	28 (4th)	38	20	26	39	24	39
Home circumstances	33 (4th)	41	20	30	42	27	40
Books in home	29 (4th)	33	22	23	37	24	30
Motivation variables							
Like school	15 (1st)	12	3	8	6	4	4
Hours reading for pleasure	24 (3rd)	35	20	21	37	15	23
Eighth grade middle school students							
Status variables							
Mother's education	21 (2nd)	20	13	12	19	17	25
Father's occupation	24 (5th)	34	19	25	39	23	31
Home circumstances	38 (4th)	45	31	27	48	28	41
Books in home	32 (3rd)	34	22	12	36	20	25
Motivation variables							
Like school	20 (2nd)	19	13	3	23	20	13
Science interest	49 (1st)	39	27	26	42	35	35
Expected education	47 (1st)	45	31	40	46	31	28
Hours reading for pleasure	23 (3rd)	26	11	7	28	5	20

SOURCE: Comber and Keeves, *Science Education in Nineteen Countries*, 1973.

tion would be strongly associated with class variables. However, in Japan it turns out that class variables explain less than 5 percent of the variance in student motivation. Possibly, the concern of many parents is counterproductive. The Fukayas (1975:18), who studied several hundred families, found that children become noticeably cool to parental attempts to motivate achievement as they move into the latter years of primary school. Some children manipulate parental zeal. Befu (1971:159) relates how children extort the best room in the house, expensive cakes and cookies for study breaks, and other privileges from their anxious parents. Although zealous parents tend to be generally successful in motivating their children, some fail abysmally and drive their children into the growing numbers of children who dislike school. Partly for this reason and partly because of egalitarian education's concern with developing strong motivation in all students, most studies of general student populations in Japan indicate only modest correlations between class background and motivation to learn.

If class does not account for much of the variation in motivation, what does? Earlier it was observed that Japan's egalitarian education is most characteristic of the primary school. From the latter years of the primary school and especially after the beginning of middle school, teachers, anxious to cover the demanding curriculum, adopt more conventional teaching methods and devote less attention to the individual student's mastery of the subject matter. Due to this shift, many students begin to fall behind, and one would expect the distribution of cognitive achievement test scores for Japanese middle school students to become more dispersed and somewhat negatively skewed—an expectation confirmed by the IEA science achievement tests (see Figure 6.4). With the shift to conventional methods, Japanese middle school teachers become more severe and judicious in rewarding student performance.

---

sional or manager with an income in excess of six thousand dollars, there is only one child, and the mother does not work. The Fukayas asked several hundred mothers of sixth grade children just what level of school performance they hoped for. Virtually all mothers said they hoped their children would be in the top half of the class; college-educated mothers expressed a desire for their children to be in the top eighth.

[7] For example, in his study of urban family structure, Oyama (n.d.:58) reports that most families agree they should spend as much money as they can on their children's education. However, it is the white-collar workers who stand out in terms of actual expenditures.

Differential grading results in differential motivation for learning and, hence, achievement. This process may transpire completely independently of any differences in social class.

These observations suggest the thesis that the most important factor influencing motivational differentiation is performance in school, and differential motivation in turn promotes differential performance. The strong association between these two variables is only modestly reduced after controlling for the influence of other factors. A major source of cognitive inequality, then, is what goes on in the school, not what impinges from without.

Achievement Tests, Grades, and Entrance Exams

The discussion thus far has focused on individual performance on achievement tests, but these tests are not what Japanese schools use to measure a student's progress. From month to month, Japanese schools evaluate students on the basis of grades. For the transitions between educational levels, entrance exams are utilized.

Grades are usually administered along a five-point scale with roughly half going to the average mark of 3, 20 percent each to 2 and 4, and the remaining 10 percent divided between 1 and 5. Teachers report that grading is one of their most difficult tasks, perhaps because of the narrow range in actual achievement. In any case, the grades that teachers do assign have a reasonably strong association with test scores.

The best evidence of this comes from the series of studies on the correlates of educational performance and cognitive achievement among middle schoolers in ten local areas conducted in 1965 by the National Institute of Education (Kokuritso Kyoiku Kenkyusho, 1966-1968). Two of these local studies report correlations between grades and a battery of four achievement tests. The correlations range between .57 and .72; comparable American studies report slightly lower correlations (Jencks et al., 1972:111 and n. 7).

Although grades are given out each academic quarter, Japanese schools do not emphasize them in promoting students from one year to the next. Once a student enters a particular primary, middle, or high school, his promotion there is virtually automatic.

Of course, in the Japanese educational system, it is not this yearly progression but rather the big leap from one school level or institution to another that has the greatest bearing on individual success. The most important of these movements is from the high school to the university. As there are great variations among universities, ambitious high school students compete to gain entrance to one of the handful of well-known institutions. Their fate in this competition is determined by their performance on the entrance exams prepared and administered by each of the universities they apply to. In addition, most students write at least two exams prior to the stage of university entrance in their attempts to gain entry into the middle and high schools of their choice. Because the alternatives at these stages are complex, they will be discussed in more detail in Chapter Eight. Here, the content of entrance exams and the kind of aptitudes required for passing will be examined.

At all school levels, entrance exams are prepared by the institutions receiving new students. These exams are invariably demanding, but in many cases they do not test the content of the instruction in the preceding schools. Often, the exams skip over ordinary problems and well-known facts to focus on esoteric questions. They test traits that may have little relation to cognitive abilities, such as the student's willingness to spend long hours studying, his attention to detail, and his fortune in covering the tested material (Dore, 1976). Most university entrance exams also strongly emphasize foreign languages, regardless of an individual's intended field of specialization.

When one analyzes the way young people prepare for these exams, it is obvious that they do not consider cognitive achievement a sufficient or even necessary ingredient of success. The folklore of exam preparation stresses effort: it is said that a young person who spends more than four hours sleeping each night is sure to fail. Long hours of diligent study are considered critical in mastering the esoteric material covered in the exams.

Students and parents doubt that the normal school curriculum provides the best orientation to exams. Thus, they put great pressure on the schools to concentrate more on exam preparation and less on whole-person education. Throughout the nation, public middle schools and high schools curtail the extracurricular activities of third year students to meet the task of exam preparation. Apart from going to school, preparation may take the form of attending extra-schools, known as *juku* and *yobiko*, or hiring tutors. It is quite common for a youth to spend a year or two after high school devoting his full time to exam preparation; in recent years, roughly 40 percent of those who gain admittance to a university have spent at least one year in the *ronin* status of full-time study (Mombusho,

1975:37). Needless to say, these special aids cost money, and it is the more affluent and education-oriented families who are most prepared to pay for them.[7]

In addition, to accommodate those preparing for university entrance exams, a number of well-known private schools exist that devote themselves almost exclusively to this goal. Tuition at most of these schools is substantial and beyond the reach of ordinary families.

This brief review of how Japanese students prepare for exams suggests that not only effort but also strong financial backing is an important aid in passing exams. To what extent do these factors override cognitive achievements? A lack of systematic data unfortunately prevents a clear answer. However, several pieces of information suggest that cognitive achievement may be subordinate to these other factors. As indicated in Chapter Eight, those who succeed in gaining entrance to the best high schools and universities are overwhelmingly from the upper and middle classes. An extensive government survey indicates that entrants to national universities tend to have higher high school grade-point averages than those who enter public and private universities (the latter are generally lower in quality). Yet 46 percent of the national university entrants had average or below-average grades (Mombusho, 1970:18-19).

More evidence comes from a Japanese study attempting to predict the academic performance of university students from several indicators of preuniversity performance. American research generally shows that high school grades are the best predictor of university performance (grade-point averages), often accounting for as much as one fourth of the variance. In the Japanese study, high school grades accounted for only 9 percent of the variance in university performance of first-year students; by the third year, grades accounted for less than 4 percent. What is more, no other predictor of academic ability (performance on an achievement test, entrance exam score) proved any more successful in predicting university performance (Central Council for Education, 1972:171). It would appear that success in university entrance and university performance are only modestly associated with preuniversity cognitive achievement.

The lack of association between school grades and entrance procedures has one salutary consequence deserving brief mention. Because grades do not have long-run consequences for individual achievement, teachers, especially at the primary level, feel somewhat at ease in assigning them for reasons other than performance. Although departures from strict, objective grading are exceptional, a number of alternatives do exist. Many teachers say they try to give every student at least one good grade each quarter to give them something to be proud of. On the other hand, they avoid giving all 5's as this would make a child too conceited. Sometimes a teacher will encourage a student by progressively raising a grade from quarter to quarter, even if the grade is incommensurate with the level of achievement. Finally, a few teachers report that, in a particularly egalitarian mood, they dispense with grading altogether and instead give straight 3's to all their students.

Differences by Sex

The focus in this chapter has been on the cognitive achievement of all children, with some attention to differential achievement by class. In many countries, sex is another variable known to have an important impact on achievement. Certainly, in Japan's old system of education, expectations of achievement for boys and girls differed as did the educational programs prepared for these two groups. However, following the war, virtually all of the formal differences in programs were removed from the official educational system, and teachers were exhorted to treat the two sexes equally. Opinions vary as to Japan's progress in this aspect of equal treatment, for, inevitably, personal standards enter into these evaluations.

At various points, this account of Japan's education (Chapter Five) has indicated how teachers and the school treated boys and girls. To recount them, class seating is arranged so that boys sit behind boys and girls sit behind girls in respective columns facing the teacher; home economics courses are directed at girls, whereas industrial arts shops are often provided for boys. Although these unequal treatments were evident, the relative equality of treatment was more impressive. In the classroom, teachers rarely referred to particular kinds of behavior as girlish, nor did they reserve heavier jobs for boys. Whether the subject matter was science or literature, boys and girls were called on with equal frequency. In one primary school, sixth grade boys and girls participated together in a vigorous soccer game. And middle school girls were as eager to enjoy the sports clubs as boys.

In achievement, there is the familiar pattern of sex "specialization" by subject. Boys are better in math and the sciences while

girls are better in the arts—yet the differences in Japan are not especially large. For example, according to the IEA study (Comber and
Keeves, 1973:248, 258) at the primary level, sex (girls were assigned
a score of 1, boys 0) correlated −.08 with science achievement in
Japan, compared with −.09 in the United States and an average of
−.11 across the fifteen countries covered. At the middle school
level, the correlation in Japan was −.28, compared with −.22 in the
United States and an average of −.20 for the seventeen countries
included.

There is sex differentiation in student achievement in Japan but
one hesitates to say it is especially large. Today, more Japanese girls
than boys complete high school, and nearly as many girls enter a
higher educational institution. Although girls are more likely than
boys to attend a junior college, a growing proportion are entering
the elite universities and fields traditionally dominated by men, especially the sciences and medicine. In view of the highly formalized
sex discrimination that characterized Japanese education through
World War II, these developments gain added significance.

CONCLUSION

Much of the research supporting mastery learning has been conducted at the classroom level. In this chapter, the discussion has
moved to the national level to ask whether the theory is useful in
predicting aggregated outcomes for thousands of geographically
dispersed classrooms. Although the internal diversity of most nations jeopardizes the value of aggregate data, this is less of a problem in Japan, as there is a centralized education system and a unified
educational tradition. As predicted by the theory of mastery learning, that Japanese primary school students achieve exceptionally
high average levels of cognitive performance as well as develop
high levels of motivation for further learning. Moreover, there is
relatively less variation around these means than in most other
societies. These generalizations hold, though with lesser force, for
Japanese students at the middle school level and, it can be supposed,
even for those at more advanced stages, such as the high schools
and universities. Family background appears to have only a moderate impact on cognitive achievement, though its relation to entrance exam success and actual educational attainment may be more
pronounced.

Japan's egalitarian schools provide society with successive

cohorts of young people who, almost without exception, have a reasonable ability in cognitive tasks and a desire to exercise this ability. Traditionally, adult society was not accustomed to receiving such capable groups of youths. It is probable that the contemporary situation, with successive cohorts of cognitively able and motivated young people entering society, places unusual pressure on the adult society. In Chapter Nine, some of the implications of this will be explored.

Figure 6.4 compared the distribution of scores of Japanese school-children on the IEA science achievement test with the distribution for all youths in the highly advanced societies. In this appendix, more detailed data on Japanese test score distributions are presented. Table A.1 presents science achievement means and co-efficients of variation and standardized "likes school" scores for each of the countries that participated in the science survey.

The mean scores for Japanese schoolchildren on science achievement at both the fifth grade primary and second grade middle school levels were the highest of all the nations in the study. The coefficient of variation for the primary school group was the lowest and for the middle school group the third lowest. Finally, concerning "likes school," the attitudinal variable that provides the best indication of student motivation, the Japanese score was second highest (again following Hungary, which reported data for only a segment of the cohort). The Tomoda study, reported in Chapter Seven, indicates that the mean level of occupational aspirations of Japanese high school students is higher than that of American students, whereas, in contrast with the American pattern, in Japan no relation is found between social background and aspiration level.

Prior to the science achievement survey, the IEA conducted a comparative study of math achievement, which produced a some-what similar ranking in terms of national means and coefficients of variation. In the tests administered to thirteen year olds, Japan's mean was highest and its coefficient of variation tied for second lowest (see Table A.2).

The Japanese youths sampled for the math study indicated a high average level of motivation toward school and toward learning math. Although, at the time of writing, intercorrelation matrices by country for all relevant variables were not obtainable, they were available for the math study. From these matrices Figure A.1 has been constructed. As argued in Chapter Four, in Japan status is a relatively unimportant predictor of achievement and has only a modest relation to motivation. However, the figure provides another illustration of the relatively strong association between motivation and achievement.

In the preparation for this field study, several informants were

TABLE A.1

MEANS AND COEFFICIENTS OF VARIATION FOR THE DISTRIBUTIONS OF SCORES ON THE INTERNATIONAL SCIENCE ACHIEVEMENT TEST

	Primary School Sample (about Age 11)			Middle School Sample (about Age 14)		
	Mean	Coefficient of Variation	Standardized Score on the Likes School Variable	Mean	Coefficient of Variation	Standardized Score on the Likes School Variable
Japan	21.7	.355	.19	31.2	.474	.20
Australia	—	—	—	24.6	.545	-.09
Belgium (Flemish)	17.9	.408	-.13	21.2	.434	.13
Belgium (French)	13.9	.511	.09	15.4	.571	-.05
Chile	9.1	.945	-.16	9.2	.967	-.22
England	15.7	.541	.05	21.3	.662	.07
Federal Republic of Germany	14.9	.497	-.18	23.7	.485	-.26
Finland	17.5	.468	-.08	20.5	.517	-.16
Hungary	16.7	.479	.35	29.1	.436	.29
India	8.5	.976	-.19	7.6	1.184	-.01
Iran	4.1	1.317	.12	7.8	.782	.13
Italy	16.5	.521	.06	18.5	.551	.01
Netherlands	15.3	.497	-.19	17.8	.562	-.14
New Zealand	—	—	—	24.2	.533	.14
Scotland	14.0	.600	.05	21.4	.664	.03
Sweden	18.3	.399	-.36	21.7	.539	-.37
Thailand	9.9	.657	.23	15.6	.519	.10
United States	17.7	.525	.14	21.6	.537	.19

SOURCE: L. C. Comber and John P. Keeves, *Science Education in Nineteen Countries*, pp. 159, 108.

Table A.2
ACHIEVEMENT TEST MEANS AND COEFFICIENTS OF VARIATION ON
MATHEMATICS FOR THIRTEEN-YEAR-OLDS

	Mean	13-Year-Olds
Australia	20.2	.693
Belgium	27.7	.542
England	19.3	.881
Finland	24.1	.411
France	18.3	.678
Japan	31.2	.542
Netherlands	23.9	.665
Scotland	19.1	.764
Sweden	15.7	.689
United States	16.2	.821

SOURCE: Torsten Husén, ed. *International Study of Achievement in Mathematics: A Comparison of Twelve Countries*, vol. 2.

NOTE: Population considered here is labelled Pop. 1a in the report.

asked the area in which egalitarian educational principles are most firmly entrenched. This led to the selection of Kyoto as the primary site for the fieldwork. Previously, in 1965, the National Institute of Education had conducted various tests of academic achievement in samples of Japanese middle schoolers in ten local areas. The means and coefficients of variation for each of these local areas is reported in Table A.3. As can be seen, Kyoto, the reputed forerunner in egalitarian education, tends to have a high mean (highest on one, second highest on two, and third on the remaining test) and a low coefficient of variation (second from the bottom on all four tests)

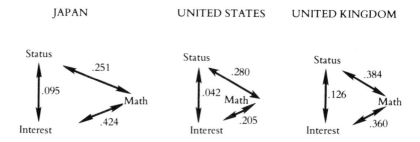

FIGURE A.1   INTERRELATIONS OF FATHER'S OCCUPATIONAL STATUS,
INTEREST IN MATH, AND TOTAL MATH SCORE

MEANS AND COEFFICIENTS OF VARIATIONS ON FOUR COGNITIVE ACHIEVEMENT TESTS
ADMINISTERED TO SAMPLES OF NINTH GRADERS

	Differential Aptitude Test: Verbal Reasoning		American College Testing Program Mathematics Usage Test		Japanese Word Association and Sentence Under-standing Test		Japanese Numerical Ability Test	
	Mean	Coefficient of Variation	Mean	Coefficient of Variation	Mean	Coefficient of Variation	Mean	Coefficient of Variation
Kyoto	25.6	.367	15.6	.474	26.2	.328	26.1	.414
Kobe	26.5	.328	17.5	.457	26.9	.312	25.9	.398
Tokyo	25.0	.384	15.9	.491	25.5	.345	24.6	.423
Saitama	20.6	.427	12.1	.504	22.2	.369	21.1	.460
Hyogo	23.0	.404	14.3	.497	24.0	.346	23.3	.438
Wakayama	19.8	.434	13.5	.585	22.3	.350	20.7	.435
Shiga	21.1	.431	13.4	.500	23.2	.366	22.3	.448
Kawasaki	23.0	.404	13.1	.481	23.8	.361	21.6	.463
Yokohama	22.3	.435	12.3	.512	22.8	.408	21.2	.467
Miyazaki	21.1	.403	12.9	.620	22.5	.373	19.9	.452

SOURCE: Kokuritsu Kyoiku Kenkyusho (National Institute of Education), *Shunendo Chosa: Chugakko Sotsugyo Jikki no Jokyo* (Initial Survey: The Situation at the Time of Graduation from Middle School). Separate reports for each of the local areas were released under this general title from 1966 to 1968.

on each of these tests. The data are insufficient on other educational outcomes, but these limited findings support the view that Kyoto's educational system is different, or at least at one extreme within the Japanese system. For the present study, it is important to note that this is the extreme with the most egalitarian outcomes, at least in terms of cognitive achievement.

All the same, it should be emphasized that the differences in mean scores and coefficients of variation for the ten Japanese districts are not great. One of these tests, the Differential Aptitude Test verbal reasoning battery, was originally developed and administered in the United States. The results for a similar age-group in America fall outside of the Japanese ranges: according to the official manual for this test (Bennett et al., 1952:26), which is based on data from tests administered to large numbers of American children, the mean is lower (18.5) and the coefficient of variation is higher (.468). Field observations in several other prefectures indicate that Kyoto may be the forerunner in Japan's egalitarian whole-man education, yet Kyoto's practices are not vastly different from what one study found in other areas of Japan. Although there is variation within Japan in terms of educational outcomes and although Kyoto is at one end of that distribution, it also appears plausible that the several Japanese districts are bunched toward one end of a hypothetical international distribution.

Chapter Seven.

THE DEVELOPMENT OF THE
EGALITARIAN SENTIMENT

Much of the current literature on schooling refers to those activities creating value change and other noncognitive outcomes as part of the "hidden curriculum." The implication is that schools are or should be only concerned with cognitive development, and that noncognitive outcomes are incidental. Indeed, American schools since Sputnik have focused with unprecedented energy on cognitive outcomes at the expense of other curricular goals.[1] In Japan, at least in the early years of schooling, the emphasis is reversed. Teachers, schools, local boards, nationwide institutions such as the Ministry of Education and the teachers' union all devote considerable attention to value education and even prepare lengthy documents outlining their plans in this noncognitive area. Although the content of the documents developed by these competing actors often differs, there is nothing "hidden" about them. The following discussion draws on some of these documents.

It is the conclusion here that the explicit efforts of Japanese schools to create new values are effective. Although Japanese schools preserve many aspects of the prevailing value system, their emphasis on the "egalitarian sentiment" is a significant departure. The three components of this sentiment that will receive attention in this study are as follows:

1. *An egalitarian orientation to jobs.* This orientation stresses the ways in which all jobs contribute to the greater good and hence are deserving of respect. Grading of jobs in terms of their importance or prestige is de-emphasized.

2. *An orientation toward individualism.* This orientation encourages the nurturance of personally conceived goals and evaluates highly striving to realize these personal goals instead of merely following the accepted way. In the work realm, this orientation toward indi-

---

[1] Japanese teachers who visit American schools express surprise at the extent to which their American counterparts neglect noncognitive education. See Bereday and Masui (1973).

vidualism leads individuals to seek intrinsic rewards and to place less emphasis on status and income.

3. *A participatory orientation*. This orientation leads individuals to participate critically in groups, associations, and other collectivities. It leads one to challenge traditional patterns of hierarchical authority in the family, the work place, the community, and the polity.

SOME ASSUMPTIONS

This account will indicate that Japanese schools devote much attention to value education. However, given the current skeptical climate with respect to school effects, one might naturally wonder whether this attention has any impact. Presumably, the final answer to this question will come when social research develops meaningful indicators for a wide range of noncognitive learning and is able to examine the relation over time between educational efforts and this learning. Present research on noncognitive learning, including that reported here, does not conform to these ideal standards.[2] However, it will be shown here that the substantial efforts of Japanese schools to change the values of young people have been accompanied by significant shifts over the postwar period in the value commitments of successive cohorts of youths. Thus, a cumulative process can be hypothesized: Japan's schools have, over time, become more determined to convey the new values, and as their graduates have moved into adult society, the schools have found increasing community support for their efforts.

Leading theories of child development assert that children enter their most significant stage of value learning after, not before, they enter school. Kohlberg (in Brown, 1965:404) indicates that the first steps toward the higher stages of moral development begin at about age seven. Piaget (in Mussen et al., 1974:448) finds that children move from heteronomous (subject to another's laws) to autonomous morality (subject to one's own laws) at age eight or so. Japanese educators are aware of these basic developmental facts, and structure an educational program geared to maximize the opportunity of the early school years. Relative to the final years of primary school and further education, the first years are not exceptionally

[2] We should also, of course, keep in mind that most of the recent studies of the cognitive outcomes of schools suffer from similar limitations. See, for example, Hanushek (forthcoming) and Luecke and McGinn (1976).

demanding in an academic sense. Much effort is devoted to establishing a cohesive homeroom unit that will facilitate moral education. The same teacher stays with this homeroom throughout the first two full school years and conducts the whole range of education from reading and writing to physical education; however, above all the stress is on moral and value education.

Relative to other school systems, Japanese schools abound in those characteristics Bidwell and Vreeland (1963) consider most conducive to a "very strong, homogeneous moral impact." A child finds his closest friends among his school mates, and generally reflecting the attitude of his parents, the child respectfully looks to his teacher for guidance. Along with the commitment to moral education is the totality of the school experience: children go to school a minimum of 240 days a year, and their longest continuous holiday from school is less than 6 weeks; even in this holiday period, children often visit their schools, as many of their extracurricular activities, such as clubs and sports, occur on the school grounds; indeed in many crowded urban areas there are no other facilities. Thus, the school is the child's central life experience. The content of this experience will now be examined, beginning with a summary of those activities that relate to an egalitarian work orientation, the first component of the egalitarian sentiment.

THE DEVELOPMENT OF EGALITARIAN WORK ORIENTATIONS

The Primary School Experience

Children obtain information from many sources during their early years, but the occupational messages are typically diluted. Television provides primary school children with a fare of fantasy dramas, such as Heidi, Snow White, and a Japanese version of King Kong, as well as comedies and pop singing (Nihon Kodomo, 1975:438 ff.). Insofar as programs depict realistic situations, many seem to feature such occupations as pilot, school teacher, policeman, or restaurateur. There is relatively little in the way of historical fiction, possibly because producers are still uncertain about the proper way to treat the past. The types of things most children read about resemble the themes found on television. It is only a minority who break away from *manga* (comic books) to work their way through the books of their school and local libraries. Doubtless, the slant in the media's message has some influence on the emerging occupational consciousness of primary school children; it probably facilitates a positive disposition to the newly developing leisure and service occupations as well as to futuristic work involving space-ships, electronics, and computers.

Still, at this stage, the media's messages seem secondary to those of the schools. Although the school's main thrust is in a different direction, parts of its curriculum reinforce the media's message of glamour and ambition. Old system Japanese texts included numerous short biographies of famous people as a way of fanning the ambition of students—Tokugawa Ieyasu, General Nogi, Pasteur, Florence Nightingale, and others (Hall, R., 1949). This is less common today. Heroes are completely purged from the social science and moral education courses. However, there is mention of exemplary figures in other courses, notably science, in which the inside leaf of texts often includes the names and contributions of path breakers.

Thus it is not surprising to read in Goodman's (1957:983) comparative study of the occupational perceptions of primary school students that,

> in Japan the boys speak of becoming a "company man" or "office man," or "president of the company," and they want to be bankers, factory or store owners, employees of a "trading company" or—better still—the founder of such a company. In the United States boys most frequently speak of becoming salesmen and of merchandising specific products (e.g. wholesale drugs, retail clothing). . . . American boys discuss with sophisticated practicality the relative merits of careers in electronic as compared with electrical, or chemical as compared with civil engineering, while the Japanese boys are more given to dreamy contemplation of great things to be achieved through a nebulous "science." Moreover, the dreams of Japanese boys soar beyond the mundane level of superior picture tubes for color TV and such other specific engineering problems as are likely to engross Americans. The Japanese is inclined toward vast humanitarian goals, to "make a machine which will protect from the dangers of atomic or hydrogen bombs," to "invent a machine to cure disease by radio-activity," or to "explore the universe." He also inclines toward scientific hero-worship, and not a few Japanese boys aspire to "win a Nobel prize, like Dr. Yukawa." Nobel

prize-winners are more numerous in the United States, but the American boys who seem to know of their existence and aspire to be like them are conspicious by their absence (1957:983).

For Japanese girls, Goodman reports a similar romantic tendency toward politics and public service as well as teaching. Although Goodman observes these fantastic dreams in Japanese youth, she does not find much difference in the average prestige level of the occupations aspired to by the youths in the two nations. If there is any difference at all, it is that Japanese boys are more likely to look to ordinary manual jobs and Japanese girls are more likely to think of becoming housewives.

Fantasy aside, these more mundane aspirations of Japanese can be related to what they are taught in the social science curriculum. This curriculum conveys to children a sense that everyone should work, and that all work is essential, both for society as a whole and for individual members. As directed by the central government's official course of study, first grade social studies texts begin with a discussion of school life and soon turn to consider the important contribution of janitors and cooks to each school's welfare. Then the texts turn to the structure of typical Japanese families, showing how the external occupations and home chores of each member are essential. Second grade texts, according to the *Course of Study for Elementary Schools in Japan*, should strive, "to enable children to realize the fact that their lives are constituted resting on the labours on the part of many of those who are engaged in the production and circulation of commodities, traffic and communications, as well as in the efforts to safeguard life and property; thus to help the children to deepen their interest in the persons who are at work, and also make them aware of the implications of the division of labour in society" (Ministry of Education, 1976, a.:34-35). The description goes on for two full pages discussing the contributions of wholesale and retail shopkeepers, farmers and food processors, foresters, fishermen, blue-collar workers, firemen, policemen, and so on. High status occupations such as doctor and government bureaucrat are conspicuous by their absence. The third grade text takes up activity in the public sector, including the facilities for water supply, sewage disposal, and health protection. The fourth grade shifts to civics; the texts convey a sense that social problems are widespread—pollution, poverty, bad health—and that individuals are expected to participate in their solution. Along with the implications of this message for political socialization, it implicitly encourages careers in public service. In the fifth grade, one again finds a concentration of work-related themes in the prescribed course:

> Have them consider the relation between agricultural production and the people's lives and the achievements of those who have been putting forth effort for an increase in production for others. . . . To guide them to understand the fact that in the forestry and the marine product industry, as well, mechanization of operations and changes in other methods of production are observed, and at the same time stimulate their interest in the conditions under which the people in the farming, mountain and fishing villages are exerting efforts in diversified forms under the conditions of the new age. . . . To guide them to consider the significance of industrial production from the viewpoint of the way of life of the people and of the industry as a whole, and at the same time lead them to deepen their grasp of the present condition of Japanese industry and its historic background (Ministry of Education, 1976, a.:47-49).

The sixth grade course shifts to a historical study of Japan's development and then to a consideration of Japan's place in the world. The final lessons focus on the third world, the role of the United Nations, and the importance of international peace. One gains the sense that the social studies texts are attempting to balance the tendency among young people to develop glamorous dreams by focusing on the everyday side of work and by showing how all occupations contribute in important ways.

Other aspects of the school routine are also aimed at encouraging esteem for ordinary work. It has been noted that schoolchildren are required to clean up their own classrooms and the school grounds and that the contributions of the janitors and cooks are often praised by teachers and the principal. Also, parents from the most ordinary homes are warmly welcomed and encouraged to take responsible roles in the parent-teacher association and the school ceremonies.

The school's celebration of ordinary work does seem to affect the way young people evaluate occupations. For example, Masashi and Kazuko Fukaya (1975:98) report that the nearly five hundred sixth grade students they sampled have reasonably accurate perceptions of the different qualities required for achieving success in politics, business, medicine, agriculture, and small business management. They understand that the doctor requires more knowledge and technique than the company president, and that both require much more than the owner of a noodle shop. Also the young people recognize that these occupations receive different rewards. These judgments are given in Table 7.1, in which their perceptions of relative income and prestige are presented on a five-point scale. Teachers are perceived as receiving relatively less income but as having more prestige than the other occupations; company presidents contribute less to society than teachers, doctors, politicians, and even farmers—though somewhat more than the owner-operators of noodle shops. Still, with respect to all these evaluations, the primary school students are not very severe in their discriminations. If one takes their answers literally, one finds they say neither that the position of owner of a noodle shop is prestigious nor that it is not—rather, they say that it is so-so. Similarly, teachers and doctors, who get the highest average prestige rating,

TABLE 7.1
SIXTH GRADERS' EVALUATIONS OF SELECTED OCCUPATIONS

Evaluation	Large Company President	Leading Diet Member	Doctor Doing Cancer Research	Noodle Man	Farmer	Teacher of Handicapped Children
Requires knowledge and new technique						
Boys	73.8	70.8	89.8	49.3	66.3	67.8
Girls	73.0	74.0	88.0	48.3	66.8	68.5
Lucrative						
Boys	77.0	76.0	64.5	52.3	54.8	38.8
Girls	76.0	75.8	63.3	54.3	52.0	41.5
Prestigious						
Boys	57.7	68.5	78.8	43.5	48.8	79.3
Girls	59.3	71.0	81.0	45.8	50.8	80.8
Important for society						
Boys	59.5	78.3	90.5	51.8	64.0	83.3
Girls	60.3	78.3	90.8	50.8	67.0	87.8
Personal choice						
Boys	33.5	45.0	45.8	32.5	26.5	37.0
Girls	35.0	29.3	38.3	25.0	22.8	55.8

SOURCE: Masashi Fukaya and Kazuko Fukaya. *Gendai Kodomoron* (Perspectives on Today's Children), p. 98.
SCALE: 100 = very much; 75 = fairly; 50 = can't say; 25 = not so much; 0 = nil.

are merely considered "fairly prestigious." Stated differently, the range between the occupations getting the highest and lowest prestige scores (doctor and noodle shop owner-operator, respectively) on a scale of 100 is only 35; Japanese adults, in a 1975 national study ranking the same occupations on a 100-point scale, showed a divergence of 46 points (see Table 7.4).

The Middle and High School Experience

As students proceed beyond the primary school their sources of information on occupations become much richer. Their television and radio tastes shift to more realistic programs, which for most boys include heavy doses of sports; surveys indicate that the average middle schooler spends nearly three hours a day watching television. Their favorite programs include comedies and soap operas, which often portray ordinary families in a positive light. The most popular programs during the year of this fieldwork had heroes in the following occupational situations: a family running a soda fountain, an apprentice potter, a teacher, a family operating a noodle shop, a doctor and his terminally ill teenage daughter, and a young aspiring airplane pilot. Also, during this period the networks offered several "specials" on the labor market: one talked about the phenomenon of over-education, which Japan, the United States, and other nations supposedly shared and a second interviewed a number of college graduates who were working in various blue- and gray-collar jobs, such as waiters and mechanics. These programs presented a thoughtful message about the decreasing returns that can be expected from advanced education and the unique rewards that are found in seemingly ordinary occupations.

Middle schoolers also begin to read much more on their own. By this stage virtually all read at least one national newspaper each day and are exposed to popular weekly magazines. These media also provide them with perspectives on occupations. Looking over back issues of these magazines, one perceives a timeworn formula. Each autumn, the magazines feature a number of scare stories about exam preparation schools and about young students driving themselves too hard. Then, in the early spring they tell who gets into which elite university, and beginning in April, they report the names of the universities attended by the new recruits to top government and business organizations. The obvious effect of this journalism is to perpetuate a belief in the elite course. Nevertheless, in recent years one can sense a new pessimism in these popular weeklies. For example, the weekly *Shukan Asahi* frequently reports on unemployed university graduates and their problems: one recent article ("Todai," Feb., 1977) discussed the large number of underemployed University of Tokyo Ph.D.'s, who, because there are no jobs, have no alternative except to work as researchers. The article concluded with quotes from several of Todai's "over doctors" (underemployed Ph.D.'s) urging young mothers to cool the educational and occupational aspirations they have for their children. Other journals, such as *Career Guidance*, have recently been established to specialize in the area of supplying young people with information on new careers. Apart from the flooded elite course, these journals give special emphasis to the semiprofessions, such as medical technician, nutritionist, physical education instructor, and so on.

In addition, as young people enter middle school they become increasingly involved in their peer groups, and as Grusen (1971:147 ff.) notes, educational and occupational plans are a major topic. While apparently no one has attempted a detailed study of the types of things young people say to each other, it can be said from this very limited observation that peer counsel is not very critical and does not attempt to confront realities. Young people seem to restrict discussion of their plans to their closest friends, and these friends usually take the role of sounding board and supporter. Friends encourage each other by saying that anything is possible if one tries. It is significant that a growing minority of those who seek entrance to college do so only because their friends are doing the same thing. Thus, peer group pressure pushes many youths into a higher educational experience and a life plan for which they are not especially well motivated or even prepared. Friends share information on prospective exam questions, preferred teachers, *juku*, and so on, with little reservation. According to several observers, their generosity is not even curbed by the thought that furthering a friend's success may thwart their own (Vogel, 1975:"Intro.").

With the increasing diversification of sources providing relevant information, the middle school's role as a source of information on occupations is probably less than that of the primary school. Actually, in the middle schools, less than a week of the second year of the social studies course focuses on "occupations and life." As in the primary school curriculum, the purpose is to teach students that work is both a right and a duty, that their labor contributes not only to their personal welfare but also to the broader society, and moreover, that the nature of work is undergoing rapid technological change. Teachers are also urged to tell students about the local agencies in charge of vocational education and training, and about the Public Employment Security Office. The text used in Kyoto City followed these instructions to the letter, though with some interesting embellishments that will take on added significance in other parts of this discussion (Ugai, 1975:29 ff.). The Kyoto text identifies technician, teacher, and artisan as typical professionals—but does not mention high status examples like doctor, lawyer, and dentist. In the text, great stress is placed on the constitutional guarantees of equal employment (Article 22). In this spirit, youths are told that they can select their occupations on their own; no mention is made of parental guidance or, for that matter, of the school's role in occupational counseling. The approved course of study for the senior high makes virtually no mention of occupations.

Although social science texts do not devote a large amount of space to occupations as such, they do take up many related activities—altogether one third of the second-year texts in middle school deal with aspects of national and international economic activity. Occupation-related topics are also taken up in other courses. In one of the schools visited, the principal and teachers were attempting to boost student images of the occupations performed by *burakumin*, a former outcaste group. So every week during the ethics period, students were provided a special course on the activities of garbagemen, leather workers, and butchers. This type of special education has become fairly common in the Kansai area, where the schools are attempting to aid in upgrading the social position of the *burakumin*. Of course, from a national perspective, this type of program is still exceptional.

By the stage of middle school, the curriculum no longer explicitly teaches students about occupations as such. On the other hand, the academic selection that begins to take place in the middle school does force students to think about their occupational future—upon graduation, will they continue in an academic course or take up one of the several vocational courses provided at the high school level. And the way in which middle school teachers discuss these alternatives with students has profound occupational implications. In the past, it is said that the teachers simply explained that the different high school courses led to differentially "valued" occupations—professional and managerial jobs at the top, clerical jobs below these, and blue-collar and artisan jobs at a still lower level; moreover, becoming a company man was presented as more desirable than going it alone or in a small enterprise. Students were told that middle school grades were the best indicator of where they would end up on the social ladder. This advice was supplemented by advice from parents, with the result that class considerations exercised some influence: upper-class parents were ambitious for their children, irrespective of their performance whereas lower-class parents were inclined to steer their children in the direction of traditional family pursuits.

However, from discussions with those teachers involved, it appears that, over the postwar period, this counseling process has undergone subtle changes. First, counselors still inform students that the respective courses require differential abilities, but no longer do they uniformly place the vocational courses below all academic courses. For example, in the Kyoto system (and in several of the other progressive urban systems) counselors are likely to tell students that many of the vocational courses require more ability than do most of the academic high schools of the private sector. In prefectures without a large private sector, they paint a somewhat different picture (as we will indicate in Chapter Eight). The main point is that counselors are no longer so emphatic in relating the ability and course alternatives in overlapping hierarchies. Second, counselors present a more flexible picture of the relative values of different occupational outcomes that are likely to follow from the different courses. Again, there are differences by prefecture, but the Kyoto area counselors claim they try to stress the intrinsic rewards of all occupations, urging students to make choices based on their own interests. Similarly, the counselors, although they bring parents into the counseling process, try to establish an atmosphere in which students can express and act on their own preferences. These messages clearly contradict the view that says the school acts to reproduce the class order.

Needless to say, the school-initiated counseling process is only one of several influences bearing on a young person's choices for further study and career. The school's message tends to oppose that of parents and the more conversational media, whereas it reinforces the views and information supplied from more progressive sources. Which among these sources is most influential cannot be determined. Still, as one looks at the actual patterns of adolescent aspiration and choice, one cannot help but be impressed with the limited impact of background factors. According to the Ministry of Education's survey of the determinants of the high school aspirations of a national sample of middle schoolers, their grade-point average is far more important than any background factor in explaining whether middle schoolers plan to go to high school or not (Central Council for Education, 1972:129). In a subanalysis, the ministry also shows how grade-point average is the principal determinant of the course individuals plan to take up. In other words, the school's message through its process of evaluating students is more influential in shaping aspirations than any of the family variables included in the study.

Unfortunately, the ministry's study does not provide the information for determining where students actually end up. Other studies suggest a complicated picture. As with high school aspirations, grade-point average is the major determinant; however, class and region also play an important role. In urban areas the best students obtain entry to "famous" schools, and one finds a definite class bias in the class composition of these schools. Beneath these best schools are the public academic and vocational schools, and for the former there appears to be relatively little class bias. On the other hand, the picture for the vocational schools is more complicated. Some very able lower-class children select these over an academic high school out of a recognition that their family circumstances will not permit them to go onto a university; hence, the vocational courses provide the quickest route to a livelihood. On the other hand, the sons from upper- and middle-class homes who fail to gain admission to a good academic high school will often choose low-quality private academic high schools rather than these vocational courses. Through diligent study in these schools, supplemented by extra-study schools, they hope to bring their grades up to the level at which they can compete for college entrance. Girls from upper- and middle-class homes are not as firmly set on college and may settle for commercial, home economics, or nursing courses. Still, here again, there is a slight bias toward the private sector. Thus, with the exception of the public academic high schools, one finds a complex pattern of interaction between social background and academic ability in determining where middle schoolers actually end up.

These comments provide the essential background for interpreting what is undoubtedly the best postwar study of the occupational aspirations of Japanese high school students. In cooperation with several leading Japanese scholars, Mary Jean Bowman collected data from over fifteen thousand public high school students and their parents in several urban and rural areas selected in such a manner as to give a fair representation of the national situation. That the students were restricted to the public sector introduces some bias, but as indicated in the discussion of high school attendance, the public schools receive a considerable diversity of students. As one offshoot of the broader study, Yasumasa Tomoda scored the ideal and expected occupational aspirations of the male students, using the weights indicated in Table 7.2. Tomoda then computed the average ideal and expected occupational scores for the males with fathers from each of eight graded status levels, as indicated in Table 7.3, and made some comparisons with similar studies in the United States. He concludes:

> Japanese students of middle and lower social class origins had much higher aspirations than did the corresponding American students. Furthermore, the aspiration scores of Japanese students of lower social class origins turned out to be slightly higher than those of the students of middle class origins. A series of tests demonstrate that the flatness or even curvilinearity of the distribution of students' occupational aspiration levels cannot be attributed to response biases. The pattern was repeated within each type of curriculum, in rural and in urban area [*sic*], including and excluding sons of farmers, and within student class-rank categories. Furthermore, the tests included examination of char-

TABLE 7.2

THE DUNCAN SCALE, THE EIGHT STATUS CATEGORIES AND THE VALUE WEIGHTS FOR COMPUTATIONS OF STUDENTS' OCCUPATIONAL ASPIRATION SCORES

Duncan Scale	Eight Status Categories	Value for Aspiration Score
80 or more	1	9.0
70–79	2	7.5
60–69	3	6.5
50–59	4	5.5
35–49	5	4.2
25–34	6	3.0
11–24	7	1.8
10 or less	8	0.5

SOURCE: Yasumasa Tomoda, "Occupational Aspirations of Japanese High School Students," p. 218.

TABLE 7.3
AVERAGE OCCUPATIONAL ASPIRATION SCORES FOR EACH FATHER'S STATUS LEVEL

Students' Average Aspiration Score

| Father's Status Level | Excluding Students in Agricultural Course | | | | | Including Students in Agricultural Course | | | | | |
| | Preferred | | Expected | | Difference | Preferred | | Expected | | Difference | |
	(M)	(N)	(M)	(N)	(Preferred less Expected)	(M)	(N)	(M)	(N)	(Preferred less Expected)	
1	7.45	40	8.15	33	−.70	7.45	40	8.15	33	−.70	
2	7.03	106	6.80	95	+.23	7.03	106	6.75	96	+.29	
3	6.91	354	6.56	327	+.35	6.90	358	6.55	330	+.35	
4	6.92	348	6.31	309	+.61	6.89	358	6.27	318	+.62	
5	6.54	630	6.04	532	+.50	6.40	749	5.74	653	+.55	
6	6.60	473	6.06	430	+.54	6.51	521	5.91	482	+.60	
7	6.63	381	6.15	336	+.48	6.62	388	6.13	342	+.49	
8	6.68	41	6.33	43	+.35	6.69	42	6.22	45	+.47	

SOURCE: Yasumasa Tomoda, "Occupational Aspirations of Japanese High School Students," p. 218.
NOTE: M = Mean; N = Number of Respondents.

acteristics of students who did not respond to the questions on occupational aspirations. Sensitivity tests (not detailed here) demonstrated also that the contrast between the Japanese and U.S. findings could not be attributed to any differences in status coding. We concluded that Japanese students' occupational aspiration levels are much less influenced by their social class origins than might be expected (1968:212).

From a comparative standpoint, this evidence on the Japanese pattern of expectations is remarkable. Yet it is precisely what one would expect from the process of egalitarian education and its subsequent reinforcement that has been described in these pages. The students' expectations are, of course, unrealistic. Many will have to settle for work other than that to which they aspire. Hence, many are destined to experience severe frustrations as they move on to the university and into their careers.

The egalitarian occupational orientations that young people acquire in school are, no doubt, altered somewhat as they move into the actual world of work; they come to a better appreciation of how different types of work are ordered in organizational hierarchies and of how they entail different privileges and rewards. Still, it is possible that some of the egalitarian lessons today's young people have learned will remain with them as they move through their careers. The 1975 social mobility survey asked a sample of adult males aged twenty to seventy to rank a list of 82 occupations as well as to indicate the criteria they placed greatest emphasis on when conducting this ranking. Young respondents, who had been educated in the egalitarian environment of postwar schools, were more likely to say that they evaluated the "general standing" of occupations in terms of challenge, style, autonomy, and skill requirement while de-emphasizing influence, income, education, responsibility and public respect. Also young people were less discriminating in their rankings. Respondents were asked to evaluate each occupation on a five-point scale from very high in general standing to very low; young people were less likely to choose the extremes. This difference shows up when we convert the evaluations to the conventional prestige scale with values ranging from 0 to 100. Table 7.4, which contrasts the average rankings for the youngest age-group and two middle-aged groups, indicates a consistent tendency for young people to regard low status occupations with greater esteem than older people and high status occupations with less esteem. The

TABLE 7.4
PRESTIGE SCORES BY AGE (PERCENTAGES)

	20-29	40-49	20-29 less 40-49	50-59	20-29 less 50-59
University professor	82.5	84.4	−1.9	83.4	− .9
Doctor	82.8	83.4	− .6	82.5	+ .3
Civil engineer	62.8	64.0	−1.2	62.0	+ .8
City department chief	58.7	61.2	−2.5	60.2	−1.5
Teacher	61.9	64.6	−2.7	62.1	− .2
Temple priest	57.6	60.3	−2.7	59.5	−1.9
Policeman	52.8	56.2	−3.4	55.7	−2.9
Manager of small shop	48.5	49.4	− .9	48.5	0
Joiner	41.7	42.9	−1.2	41.1	+ .6
Barber	47.3	45.2	+2.1	42.4	+4.9
Auto mechanic	42.7	43.6	− .9	42.3	+ .4
Railway station employee	44.0	44.6	− .6	45.2	−1.2
Carpenter	45.1	45.3	− .2	45.8	− .7
Owner-farmer	43.6	44.7	−1.1	45.8	−2.2
Truck driver	40.0	40.9	− .9	42.3	−2.3
Lathe operator	34.0	38.8	−4.8	38.3	−4.3
Clerk in small shop	36.2	35.3	+ .9	33.9	+2.3
Spinner	33.8	33.4	+ .4	28.8	+5.0
Insurance agent	34.4	37.2	−2.8	37.6	−2.2
Typist	48.8	48.9	− .1	45.9	+2.9
Fisherman	37.4	34.8	+2.6	36.7	+ .7
Baker	37.4	36.6	+ .8	35.2	+2.2
Tenant farmer	30.2	29.3	+ .5	27.4	+2.8
Road construction	26.0	28.1	−2.1	27.8	−1.8
Street salesman	29.4	27.4	+2.0	26.5	+2.9
Coal miner	29.1	28.9	+ .2	25.3	+3.8
Charcoal maker	25.3	24.4	+1.1	20.9	+4.4

SOURCE: 1975 Social Mobility Survey.

egalitarian occupational socialization of the younger group constitutes at least part of the explanation for this difference.

THE ORIENTATION TOWARD INDIVIDUALISM

It should be emphasized that the Tomoda analysis of occupational
aspirations is based on data collected in 1966. It is uncertain whether
a survey conducted today would yield the same results. Several of
the factors underlying this surprising evidence have undergone important changes over the past decade.

As the postwar educational system initially developed, young people were provided relatively little guidance concerning their abilities or how these abilities related to different occupations. Thus, many young people had not subjected their occupational ambitions to a serious evaluation even as late as the final years of high school. Partly due to this lack of information, many young people had romantic and somewhat unrealistic orientations to the world of work. Gradually, this situation has changed (as indicated in some detail in Chapter Eight). A number of testing services have been established to help young people gain a better understanding of their abilities, and several new career guidance magazines are in circulation. Furthermore, it appears that the postcompulsory school system has become somewhat more differentiated and selective than it was in the early sixties. Since 1962 a large group of five-year technical colleges have been established, and within the private postcompulsory sector, one finds a growing division between "famous" and ordinary schools. All these developments assist young people in thinking more seriously about occupations at an earlier age, and this probably results in greater realism. Yet, there is a class bias in educational achievement, and many of the sources that provide advice on career planning link educational to occupational achievement. Thus, this new realism may bring about a stronger relation between class position and occupational aspiration.

On the other hand, two tendencies that were present in the sixties but have become much more evident since tend to counteract the stratifying effect of the new information. First, egalitarian education promotes the motivations of all children. With each year, this egalitarian education has become more widely adopted; other things being equal, the diffusion of these practices would lead to a steady decline in the stratification of the motivations of young people, at least up to the time when they complete their primary school education. Still, one cannot say whether the availability of realistic information subsequently neutralizes the primary school's leveling effect or not.

Second, the new tendency toward individuation, which, among other things, involves a more selfish or self-actualizing orientation to work and life, motivates young people increasingly to place a higher value on their own personal satisfaction than on worldly success. Among the many consequences of this individualistic orientation is a disposition to adopt a more critical attitude toward occupations. There is growing evidence that youths are beginning to devalue the traditional rewards of status and income and to place more importance on considerations such as freedom from control, challenge, and style. Some evidence on this shift was provided in connection with the discussion of occupational ranking. These new work orientations also affect the way a contemporary sample might respond to an occupational aspiration survey. Rather than make choices simply in terms of status, they would also use personal preference, thus complicating the traditional class-ability-aspiration linkage.

It is difficult to determine the origin of this tendency toward individualism, compared with other emerging values. Postwar child-rearing, with its impressive level of maternal devotion, may contribute to an individualistic desire for gratification and fulfillment. The schools and public institutions give much lip service to individualism. For example, in the middle school texts great stress is placed on the individual's right to choose his job. Looking at other parts of the school curriculum, one finds that history books champion the courage of individuals who have stood up for ideals, even in the face of opposition. However, the mass production-like character of schools does not allow much opportunity for individualized instruction or other means of encouraging individuality.

As youths mingle with their friends, however, their individualistic sentiments receive more generous support. Friends discuss how they can meet and even marry a particular individual whom their parents do not favor. Today's youths spend a lot of their time alone. Families are small, so many young people do not have a brother or sister. The pressures to study have escalated, so that much of their free time is spent poring over books. These private experiences may also nurture individualism.

Perhaps the best indicator of the emerging orientation toward individualism comes from a question on life goals that has been repeated at five-year intervals since 1953 in a series of Japanese national character surveys conducted by the National Institute of Mathematics. This institute is one of Japan's more respected social science research institutes, and each of these surveys has included a large representative sample of at least two thousand people, so the findings can be considered reliable. The life goals question goes as follows:

There are various views about one's way of life. Of those listed here, which one would you say comes closest to your feeling?
1. **Work hard and get rich**

2. Study earnestly and make a name for yourself
3. Don't think about money or fame; just live a life that suits your own tastes
4. Live each day as it comes, cheerfully and without worrying
5. Resist all evils in the world and live a pure and just life
6. Never think of yourself; give everything in service of society (National Institute of Mathematics, 1975:512).

The third response—"just live a life that suits your own tastes"—is the most individualistic, self-actualizing response, and as we can see from Table 7.5, it is the response that has become progressively more common for young people.

TABLE 7.5

YOUNG PEOPLE (AGE 20-24) SELECTING THE LIFE GOAL "LIVE A LIFE THAT SUITS ONE'S TASTES" (PERCENTAGES)

	1953	1958	1963	1968	1973
Young people	34	38	45	51	53
Total sample	21	27	30	32	39

SOURCE: National Institute of Mathematics, *Nihonjin no Kokuminsei* (The Japanase National Character), vols. 1 and 2.

In another set of surveys, young people between the ages of eighteen and twenty-one were asked what sorts of criteria were important in their selection of jobs (Table 7.6). In 1956, the majority of the respondents selected the ambitious response—"because of the possibility of future growth and high security"—while less than two fifths mentioned the more individualistic response—a job "suited to his or her ability and liking." By 1971, these relative proportions had been reversed—nearly two thirds of the young job seekers preferred the individualistic response, whereas the ambitious alternative was selected by only one fifth.

This trend toward individualism has caused much concern among certain elements of Japan's business and industrial leadership. They fear contemporary young people may be losing the strong work and company commitment values that have played such a vital role in Japan's economic growth. Because of this concern, they have commissioned a number of studies to probe more deeply into the emerging orientations of youth. One of the more interesting involves a survey of attitudes toward education, work, and society of youth in eleven nations. Possibly, the investigation

TABLE 7.6

JOB MOTIVATIONS OF YOUTHS IN JAPAN

Reason for Preferring a Given Job	1971	1956
The salary is high	5.9	1.2
Inherited from parents	0.8	0.4
Suited to his or her ability and liking	64.4	39.6
The possibility of future growth and high security	17.2	52.5
Needed by the society	4.0	5.6
The school prestige	0.4	0.5
No particular preference	6.7	0.2
No answer	0.6	0.0

SOURCE: Japan Research Center, *Wakamono Ishiki Chosa* (Analysis of the Psychology of Youth in Japan).

hoped to discover that although deficient in the traditional commitment to hard work and ambition, Japanese youths were still superior in these respects to the youths of other advanced societies. Insofar as the survey's sponsors believed the results of this survey—conducted by Gallup International—they were surprised. For example, Japanese young people were exceptional in their overwhelming approval of the opinion that "it is important in this world to take it easy and not to work too hard." When asked what they looked for in school, Japanese young people were more likely to say they wanted a good education than to pick an instrumental reason such as "improving their chances of obtaining a good job and marriage." Similarly, when asked, "Why do you think man works?" Japanese youths were least likely among the young of the eleven nations surveyed to choose the instrumental response "to earn money"; rather a large percentage chose the more individualistic response "to find self-fulfillment."

The various pieces of information do suggest that contemporary youths have developed a new orientation to life that is more inward looking and less concerned with extrinsic rewards and social achievement. Although this new tendency is labeled here an emerging individuated orientation, this may lead to some misunderstanding. Unquestionably today's young people are more concerned about personal growth and satisfaction and hence are more individualistic. On the other hand, this does not mean that they reject group life or avoid involvement in large collectivities. To the contrary, today's young people appear just as positive as ever about group life. They mention love and friendship as among the values they consider most important. They enjoy school club activities and other opportunities for collective endeavor, such as school trips. And as they move into work, most mention relations with coworkers and bosses as a major personal concern. Thus, the new individualism does not mean a rejection of taking part in groups; rather, it seems to involve a new orientation to the group. The group is viewed as a collection of individuals, each of whom is seeking self-fulfillment. A group is appreciated insofar as it is responsive to individual needs. In contrast, a group that imposes rigid and nonnegotiable demands on its individual members is disliked. One can see how this contingent view of group life relates to the third emerging orientation, the new skepticism toward authority and established politics.

ORIENTATIONS TO DECISION MAKING AND POLITICS

Another of the striking developments of the postwar period is the new cynicism about decision making and politics on the part of young people: they emphasize participation rather than authority, cooperation rather than control. These preferences are at the core of the egalitarian sentiment, and traces of this new orientation can be seen in the child-rearing patterns typical of *sarariman* families.

The school also plays a central role in the promotion of the participatory orientation, especially through its formal curriculum. The constitution and virtually every other law and regulation affecting the educational system place much emphasis on the need to promote democracy and a critical attitude toward authority. According to the official *Course of Study for Lower Secondary Schools*, the first objective is "to have the pupils take proper cognizance of the significance of individual dignity and respect for human rights, and particularly the relationship of freedom and rights with responsibilities and duties, thereby deepening their understanding of democracy and cultivating their basic cultural nature essential as citizens who are to exercise the people's sovereignty" (Ministry of Education, 1976, b.:64).

Later, in a discussion of teaching about elections and political parties, teachers are told that "pupils should be led to understand that a democratic government is superior to a dictatorship, take note of the drawbacks which the former is easily subject to, increase consciousness that sovereignty resides in the people, and foster the desire and attitude of defending and developing democratic government" (p. 53). At the same time, this official guide admonishes teachers against going overboard. It warns of the danger of promoting an "overly critical attitude in students or of failing to recognize the achievement of efforts and progress in the past." Above all, the approved course of study urges teachers to be as objective as they can and to help pupils develop the ability to make impartial judgments.

These official concerns are developed against a background of frequent charges and countercharges from both the right and left about misuse of the schools for political purposes. These charges have a substantial basis. No small number of leftist-inclined teachers use the classroom as their personal soapbox. On the other hand, there is a definite manpower and traditional morality bias in official educational policy. These accusations and their disavowals can be understood as a further extension of the ongoing battle over the schools.

However, even if the teachers were not biased toward a new orientation to decision making, one senses that the texts used in today's classrooms would relay the message. In the primary school social studies texts read for this study, several progressive themes were sounded concerning questions of social class and authority. For example, these texts established an explicit link between the authoritarian nature of the old political regime and Japan's involvement in World War II. Repeatedly, the social science and literature texts stressed the danger involved in leaving decisions to leaders. Similarly, the texts emphasized the people's role in shaping local government decisions. Huthwaite concluded from a thematic analysis of children's books used in and outside the classroom that "the most common values found in folk literature were courage, cleverness, loyalty, and cultural pride. The most common values found in realistic fiction were cooperation, kindness, independence, honesty and love of nature" (1974:107). Hierarchical loyalty was evident in the folk literature, but it was virtually absent in fantasy and realistic literature. Indeed "none of the sample books of realistic fiction recommended loyalty to a superior, allegiance or blind loyalty. Authority was questioned and even defied on occasion." Huthwaite concludes that "hierarchical relations are much less frequently stressed in contemporary texts than cooperative horizontal relations" (p. 110).

Moving up to the texts for middle and higher schools, these egalitarian and participation themes are much more elaborated, almost to the point of ideological statements. Ienaga's text on modern Japanese history is the best-known example because of the sensational controversy it has generated. The Ministry of Education, which has claimed the authority to screen texts before they can be permitted in classrooms, ordered Ienaga to make certain alterations in his history text so as to achieve a better "balance." Ultimately Ienaga complied, but at the same time he decided to take the ministry to court for its undemocratic act of censorship. On the first round he won, but the ministry appealed, and now the decision by the Supreme Court is pending (Duke, 1972). Whatever the outcome, the controversy itself represents a special lesson in contemporary attitudes toward authority for today's young people.

Ienaga's text is conspicious for its effort to present a people's history. In the premodern period the focus is on the peasants from whom came "the productive labor to support feudal society." The Tokugawa regime's exploitative policies are said to have increased "the poverty of needy peasants and lower class city people" and created a feeling of "serious social insecurity." Thus, according to the text, the Meiji revolution was initiated by lower samurai who perceived this trend among the people. Fully three pages are devoted to the Free People's Rights Movement of the early Meiji period. As the text moves into the industrial era, considerable attention is devoted to the *zaibatsu* and other upper-class interests, who gradually steer the unsuspecting people into war. The growing impoverishment of the laboring classes is underlined, and as at earlier points, most of the illustrations are of representatives from these classes. The heroes Ienaga discusses are predominantly "outs" rather than "ins." In contrast with old system texts, military figures are left out altogether, and the barest attention is given to the military events of World War II. On the other hand, detailed attention is given to the horror of the war for the people: the immeasurable loss of life and property, the hard conditions of life without adequate food or sleep, the use of human torpedoes, the involvement of schoolchildren in war production. The popular themes continue in the postwar period, combined with an anti-American analysis of the cold war. Especially as the text turns to the present, students are warned of the dangers of pollution, cultural standardization, the lack of social security, the growing power of large corporations, and the injustices of corporate employment policies, which, among other things, are said to discriminate against women.

Local school boards have a number of modern history texts to choose from in addition to Ienaga; however, those who have read the full spectrum suggest that the Ienaga text is not atypical. In other words, despite government censorship, there appears to be a consistent leftist bias in upper-level social science texts, against authority and unsympathetic to the contributions of all but the popular classes.

Japanese youths tend to get a similar message from most of the other sources they consult. Most notable are the newspapers, which, over the postwar period, have taken a consistently critical attitude toward establishment politics. The newspapers seemingly delight in exposing instances of official corruption and political misconduct. They provide extensive and generally sympathetic coverage of popular movements, such as the student revolt of the late sixties, the farmers' campaign to keep their land from being claimed for the Narita Airport project, or the various local campaigns against industrial pollution. Similarly, most of the popular weekly journals indulge in a little muckraking at the expense of established authority. These sources exposed former Prime Minister Tanaka's questionable dealings in land speculation and supplied most of the early leads on the Lockheed scandal.

As can be seen, Japanese youths are exposed to a fairly consistent diet of material critical of the established institutions. This material tends to be approved by their teachers and peers. For example, Krauss (1974:63) notes in his study of the political socialization of young radicals that high school teachers were among the most seminal influences in their development. On the other hand, youths do not often hear articulate defenses of establishment politics or of traditional authority patterns. Parents, who would be the most obvious source of a contrary view, report that they rarely talk politics with their children. And when parents do, they often give their children the impression of being poorly informed. The intense involvement of young people in their peer society insulates them from extensive contact with other adults who might be better informed.

Finally, the actual structures in which young people live and play have striking egalitarian tendencies at least by traditional standards. The modern family, as noted above, encourages children to participate in family decision making and, increasingly, to make decisions on their own. Within the family, the language of address has become democratized: parents are "mama" and "papa" rather than "respectful father" (*otosan*) and "honorable mother" (*okasan*). In the schools, teachers attempt to maintain order, but at the same time they encourage pupil participation. The same can be said for the school as a whole, where students are allowed to assume responsibility for functions as diverse as operating the public address system or cleaning the school grounds. From middle schools on, students form self-government associations, which, among other tasks, establish and enforce the rules of everyday student conduct; the principal's role in this area is limited to dealing with the behavior of serious troublemakers such as delinquents and persistent truants. Peer group interaction patterns, including student clubs, also have a decidedly democratic tendency.

Thus, Japanese youths are exposed to a selectively egalitarian set of messages and examples relating to decision making. These egalitarian messages, continuously reinforced during the school years, lead youth to develop expectations concerning the proper way to make decisions that stand in considerable contrast with the prevailing norms. Some of the best evidence on these developmental patterns comes from political socialization research. Massey in his *Youth and Politics in Japan* (1976) presents a number of tables showing that middle school youth share attitudes to authority and the established political institutions that are close to those of adult Japanese. However, as youth proceed into high school, a gap emerges, which becomes very large by the third year (grade twelve). Young people prove to be much more suspicious of the integrity of politicians and government leaders: 41 percent of adults and 40 percent of the second-year middle schoolers disagreed with the suggestion that "most Diet members are trustworthy, honest men who do not get involved in things like graft"; however, 58 percent of tenth graders and 72 percent of twelfth graders doubted the integrity of the Diet members; similarly, in contrast with 55 percent for the parents, 78 percent of the twelfth graders said they believed "a good many people in the government are dishonest and involved in corruption." Young people are more likely to view political institutions as self-serving or oriented to a narrow range of powerful interest groups, and are much more insistent that these institutions open up to allow full participation by the people. These same tendencies are identified in a larger study by Okamura (Massey, 1976:24), in which it is shown that third-grade primary school students tend to have a positive image of the emperor and the prime minister as leaders of the nation; by the end of middle school these attitudes are reversed: middle schoolers look positively on the people and feel they should run the government.

One of Massey's questions is taken from the aforementioned national character surveys: "If we get good leaders, the best way to improve the country is for the people to leave everything to them rather than for the people to discuss things among themselves." Only 46 percent of the adult sample disagreed with this opinion, whereas 66 percent of the second-year middle schoolers (eighth graders) were opposed; among tenth graders, 76 percent disagreed, and by the last year of high school this figure was up to 81 percent (Ibid., p. 44). When one looks at the trend in responses of young adults to this question from 1953 to 1973 as reported in the reports on national surveys by the National Institute of Mathematics (see Table 7.7), one finds a very decided trend toward an increasing reluctance to "leave everything to leaders." In 1953, whereas 38 percent of the general population opposed leaving everything to leaders, 54 percent of young adults twenty to twenty-four years old were in opposition. Over each successive five-year period, the proportion of young people opposed steadily increased, so that in the 1973 survey 74 percent disagreed with the proposition. This is obviously a substantial shift in opinion toward believing that the people should play a more active participatory role in national politics.

The national character surveys also included an interesting question concerning respect for the authority of teachers: "Suppose that a child comes home and says that he has heard a rumor that his teacher has done something to get himself into trouble, and sup-

TABLE 7.7

CHANGING ATTITUDES TO THE AUTHORITY OF POLITICAL LEADERS AND
SCHOOLTEACHERS (PERCENTAGES)

	1953	1958	1963	1962	1973
Young adults (aged 20-24) opposed to relying on political leaders	54	60	58	63	74
All adults (20+)	38	44	47	51	60
Young adults (aged 20-24) who agree it is better to tell teacher did wrong	50	45	58	55	64
All adults (20+)	42	41	50	52	54

SOURCE: National Institute of Mathematics, *Nihonjin no Kokuminsei* (The Japanese National Character), vols. 2 and 3.

pose that the parent knows this is true. Do you think it is better for the parent to tell the child that it is true, or to deny it?" Respondents who answer "deny it," it can be reasoned, believe there is some virtue in protecting the teacher's authority even when the teacher has violated the public trust. On the other hand, those who say "better to tell it is true" might be regarded as having less respect for the authority of teachers. As can be seen from Table 7.7, there was a definite (though not as dramatic) increase between 1953 and 1973 in the proportion of respondents who, in selecting "better to tell it is true," indicate a willingness to challenge established authority. This second question is particularly interesting as it seems to generate a psychological conflict in young people. On the one hand, having only just completed school (some are still attending a university), they are accustomed to respecting teachers; on the other hand, the young people feel a general distrust of established authority. In the immediate postschool years, latent respect for teachers outweighs antiauthority attitudes, but as they grow older, young people seem to overcome this conflict; thus, their willingness to affirm that the teacher did wrong actually increases (see Table 9.4). The figures presented in Table 7.7 on this question, then, may not fully represent the young people's antiauthority sentiment.

EDUCATION BECOMES A CONSTANT

The three changes in consciousness considered here—toward a more egalitarian orientation to jobs, a greater individuation, and a greater participation—have become progressively more evident as each new cohort of postwar students has graduated from the schools. Behind these changes in outcomes is the wider acceptance of the egalitarian educational ideal. With each passing year, the proportion of teachers educated under the new system and hence familiar with the egalitarian ideal has increased; also, the influence of the teachers' union has diffused more widely throughout the various regions of Japan.

Young people receive their most systematic introduction to these new orientations in the primary schools. Subsequent stages in the educational process mainly reinforce the lessons of the primary school. In earlier periods in Japanese history, due to the discontinuities between the morally restricted atmosphere of the primary school and the remarkably free atmosphere of the university, level of educational attainment proved to be a very powerful predictor of personal values. Unlike in many European societies, Japanese with a university education, especially those in white-collar jobs, had the most progressive and reformist orientations, whereas the lesser-educated manual workers were more conservative and tradition bound. With the liberalization of the primary school and its pivotal role in postwar socialization, one could expect these differences by educational level to decrease. Again, data from the national character surveys, provide persuasive evidence to this effect. Whereas in 1953 an individual's educational level proved to be the most consistent predictor of his response pattern, by 1973 for many questions there were but modest differences by educational level. In contrast, age and sex had become more effective differentiators of individual consciousness. For example, in the 1953 survey, for the youngest cohort (twenty to twenty-nine years old) there was a 13 percent difference between university educated and middle school educated in frequency of affirmation that "the Prime Minister should go to Ise"; by 1973, this difference had disappeared. Decreases in spread by educational level are found for most of the other questions of the national character survey that were mentioned earlier in this chapter (National Institute of Mathematics, 1975:187 ff.).

Thus, over the postwar period, especially for those personal orientations making up the egalitarian sentiment, the value of educational attainment as an explanatory variable has gradually declined. With the increasing adoption of the goals of egalitarian education at the primary school level and their consistent reinforcement at subsequent stages of the educational process, young people indicate ever greater acceptance of the egalitarian sentiment, regardless of their level of educational attainment. For the cohorts coming out of today's schools this sentiment is a matter of course rather than a matter for consideration. Although at one time an important variable influencing an individual's values, educational attainment is today virtually a constant.

Conclusion

There is abundant evidence to suggest significant continuities in the main value themes of modernizing Japanese society. However, in this study the focus is on change, and in this chapter three value clusters where postwar change has been the most dramatic have been identified. As shown here, these value changes can be plausibly related to what is explicitly taught in Japan's schools; these values have become more evident as each new cohort of postwar students had graduated from the schools. By and large the evidence for a class effect independent of the schools' effect on the egalitarian values of young people is weak. Insofar as families from different classes once achieved differential socialization with respect to these clusters, the contemporary absence of class effect also deserves notice.

It is the contention here that Japan's schools are more effectively structured to realize value education, whether to preserve or change the trend in value commitments of successive cohorts, than the schools of most other educational systems. As will now be shown, these value changes provide the evaluative basis for the postwar shift toward greater social equality.

Chapter Eight

THE EXAMINATION COMPETITION

Transitions across school levels in the Japanese educational system are marked by entrance exams.[1] Japanese people believe that their individual life chances hinge on success in these exams. Thus, families devote a surprising proportion of their resources toward assisting their children in exam preparation, and children devote long hours day after day to study. Over the postwar period the number of children seriously committing themselves to exam preparation has steadily increased, whereas the number of openings at the elite schools has scarcely changed. Necessarily, competition has intensified, raising several questions about the examination system:

1. *The quality of adolescent life.* Mass media accounts of the examination competition claim that it is causing a steady deterioration in the quality of adolescent life. What is the evidence that supports these claims? Is a contrary view tenable?

2. *Equity.* Has the growing participation of lower-class youths in the educational system brought about any improvement in their rate of successful entry into higher educational institutions? Into the elite institutions?

3. *The implications for egalitarian values.* Competition is conventionally viewed as a process in which individuals are pitted against each other in the pursuit of some limited and valued goal. In that competition leads to the objective ranking of people, it can be reasoned that it also leads to a situation in which individuals internalize these rankings and see themselves as superior or inferior to others. Intensified competition should accentuate this tendency toward subjective ranking—exactly the opposite of what is achieved in egalitarian socialization. Thus, one arrives at a question of great relevance for the transformation thesis proposed by this discussion.

[1] Thomas Rohlen, who has been conducting a field study of several Kobe high schools, was especially generous and helpful with his comments. Table 8.3 is similar to one he has published elsewhere (1977).

Which value trend, subjective ranking or equality, is more evident
in the thinking and behavior of today's young people?

THE INCREASING NUMBERS INVOLVED SINCE WORLD WAR II

As a background for a consideration of these questions, several related developments that have influenced the nature of competition
should be first reviewed. The most prominent trend in the postwar
labor force has been the expansion of the organizational sector, particularly the increase in white-collar jobs. In 1950, 4.3 million
people, or 11.9 percent of the labor force, were involved in white-
collar work. By 1970 the figures were 9.9 million and 18.7 percent,
respectively (see Table 3.4). Roughly speaking, within twenty years
the number of jobs requiring individuals with some level of higher
education doubled. The growth in the white-collar sector not only
signified new jobs, but it also provided a new impetus to the demand for higher education. Because white-collar families lacked a
family enterprise and property, they depended on education as the
sole means of easing their children into adult roles.

The Occupation reforms responded to this growing demand for
highly educated manpower by extending compulsory education
and easing the standards for the establishment of universities. The
immediate impact of the reforms was to quadruple the number of
university places (a doubling of those applying to all higher educational institutions).

Moreover, the reforms fostered a social situation in which a
much larger proportion of the population could think of going to a
university. Apart from the structural reforms of extending compulsory education, increasing the number of comprehensive high
schools that prepare youth for college, and lowering the fees at pub-
licly supported high schools and universities, the shift toward
egalitarian education (higher mean level of cognitive performance
with less variation) provided more youth with the intellectual resources essential for higher education. This shift achieved much the
same result in terms of individual motivation. Finally, economic
growth and the trend toward income equality enabled a growing
proportion of families to think of sending their children to a university. In 1951, when asked what steps they would take if they had a
college-age son, only 22 percent of the adult population said they
wished to send their son to a university. By 1960, the proportion

had risen to 38 percent, and by 1973 it was 70 percent. In addition, with the democratization of sex roles, 53 percent of all adults said they wanted to send their daughter to a university or junior college (Kojima, 1975:83).[2]

THE UNALTERED POSITION OF THE ELITE UNIVERSITIES

Although the Occupation's reforms and postwar economic growth spurred the demand for higher education, they also enhanced the competition among youth to enter elite universities. As already noted, the old system was characterized by heavy competition to gain entry to an elite university. The Occupation opposed the elitist spirit engendered by this competition, and promoted several reforms aimed at mitigating it.

Reasoning that a reduction in the distinctiveness of the elite universities would lead young people to choose from a wider pool of institutions, one of the Occupation's goals was to level the university hierarchy. To achieve this, the central government was pressured to reduce the differentials in its financial allocations to universities. For a few short years, the government complied with this request; thus, for example, the University of Tokyo's budgetary share shrank to about 8 percent of the total allocated to all national educational institutions. However, by the mid-fifties Tokyo's share was once again increasing, and by the late sixties it was up to 15 percent of the total. Thus, the Occupation reforms failed to significantly alter the government's habit of favorable treatment of elite universities.

Moreover, the Occupation failed to alter the most central element sustaining the examination system: the link between the prestigious employers of the organizational sector and the well-known universities. Although the employers were concerned with the financial difficulties of some of the elite universities and openly expressed their belief that the quality of education was declining, they nevertheless retained their confidence in the ability of elite universities to attract the most able students. Moreover, believing they could provide sufficient on-the-job training to make up for the deficiencies in the education provided by the universities, the major employers continued to show preferential treatment to

[2] The author has co-edited a related volume that explores in considerable detail the postwar expansion of Japanese higher education and its consequences. See Cummings, Amano, and Kitamura (1979).

graduates of the elite institutions. Keidanren (The Japan Federation of Corporations) reported in 1957 that 270 out of the 321 member corporations responding to its survey said they limited their white-collar recruitment search to graduates from a preferred group of universities; 61 of these corporations considered the graduates of five schools or less, and over half looked at graduates of no more than ten schools (Shimizu, 1957:123). The central government, although maintaining that its civil service exams were open to all, continued to recruit over half the new members to its higher civil service from the University of Tokyo alone. Aspirants to higher education were well aware of these patterns and, insofar as they were ambitious, focused their efforts on admission to a well-known university.

PROLIFERATION OF SPECIAL ROUTES

Traditionally, there were special routes open to Japanese families who wished their children to have the highest chance of success in the university competition. For those who wished to see their children enter the Imperial University of Tokyo, the most certain and prestigious route involved passing the exams for and studying at the First Middle School and the First Higher School, both located in Tokyo. Because of the stature of these schools, families from both local and outlying areas sent their children to compete for entrance. Alternatively, ambitious families might focus on the Second or Third higher schools of the public sector or on certain of the private schools. Gakushuin (The Peer's School) accepted an elite clientele, many of whom went on to pass the exam at the Imperial University. To secure admission to the well-known private universities, children were often sent to the attached middle and higher schools. Thus, within the already highly selective old system, one could find an even more exclusive set of elite tracks toward which the more zealous parents steered their children.

The Occupation reforms, along with attempting to level the university hierarchy, also eliminated several of these elite secondary schools, especially those in the public sector. The First Higher School became a part of the University of Tokyo, the Second Higher School was incorporated into Tohoku University, and the Third Higher School was joined with Kyoto University. The private elite schools remained largely intact. Due to these early postwar changes, ambitious parents could not determine which public sector schools were worthwhile and often could not afford the tuition of the private schools. As a result, bright children accompanied average children to the public schools, and the entering classes in elite universities came from a variety of high schools.

This new reform at first generated much uncertainty. Parents could not decide which schools would provide the best opportunities for their children. And students were unclear about the areas of study in which they should devote the greatest effort. However, soon the newspapers and mass weeklies began featuring articles on these subjects, and several companies began publishing useful guidebooks. (The most famous among these companies today is Obunsha, which publishes *Keisetsu Jidai*, a periodical with a massive volume of detail about all of Japan's higher educational institutions, as well as a diversified series of cram books for high school and university entrance exams.)

With the greater wealth of information available from the late fifties, zealous parents began to search for special schools and strategies that might provide their children with an advantage. The traditional strategies were to hire private tutors and to enroll in a *yobiko* (preparatory school); needless to say, both of these institutions have prospered over the postwar period. Today over one third of the students at such elite universities as Todai and Kyodai have a tutorial job. The most famous *yobiko* enroll over twenty thousand students annually in classes designed exclusively for entrance exam preparation.

Nevertheless, these short-run cram programs are not considered as effective as continuous involvement in a quality day-school program, such as that formerly provided by the elite national higher schools. For those with enough money, one of the obvious substitutes for the elite higher schools are the traditional private school systems such as Doshisha in Kyoto or Keio and Aoyama Gakuin in Tokyo. During the fifties, the caliber of students entering these systems and especially their high schools rose. To capitalize on their new attractiveness, many of these schools made efforts to improve their performance in preparing students for the exam competition. The Doshisha provides a representative example. In contrast with its earlier permissive stance, Doshisha began to flunk students in the early fifties who failed to achieve a certain academic level; by eliminating the weaker students, Doshisha's reputation for placing its graduates in good universities was enhanced. Moreover, to reassure anxious parents, Doshisha allowed the top half of the high school senior class to enter one of the system's universities or junior colleges without a regular entrance examination.

Despite these modifications, the broad educational objectives of many of the traditional private schools as well as their complex financial commitments placed limits on their response to the new market. Thus, alongside the traditional private schools, several famous exam-oriented private schools rose to prominence. The most outstanding example today is Nada High School of Kobe, which has managed year after year to place virtually its entire graduating class in well-known universities. Altogether, there are a dozen of these schools, which, by virtue of their ability to select outstanding students and their freedom to provide accelerated programs—for example, twelfth grade math and science by the end of the ninth grade—push many students toward success in the exams. Because these schools have such excellent educational programs, their students rarely seek the aid of tutors or other examination props and often find the time for extracurricular activities. However, the tuition at several of these schools is steep and admissions are highly selective.

Where they exist, the attached schools of national universities are another set of alternatives. Ostensibly, these schools were established to provide a setting for educational experiments. Today, however, they do little experimental work and simply pursue quality education. Blessed with exceptionally talented teachers and budgets several times that of a normal public school, the attached schools achieve exceptional results. Year by year, their graduates have improved their positions in the exam competition. In the 1976 competition, these schools ranked second, third, and fourth in the number of students sent to Todai and fifth and tenth for Kyodai (*Shukan Asahi*, April 9, 1976, p. 131).

These two types of special school are located primarily in urban areas and, hence, not readily accessible to the majority of Japanese children.[3] Thus, in response to public pressure, local school boards in several prefectures have taken steps to restructure the public

[3] Still, the reputation of these schools is such that many parents from distant places send their children to sit for the entrance exams. An annual chartered flight takes children from Hokkaido, Japan's northernmost island, to sit for the exam of Nada high school—located 800 miles distant. In 1976, 61 percent of the students attending LaSalle High School of Kagoshima, a city located on the southern tip of Kyushu island, came from a different part of Japan. See "Shiritsu Yumeiko no Fukei Shirabe" (1976:153).

school system in order to help local children prepare for the exams. The usual strategy is to modify the Occupation's neighborhood school principle (small district system) by grouping several high schools into a "middle" (2-6 schools) or "large" (7 or more) district, and by establishing a hierarchy among these schools. At the top school of a given district, a special accelerated program is offered to those students who obtain high grades during their middle school days and excel in the district-wide high school entrance exam. In 1956, only two of Japan's prefectures used the large district, but by 1960 this type of district was implemented in seventeen prefectures. In 1967, thirty-three prefectures employed this principle (Sasaki, 1976:58).

The Juku Boom

To place their child in one of the attached schools, parents found it necessary to begin planning the child's education at birth. Many of the attached schools admitted the majority of their students at the kindergarten or primary school level, allowing only modest numbers to transfer in thereafter. Moreover, although the schools were national in name, they generally restricted entrance to students living within a certain commuting distance. To overcome these obstacles, interested parents had to locate their homes nearby and restrict their mobility until after their children matriculated—a step that no small number actually took.

In contrast, the well-known private schools place fewer non-monetary barriers on entry. Most admit students by examination at the point of passage from compulsory education (though Azabu Gakuin and Kyodo admit most students at the end of primary school). Also, these schools tend to accept students without regard to residence: in 1976, 61 percent of the students attending LaSalle High School in Kagoshima were from other prefectures, whereas 26 percent of the students at Azabu Gakuin Middle School came from outside the Tokyo metropolitan area.

To prepare their children for the exams to these schools, many parents resort to the same tactics that are common at the university entrance stage—hiring special tutors and sending their children to special extra-study schools known as *juku*.

Another development that has contributed to the expansion of *juku* is the demanding curriculum of the public schools. In response both to parental demands for accelerated education and a "scientific" conviction that children were capable of learning more, the central government in 1968 sharply upgraded the difficulty of the curriculum as specified in the official course of study. For example, first-year students in Japanese language were now expected to memorize 76 characters, 30 more than before the reform; second-year students were expected to know 221, an increase of 70; by the sixth grade, students were expected to memorize 996, 115 more than had been previously required. In math far more difficult problems were assigned after the 1968 reform (see Table 8.1).

Although this accelerated curriculum was designed to accommodate the brighter youths, it has proved too challenging for the slow learners. Teachers generally try to pull the slow students

TABLE 8.1
ASPECTS OF TYPICAL FOURTH GRADE ARITHMETIC TEXTS

	1958 Course of Study	1970 Course of Study	An American Commercial Text
Number of teaching units (chapters)	17	25	13
Pages in text	260	254	410
Pages devoted to multiplication	52	8	64
Typical multiplication problem	64 × 58	3547 × 4398	807 × 98
Typical division problem	8742 ÷ 6	24702 ÷ 537	4192 ÷ 90
Largest number explained	10,000	100,000,000	10,000,000
Largest number in a problem	34567 + 17506	5000 million ÷ 10,000 (to do in one's head without pencil or paper)	8,424,826 ÷ 2,937,939
Fractions	which is larger ½ or ⅓?	Addition and subtraction of fractions	Addition and subtraction of fractions
Geometry	Draw triangles, quadrilaterals	Draw, compute perimeter, diagonal, surface of triangles, quadrilaterals	Same as Japan, 1970

SOURCE: Motofumi Makieda, *Nihon no Kyoshitachi* (Japanese Teachers), p. 214; the American text is *Holt School Mathematics*.

along; in some schools, especially those for minority groups, a special program of review classes and supervised study is set up for the evenings. However, given the pace of the officially prescribed curriculum, most teachers find it impossible to reach everyone in their classes. The students who do not learn in school have to learn elsewhere to keep up in the middle and high schools and to compete for university entrance. Their parents, thus, often send them to an extra-study school.

In other instances, parents who have special plans for their child's education, such as admission to one of the well-known private middle or high schools, send the child to a *juku* for special advanced instruction. Some *juku* actually specialize in preparing their students for entrance to particular schools or universities. An unusual example is one *juku* that specializes in preparing youngsters to become doctors. This predoctor *juku* attempts not only to provide its charges with the knowledge it will need to pass the exams but also with the mannerisms appropriate to the profession. Thus, each day the young students, many of whom are still in primary school, wash their hands upon entrance to the *juku*, don white robes and a stethoscope, and proceed through a routine that may include anything from the review of normal school work to an animal dissection. The typical *juku* session ends at eight in the evening with the young trainees tired and hungry, just as they can expect to be a few years later if they succeed in becoming interns at a medical school.

One survey concluded as follows: "Extracurricular studying has become an indispensable element in the daily life of today's children. A July 1972 survey of fifth-grade students showed that 80 percent of the boys and 86 percent of the girls were taking outside lessons. It is far from uncommon for a child to be getting extra tutoring on Monday, Wednesday and Friday, and lessons in painting on Tuesday, piano on Thursday and swimming on Saturday" (Kondo, 1974:15). This particular survey surely overstates the degree of utilization of *juku*. No other survey, even in the Tokyo area, where academic competition is most intense, reports such a high proportion of fifth graders taking outside lessons. Moreover, the phrase "outside lessons" fails to distinguish between participation in exam-oriented activities and others such as piano lessons, calligraphy, judo, and so on; indeed, only 26 percent of these Tokyo fifth graders were involved in academic extra-lessons. Surveys in other areas report quite diverse proportions. Table 8.2, which presents the results for a national survey conducted by the Ministry of Edu-

TABLE 8.2

STUDENTS ATTENDING JUKU BY GRADE LEVEL AND CITY SIZE (PERCENTAGES)

City Size	Primary School						Middle School		
	1	*2*	*3*	*4*	*5*	*6*	*1*	*2*	*3*
Over 100,000	3.7	5.3	8.1	14.6	24.2	33.3	43.9	44.6	45.0
30,000 to 100,000	3.8	4.9	8.4	10.8	16.3	24.8	38.5	39.3	36.6
8,000 to 30,000	1.6	4.1	5.7	7.6	11.6	16.5	29.1	29.6	27.1
Less than 8,000	1.0	0.4	3.2	2.7	5.3	5.7	13.4	11.9	9.9
Total population	3.3	4.8	7.5	11.9	19.4	26.6	37.9	38.7	37.4

SOURCE: Mombusho, *Zenkoku no Gakushu Juku Kayoi no Jitsuyo* (National Pattern of Juku Attendance: Interim Report of the 1976 survey), Tokyo: Gyosei, 1977.

cation, suggests the following generalizations on *juku* attendance: (1) relatively few students take special studies through the first years of primary school; (2) the number increases to about 25 percent near the completion of primary school in preparation for middle school entrance exams; and (3) once in middle school, the number gradually increases to about 50 percent by the third year in preparation for the high school exams.

Not only are large numbers of children going to *juku*, but in the last few years it is reported that several thousand have created a new class of *ronin*. Failing entrance to their preferred high school, these youths have decided to devote another year to preparation, rather than settle for a second-class high school. Although the institutions today are nominally the same, they are becoming just as stratified as during the old system.

Actually, the exact number involved in the *juku* and high school *ronin* phenomena is unimportant. The relevant point is that public opinion believes that the number is astronomical, and that the quality of youthful life is in jeopardy.

THE QUALITY OF ADOLESCENT LIFE

The growing public concern with the examination system is based on the fear that the involvement and competition it generates has caused a decline in the quality of adolescent life. Various sources report the ill effects of the examination system. Young children report being lonely after school because most of their playmates attend a *juku*. Parents report that their children have become so accustomed to organized activities, whether at the *juku* or school, that they forget how to play by themselves. Almost 40 percent of all sixth graders now wear glasses—over double the proportion of twenty years ago.

Principals at academic high schools report that many of their club activities have been abandoned by the students. Surveys of the time budgets of young people indicate a growing amount of time devoted to studies and declining amounts to exercise and leisure. The annual survey of physical health conducted by the Ministry of Health shows that Japanese children are becoming taller and heavier (thanks to improved diet) but have less endurance and strength. One testimony to this decline was the failure of Japan to win gold medals in the 1976 Olympics—excepting in traditional fields of strength such as judo, women's volleyball, and gymnastics—even though it fielded one of the larger teams.

Although the exam system is responsible for many of these trends, some qualifications are in order. Some of the trends, such as the growing incidence of myopia and declining physical endurance, can be just as easily attributed to other factors: for example, the increasing proportion of youths living in urban settings where physical education facilities are scarce, and the changing quality of the adolescent diet. Also the incidence of these problems is related to the school course followed by young people.

As noted, increased academic competition has resulted in an unofficial redifferentiation of academic tracks. At the top are the well-known private and university-attached high schools, which select the brightest from each adolescent cohort. The classroom pace at these schools is more accelerated than in the ordinary high schools; yet, because of the intellectual aptitudes of the select students, the pace does not constitute a burden. Moreover, the high quality of the schools' education programs obviates the need to attend *juku* or other extra schooling. Most of these advanced schools have a reasonably active program of club activities, and many of the students in these schools find time to develop rich friendships. The major constraint encountered by the students is the commuting time between home and school. Many spend well over an hour a day on the train. More importantly, the homes of school mates are widely dispersed, making weekend visits and summer outings difficult to organize.

Somewhat distinct from the elite track is the large number of lesser private high schools that are attached to, and guarantee their graduates entrance into, second-class private universities. At these high schools one is also likely to find an active club life. Indeed, some promote this aspect of their program through the active recruitment of outstanding athletes and the energetic support of sports. This is done in an effort to attract new students and thus insure a sufficient number to enable the school to cover its costs.

The second major track that remains relatively sheltered from the exam system pressure is the vocational high school system. Technical colleges, which combine three years of high school and two years of college, may be included in this group. Once a student enters a school in this group, he essentially removes himself from the competition for higher education. Most of these vocationally oriented schools also maintain a vigorous club system, which manages to involve many of their students.[4]

Apart from the above groups, there remains the much larger group of public and private academically oriented high schools. It is on the students of these institutions that the academic pressure has largely fallen. Two decades ago, when academic competition was not so intense, students in the academic courses of public schools were able to enjoy a full school life, devoting energy to both their studies and a wide variety of school club activities. The athletic clubs thrived, even at the academically oriented high schools, and in the national meets they were often able to meet the competition. The baseball teams of public academic high schools won or placed on several occasions in the national finals. However, beginning in the sixties, the teams from vocationally oriented schools, especially the commercial schools, started to dominate the national competition. Similarly the industrial high schools began to dominate the national soccer competition (Shinbori et al., 1975). Although probably still capable of training to a competitive level, the youths at the public academic high schools no longer felt they could devote the time. An hour of sports meant an hour away from the books. The increasing academic competition has gradually eroded the extracurriculum of the public academic high schools.

Japan's high adolescent suicide rate is often associated with the examination competition. Actually, the high adolescent suicide rate predates the inception of the modern university system, suggesting that there are enduring features of Japanese social structure that cause youths to encounter exceptional problems in their transition

---

[4] However, the students in vocational schools tend to have higher delinquency rates. In part, this can be explained by background factors such as coming from a low income home or a broken family. However, frustration related to reduced opportunities for achievement also must play an important role.

from adolescence to manhood. Nevertheless, as Figure 8.1 shows, during the fifties the traditionally high suicide rate increased to an unusually high rate, even for Japan. Probably, this was caused by the short-range uncertainty, as parents and children adjusted to the new system. Although adolescents have made the adjustment, the increased competition is causing new difficulties for younger children; hence, the latest development is the increase in the suicide rate of pre-middle school youth.

Equality of Educational Opportunity

The exam system is much maligned because of the great pressure placed on Japanese youths to study long hours and on Japanese parents to spend heavily on their children's preparation. Although the exam system fosters inegalitarian tendencies, it is also important to note its fundamental egalitarian nature. The single criterion of admission to a preferred school is examination performance; a student's background and wealth are of little importance. At the elite institutions there are no exceptions. The exceptions begin to occur only as the reputation of a school declines.

In contrast with Japan's rigidly universalistic admissions standards, standards elsewhere are tempered by money and influence. In America, for example, a generous contributor to Harvard can expect that his child will be admitted, even if not fully qualified. The Ivy League schools promise to accept a certain number of graduates from the New England preparatory schools, even if these applicants do not measure up to all the admission standards. These practices are maintained to preserve the character, not to speak of the endowments, of America's great private universities and colleges. Some say that America can afford this small degree of particularism because universalism is firmly institutionalized in most of its social institutions. Nevertheless, these practices contradict the claim that everyone is equal in America. The elite public schools of the United Kingdom provide an even more conspicuous example of particularism.

Government leaders in Japan point with pride to the universalistic character of their exam system, suggesting it as a guarantee of equal opportunity. In this vein, a recent white paper prepared by the Economic Planning Agency's Bureau on the Quality of National Life (1974:175-176) drew on social mobility surveys conducted in several advanced societies to demonstrate that Japan's

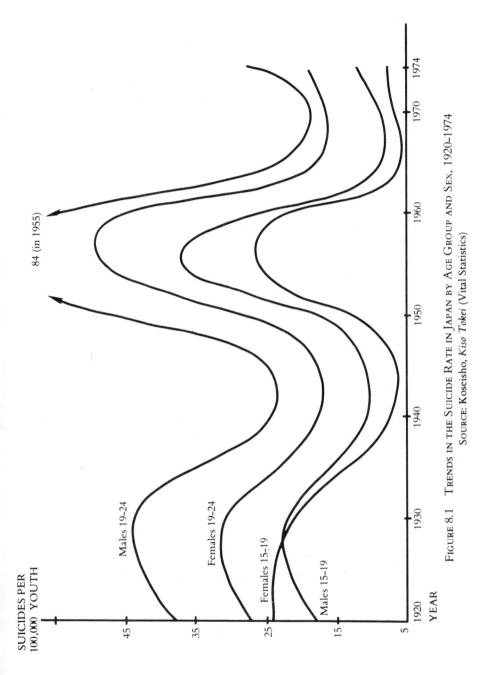

SUICIDES PER
100,000 YOUTH

YEAR

Males 19-24

Females 19-24

Females 15-19

Males 15-19

84 (in 1955)

FIGURE 8.1   TRENDS IN THE SUICIDE RATE IN JAPAN BY AGE GROUP AND SEX, 1920–1974

SOURCE: Koseisho, *Kiso Tokei* (Vital Statistics)

elite class is the most open of all. However, this particular conclusion, and for that matter the entire question of equality of opportunity in Japan, needs to be subjected to more rigorous analysis. Restricting the discussion to the question of equality of educational opportunity, the following observations seem appropriate.

1. One issue concerning equal educational opportunity is the total number of places available for young people in the educational system relative to the total number of young people. From this point of view, the Japanese system has become progressively more equal. Since World War II, it has provided sufficient places to educate all youths for nine full years of basic compulsory education. Moreover, the number of places for high school and university education steadily increased so that, by 1975, 92 percent of all high school-age youths and 38 percent of all college-age youths were enrolled in the respective schools. In terms of provisions for attendance, contemporary Japanese education may provide greater opportunity than any other system in the world. Also, the average number of years of school attendance for Japanese adults is among the highest in the world.

2. A second issue is the extent to which children from different social backgrounds are successful in taking advantage of the available opportunities. Until recently, governments did not collect data relevant to this question, making it difficult to arrive at a very satisfactory answer. However, the question may be addressed from a longitudinal perspective by examining age-group data from Japan's most recent social mobility survey. In the 1975 national mobility survey, age-groups are sufficiently large to provide reasonable approximations to successive cohorts born from the turn of the century to 1951–1955. In Figure 8.2, these estimates of average years of educational attainment over time by father's background are presented. There, one can see the steady increase in the average educational attainment for each successive cohort: the oldest cohort, born 1910 or earlier, had an average educational attainment equivalent to today's middle school level (approximately nine years); the youngest cohort, born between 1951 and 1955, had an average attainment somewhat in excess of the high school level (approximately thirteen years).

The relative attainment of and gains in educational level varied widely by social class background. Children of elites have always been the best educated and thus have had little room for further gains. Those born 1910 or earlier attained, on the average, some-

Educational attainment

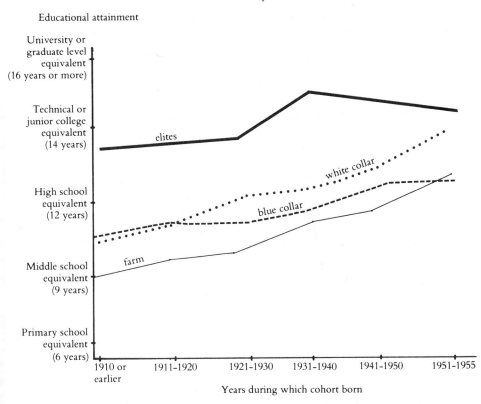

FIGURE 8.2 MEAN EDUCATIONAL ATTAINMENT BY COHORT AGE GROUPS FOR FOUR
OCCUPATIONAL CLASSIFICATIONS TABULATED FOR JAPANESE MALES OF 1975

what more than a high school education (approximately thirteen
years); the youngest elite group, born forty to forty-five years later,
improved on this average attainment only by approximately one
and a half years. The number in the sample with elite backgrounds
was comparatively small, however, so percentage figures are potentially misleading.

In contrast, children from blue-collar backgrounds born at the
turn of the century obtained, on the average, a middle school education, with only 16.7 percent attending a higher educational institution. Although the opportunities for educational upgrading were
available to this class, relatively few took advantage of them.
Neither their average level of educational attainment (middle
school for the oldest cohort, high school for the youngest—a gain

of only two years of school attendance) nor the proportion attending higher educational institutions (16.7 percent for the oldest cohort, 20.6 percent for the youngest) showed notable improvement.

Relative to the children from manual families, those from farm backgrounds have made somewhat greater advances. In fact, starting from lower levels on both indicators, farm children have surpassed children from blue-collar backgrounds in average level of educational attainment and proportion going on to a higher education institution. However, the gains for the children from white-collar backgrounds are the most impressive of all. Whereas only 7.6 percent of the oldest cohort attended a higher educational institution, the proportion rose to 50.0 percent for the most recent cohort. Simultaneously, the average educational attainment increased from slightly more than the middle school level (about ten years) to just below junior college level (nearly fourteen years).

Thus, looking at long-term trends in educational attainment, one finds significant differences in the extent to which specific classes have responded to the increasing availability of educational opportunities. The gap separating the children of the elite from the rest has narrowed somewhat. On the other hand, the gap between the children of white-collar and blue-collar families has considerably widened, whereas that between white-collar and farm children has increased somewhat. Other data not presented here indicate that the children from modern sector, white-collar managerial and professional homes have made the greatest gains in their educational attainment.

3. The high educational attainment of elite children and the rapid gains of children from white-collar homes are sustained by the exceptional level of familial support. A number of small-scale studies show that such support motivates children with only average abilities from these backgrounds to continue school, whereas more talented children from farm and blue-collar backgrounds forego further education. As one illustration, Ushiogi et al. (1972) identify those factors associated with dropping out after middle school in rural Gifu prefecture. In the year of this study, 1972, only 14.3 percent of all middle school graduates decided to forego further study; children from agricultural and blue-collar backgrounds predominated among those with low grades and those who dropped out. However, focusing only on those with respectable grade averages of 3.0 or above, one finds a definite bias for upper-class children to

persevere whereas lower-class children drop out—10.3 percent for children from farm homes and 8.4 percent for blue-collar children compared to 1.7 and .4 percent for white-collar and managerial children, respectively. On the other hand, 76.9 percent of white-collar children with low grades went on to high school, whereas only 57.4 percent of the blue-collar children with low grades continued. These class effects, which are independent of demonstrated ability, become even more exaggerated at the stage of university entrance. Clearly, something the upper classes provide their children compensates for ability, even in an educational system where ability is said to be the sole criterion for success.

Unquestionably, upper-class families can provide their children with the home circumstances most conducive to systematic and undisturbed study in preparation for the exams; also, upper-class families are better able to afford tutors and other educational aids. In contrast, children from lower-class homes feel much greater pressure either to excel in school or to leave. They cannot afford the time to devote themselves to the advanced study often required for entrance exam success. Thus, they tend to withdraw even when they have ability.

4. Although the discussion thus far has focused on general trends in educational attainment, it is also important to consider the class trends in entrance to the small group of elite educational institutions (especially the University of Tokyo) that are believed to constitute the gateways to distinguished careers in public service, big business, and the professions. Although educational opportunities in general have rapidly expanded over the postwar period, the size of many of these elite institutions has remained relatively constant. The Law Faculty of Tokyo University, the most elite among the elite paths, has increased its number of places for entering students by only 20 percent over the postwar period. The University of Tokyo as a whole has expanded by only 50 percent, and much of this growth has been in the technological specialties, which normally do not lead to elite careers. Other elite universities, especially in the private sector, have expanded at faster rates. Still, as a general statement, it is correct to say that the number of openings at the top has increased but slowly, whereas the number of aspirants has increased rapidly. Perhaps the most important question in a consideration of Japan's educational opportunity is who wins in the competition for these places in the elite universities.

There are obvious reasons why the children of the privileged classes should achieve the highest rates of success in this competition. It is generally regarded that the consumption of various forms of extra-education, such as attendance at *juku*, special high schools, *yobiko*, and lessons from household tutors, aids in the preparation for the difficult entrance exams of the elite universities. However, these extra-educational programs are not cheap, and their costs have actually increased at a faster rate than the standard of living. A recent publication reports the following amounts that parents had to pay (in 1976) to get their children into several of the better-known private schools: Y740,600 (about $2469) at Tamagawa Gakuin; Y695,500 ($2318) at Ueno Gakuen; and Y665,700 ($2219) at Azabu Gakuen (*Asahi Shinbun*, Feb. 7, 1976). Monthly fees and tuition at these schools run around Y30,000 (about $100) or something like one fourth of the average monthly family income in Japan. Admittedly, other schools are not so expensive. Nada and Koyo, two of the outstanding, charge about half as much; still, this is a substantial sum.

Clearly, not all families are able or willing to afford these avenues. Local areas differ widely in the average amount families pay for these services. Looking only at payments for tutors and academic *juku*, we find that the 1972 average in Wakayama (Y9713) was sixteen times the average in Fukushima (Y620). In general, the average was highest in the more central cities and those places noted for their educational zealotry, such as Tokushima. This trend would be more sharply indicated by expenditures for private middle and high schools, which tend to be located in and receive students from the large urban areas.

There are also substantial differences by parental income and status. Expenditures tend to increase with income. Roughly the same trend exists for status; however, it is the highly educated families dependent on salaries for their incomes, rather than the self-employed and the independently wealthy, who spend the greatest proportion of income for education.[5] These families are especially zealous in providing support for their children's education, for they realize that their children's access to the career lines that will maintain the family's social status depends on educational success.

Although the well-known private middle and high schools use

[5] According to one report, some white-collar parents spend from 30 to 40 percent of their income on their children's education; see Tsuru (1969:164).

universalistic exams to select entrants, the high tuitions they charge tend to restrict the range of applicants. Within this limited group, extra-schooling and preparation for entrance examinations is associated with parental income. The best schools no longer officially release information on student backgrounds, but reports from the independent weeklies suggest they admit a highly select group. For example, one weekly reports that over 25 percent of the third-year students at LaSalle Middle School were the children of medical doctors. The same article indicates that the fathers of over half the students at Azabu Gakuen were either managers or bureau chiefs of private companies, while another 15 percent had fathers in the higher civil service (*Shukan Ashahi*, March 23, 1976, p. 153).

Turning to the university level, there is rather clear evidence that a growing proportion of students come from higher income groups, despite the fact that the university system has vastly expanded over the past two decades. Among the national universities, which charge a modest tuition and include many of the best-known institutions, the proportion of students with family incomes in the upper two fifths increased from 45 to 60 percent between 1961 and 1976 (Table 8.3). Moreover, data released by the University of Tokyo indicate that a growing proportion of its entering student body comes from high status families (see Table 8.4). The most notable trends are the increases in the proportions from the homes of private sector executives (from 3 to 6 percent between 1959 and 1970) and private sector "employees" (from 31 to 39 percent); in 1970, two thirds of these employees were managers.

Since 1970 the university has not officially released data on the social background of its entering students, but the newsweeklies have conducted their independent surveys, and these suggest a continuation of the above trends. One weekly said that 17 percent of the entering 1976 class came from families whose head was a company president; an additional 26 percent were from private sector managerial families. Only 2 percent had fathers in agriculture, and not even 1 percent were from blue-collar families (*Shukan Gendai*, April 8, 1976). Needless to say, the trend toward higher social status backgrounds among University of Tokyo students cannot be dismissed as some simple function of an upgraded occupational system. Although it is difficult to determine the exact magnitude of the trend, it is evident that the intensified educational competition of the postwar period has led to less equality of opportunity to gain access to the most prominent high schools and universities.

TABLE 8.3
STUDENTS FROM EACH OF FIVE STRATA OF HOUSEHOLDS
BASED ON INCOME DIFFERENCES (PERCENTAGES)

	1961	*1965*	*1970*	*1974*	*1976*
National universities					
1	19.7	16.3	17.3	14.4	12.7
2	20.2	15.1	13.9	11.2	12.3
3	15.4	18.6	17.7	16.0	15.1
4	18.5	22.5	21.2	24.3	24.5
5	26.2	27.6	29.2	34.1	35.4
Private universities					
1	6.4	4.8	5.8	6.1	5.6
2	9.2	6.8	6.1	6.5	7.7
3	12.3	11.1	13.3	11.6	10.6
4	19.2	20.9	22.3	21.2	25.4
5	52.9	56.4	52.5	54.6	50.7
Total—all four-year universities					
1	11.0	8.3	8.5	8.0	7.2
2	13.1	10.4	8.0	7.5	8.7
3	13.5	13.4	14.4	12.6	11.6
4	19.1	21.7	22.0	21.8	25.2
5	43.2	46.2	47.0	50.1	47.3

SOURCE: Mombusho Gakusei Seikatsu Chosa reported in *Kōsei Hōdō* published monthly by the Gakusei Hodoka of the Mombusho.

NOTE: Each stratum represents 20 percent of all households in Japan, (1) being the lowest income stratum.

THE EXAMINATION SYSTEM AND THE
EGALITARIAN SENTIMENT

The apparent trend away from equal educational opportunities is a matter of considerable interest; yet, in terms of the broader thesis here, linking education to equality, it is beside the point. The real issue concerning the examination system is its effect on the way Japanese youths think. Does participation in the system reinforce or erode the egalitarian sentiment?

In considering this question, it is important to emphasize some obvious aspects of the Japanese school system. Virtually all Japanese youths attend public primary schools, in which egalitarian education is most intensively provided. For most youths, the efforts

TABLE 8.4

DISTRIBUTION OF THE OCCUPATIONS OF THE FATHERS OF
UNIVERSITY OF TOKYO STUDENTS, 1959–1970 (PERCENTAGES)

Occupation Groups	*1959*	*1961*	*1962*	*1964*	*1965*	*1967*	*1970*
Salaried employees in							
public service	24	26	28	28	22	23	22
Managers	—	—	—	—	—	15	15
Nonmanagerial	—	—	—	—	—	8	7
Salaried employees in							
private enterprise	31	34	32	31	34	35	39
Managers	—	—	—	—	19	25	26
Nonmanagerial	—	—	—	—	15	10	13
Small business owners,							
executives	18	18	15	17	18	17	14
Large and medium							
business executives	3	2	3	6	5	4	6
Self-employed	10	7	9	8	10	9	10
Agriculture	5	5	5	3	3	6	3
Other	9	8	8	7	8	6	6

SOURCE: Tokyo Daigaku Koseika, *Keizai Seikatsu no Ryūnen Henka*: 1958–1970
(Trend analysis of the economic conditions of student life: 1958–70).

and "lessons" of the exam system, which are experienced by growing numbers of students, do not begin until the last year of middle
school. The priority of egalitarian education suggests that it plays a
fundamental role in socialization. Of course, immediately after
World War II, egalitarian education was not that widespread in the
primary schools. However, as egalitarian education has become
more typical, its impact on the socialization of youth naturally has
become more pervasive.[6]

To some degree, the extensive postwar participation in the
examination system can be attributed to egalitarian education. This
style of education has provided a greater proportion of adolescents

[6] Those who succeed in the exam competition are just as likely to have been exposed to the public school's egalitarian education as those who fail. Noritsugu
Ishido, a graduate student at Kyoto University and my assistant, investigated the
school histories of Kyoto University's Class of 1979 and found that 95 percent had
attended a public primary school, 75 percent a public middle school, and 71 percent a
public high school. Excepting the middle school statistic, these figures closely correspond to those for the same overall age-cohort, nationwide.

with the cognitive and motivational resources to continue school beyond the compulsory level. At the same time, it can be asked whether extensive participation in the processes of preparation for the examinations leads to the acquisition of values that run contrary to the moral component conveyed by egalitarian education.

Finally, in a consideration of the exam system's effects, it is important to distinguish between lessons taught by Japanese education in general and those taught by the exam system. By comparative standards, Japanese youths tend to have an exceptional ability for concentration, for attention to detail, and for discipline. Although these traits are reinforced by the exam system, it should be appreciated that they are first developed in primary school. The basic issue concerns not these traits, but rather the extent to which the exam system encourages the individualistic competitive orientation (outlined at the beginning of this chapter) and weakens the commitment of young people to equality.

If the increasing level of participation in the exam system leads growing numbers of adolescents to internalize individualistic competitive values, several consequences should follow. These include: widespread experience of a sense of personal failure and, hence, presumably, a growing incidence of suicide; participation in "worthless" activities such as delinquency; and a growing divergence in the ways of thinking between those who succeed and those who fail, especially with respect to feelings of elitism, attitudes about welfare, and related egalitarian items. However, there is little evidence of the predicted outcomes.

The significant downturn in adolescent suicides since 1955 has already been discussed. Moreover, by the seventies only a fraction of such suicides could be related to problems in school or examination performance. The more typical causes were alienation, mental illness, and quarrels with parents or friends. The single development consistent with the predictions from the individualistic competitive model is the recent rise in the incidence of preteen suicides, a growing (though still small) proportion of which is caused by anxiety over admission to middle school.

In a discussion of these trends, Kato (1974:374) notes Henry and Short's famous hypothesis of an inverse relation between suicide and homicide and suggests that adolescent aggression in Japan may be turning outward from self-destruction toward acts against others. Indeed, from the mid-fifties through the mid-sixties, there was a steady increase in various juvenile delinquency rates, which some observers link to the exam system. However, they do not suggest that increased delinquency is a displacement of the earlier individualistic tendency toward self-destruction. Iwai presents several suggestive quotes from delinquents he interviewed: One sixteen-year-old delinquent said:

"School is useless. All they teach is how to study; they are not interested in anything else."

Another boy: "My family is poor, and won't let me go on school outings. This makes me ashamed in front of my classmates. My parents couldn't care less about school. I'm stupid, so whatever I do I get into trouble with the teachers. I don't like being the underdog, so I take it out on the people around me. I was being determined not to be looked down on and that made me this way."

An 18-year old member of a group which had been threatening people in the street explained his feelings thus: "I was caught, but I don't regret what I did in the least. The others in my school will graduate, move up to higher schools, and give themselves a foundation for going out into the world. Because I've come straight out into the world I don't count for anything. So I get together with my friends and push people around. Hard, sharp and quick, that's how I feel" (1974:387).

The impression that one gains from these quotes is that youths turn to delinquency out of a sense of generalized frustration with the examination system and the ways in which it constrains and directs their daily routines. Moreover, some youths seem to believe that through delinquency they can demonstrate equality with those who do well in school: "The others in my class spend all their time working; I've no hope of catching up with them. But I do have some pride. If I can, I want to be able to talk to them as equals in some way or other. So I decided that if I couldn't do it by being as clever, I'll do it by being as strong as they were" (Iwai, 1974:387).

The Iwai report suggests that dissatisfaction with school and the exam system is a minority feeling and that such dissatisfaction is a factor in delinquency. Although this interpretation may have been appropriate up to the mid-sixties, it has since become dated.

On the one hand, one finds that since 1965 the delinquency rate in Japan has declined, and that there is no longer a clear association between delinquency and school performance—or with most of the other structural variables normally associated with delinquency, such as broken family and impoverished home (Japan Institute of International Affairs, 1975:154). On the other hand, adolescent dissatisfaction with the examination system has become much more widespread and seems now to be essentially unrelated to school performance. Table 8.5 presents the cross-tabulations between edu-

TABLE 8.5
ATTITUDES OF JAPANESE YOUTHS TOWARD THE EDUCATIONAL SYSTEM

| | Educational Attainment | | | |
	Middle School	High School	Higher Education	Total
Schools overemphasize exams relative to human qualities	74.1	71.0	73.2	71.4
Regardless of qualifications, the social prestige of one school counts more	66.4	61.5	66.2	63.2

SOURCE: Sorifu (Prime Minister's Office), *Sekai Seinen Ishiki Chosa Hokokusho* (Report on the International Survey of the Consciousness of Youth).

cational attainment and attitude toward the exam system for youths aged eighteen to twenty-four in 1974, reported in a survey by the Japanese Prime Minister's Office. Seven tenths of all youths agree that "present day schools tend to evaluate students merely on the basis of examination results and give little attention to their human qualities" and that "it is accepted by most people that regardless of your qualifications, the social prestige of the school you graduate from will influence your job opportunities and future." There is virtually no variation by level of schooling in the pattern of response to these questions. In addition, 46 percent of all Japanese students express dissatisfaction with their school experience. This same survey was administered to youths in ten other nations, and in no other country was the level of dissatisfaction so high. These feelings are common even among those who excel in the examination system, perhaps more so. Based on his experience teaching entering students at the University of Tokyo, Orihara (1967) concludes there are two types of reactions to the exam system. The positive reactions, which make up the minority of the responses and are found mainly in students from the well-known high schools, are consistent with the individualistic competitive model: they include feelings of "fulfillment" from the exam preparation, "joy" from improved class ranking, and "superiority" in admission to Todai. But the negative reactions are more common: for example exam preparation is often viewed as a "miserable experience I'd just as soon forget—the sooner the better." Or as another student puts it:

> Tests, tests, tests. . . . They have dominated our student days. They have kept us from taking the time to think about our society or the meaning of our own lives. . . . Preparation for the college entrance exam has been a jealous mistress robbing us of the time to think about these problems. And even what we should have been able to regard as a haven from this robbery—our homeroom—was never a place where we could fully relate to each other as human beings. An education stressing competition and inculcating false values, has, unawares, created a kind of person who thinks only of himself and is uninterested in others (Orihara, 1967:229).

It seems difficult, using the individualistic competitive model, to account for the growing sense of dissatisfaction or to explain why the feeling is equally shared by those who succeed and those who fail. Also, insofar as this dissatisfaction is individually experienced, it could be expected to be accompanied by an increased tendency toward individualized reactions. But, as already noted, the incidence of the most extreme form of individual reaction, self-destruction, has significantly declined. And, following a gradual increase up to 1965, the incidence of the milder form of juvenile delinquency has also declined.

Of course, one should not neglect the impact of recent structural developments such as the increased availability of information, the elaboration of less demanding options after high school, and the growing rationality of individual approaches to the exams. These may help to limit the mounting competitive pressure, but they hardly seem sufficient to account for the reversal in the suicide and delinquency trends.

It appears that the egalitarian sentiment is the crucial factor underlying these reversals. As pointed out above, egalitarian education was first introduced after World War II. In the beginning, egalitarian education was not that widely understood or practiced, but with time it became more systematized. Presumably, its success in inculcating the egalitarian sentiment also became more widespread. This sentiment instructed youth to view the examination experience not as determining individual success or failure but rather as offering channels to different adult roles. The response of young people gradually shifted from individualized frustration to collective protest.

The major development among youths after 1965 was widespread student revolt at institutions of all quality levels, but especially at the better-known national and private universities. By the end of the revolt, even some groups of young blue-collar workers were involved. The revolt focused on a great diversity of issues, but according to Michio Nagai, the prominent commentator on educational affairs, its major concern was with the university system and all it stood for.[7]

In this reaction, one can witness the powerful influence of the egalitarian sentiment. Both those who had succeeded and those who had failed by conventional standards were saying they resented this educational process that forced them into different strata of the adult world. They wanted it terminated. If necessary, they were willing to destroy adult society in order to build a new social structure consistent with their egalitarian values. By the late sixties, youths felt their movement had gone a considerable distance toward the realization of this revolutionary goal. Ultimately, of course, the authorities were able to break the back of the student revolt and to return the campuses to their normal routines. However, there is little evidence that the basic dissatisfactions of young people have dissipated since then.

Insofar as this interpretation of recent events is well founded, it casts serious doubt on the individualistic competitive model. Of course, the model cannot be dismissed altogether. Clearly, there are still some youths who remain positive about the examination system and the lessons it teaches. But for the majority, the following orientation is more characteristic: "Broadly speaking, there are two ways to study for the exams. One is to be conscious of the countless other students throughout the country involved in the same struggle; then you have to picture yourself competing with them. The other is to perceive the exams as your personal enemy and make up your mind to expend every effort on preparing to conquer the foe; then you have to resign yourself to the results. I fit more or less into the latter category" (Orihara, 1967:235). This student has come to realize the success that can be obtained through the exam system. For him, and, apparently, for a growing proportion of Japanese

---

[7] This is a personal communication, which is summarized in Cummings (1972).

youth, this success is not worth the high price; they can be content with less in the material world so long as it provides the opportunity for personal growth and challenge. If they are fortunate enough to succeed, they will feel pleased but not necessarily superior; some will even feel guilty, because they made it, whereas others who seemed to be more qualified failed.

Of course, more than egalitarian education lies behind this new preference of young people for personal growth over worldly success. It is important to recall some of the changes in family structure and child-rearing mentioned in Chapter Four. Given these changes, one might expect that children are becoming more autonomous and, hence, analytical about their motivations. This has helped them to appreciate the extent to which they are being pushed into the exam system by external, rather than internal, motivations—by the influence of parents, first, and also by that of peers. Growing numbers of youths are beginning to acknowledge that college and fame are not goals they themselves have decided on. This realization allows them to accept failure more easily.[8]

CONCLUSION

Earlier chapters focused mainly on the achievement of egalitarian education in the lower-level schools. However, do the effects of this education persist as youths move up to the higher levels of the educational systems? This chapter tried to answer that question; it concentrated mainly on the adolescent stage, during which youths move through high school and into either college or the labor force. This stage is characterized by heightened academic competition, and as discussed here, this competition has important consequences in three areas—the quality of adolescent life, the equality of opportunity for advanced education, and the persistence of egalitarian values. As to the first outcome, the evidence presented here casts doubt on the view popularized by the mass media that today's youths suffer grievously from the examination system. There are both positive and negative outcomes for individuals in this transitional experience. On the question of equity, it appears educational opportunities, broadly defined, are becoming more equal. How-

[8] Taking a viewpoint similar to this, Kiefer (1970) portrays the exam system as a separation ritual. It teaches youths that the adult world and the world of their homes operate on different principles, the one "dry" and demanding and the other "wet" and supporting.

ever, opportunities at the elite institutions seem, if anything, to be becoming less accessible to ordinary youth. Finally, with respect to the transformation thesis, there is evidence that the examination experience, rather than eroding egalitarian values, actually appears to reinforce them—at least for most youths in most respects. Chapter Nine will follow these young people as they move into the labor force.

EQUALIZING SOCIETY

The analysis up to this point has established that the schools, in conjunction with other socialization agents, are creating a "new youth." A growing proportion of young people affirm egalitarian, individuated, and participatory values that clash with the traditional expectations of Japan's adult institutions.

There can be little doubt that Japan's young people experience difficulty in adjusting to the adult world. This is illustrated in a 1973 survey (conducted by Gallup International) of representative samples of youth in eleven societies. On each relevant question (see Table 9.1 and Sorifu, 1973) Japanese youths were far more likely to

TABLE 9.1

A COMPARISON OF THE PROPORTION OF DISSATISFIED JAPANESE YOUTH
WITH THE PROPORTIONS IN OTHER ADVANCED SOCIETIES

Dissatisfaction	Japanese Youth	Country with Next Highest Level
With nation's provision for the rights and welfare of the people	88.5	54.4 England
With society	73.5	35.7 United States
With school	45.2	29.0 France
With employment	40.0	24.8 France
With family life	30.6	10.9 France
With friends	15.8	8.0 France

SOURCE: Sorifu, *Sekai Seinen Ishiki Chosa Hokokusho*, 1973.

express dissatisfaction than the youths of other societies. They are especially outspoken on the questions relating to adult institutions: 88.5 percent of the Japanese youths said that their "country does not sufficiently protect the rights and welfare of the people," compared with only 54.4 percent for the youths of economically distressed England, who were the second most discontented. Similarly, 73.5 percent of the Japanese youths said they were dissatisfied with society, compared to only 35.7 percent for the American youths, who were second. Although the differences were not as great, Japanese youths were also the most disgruntled about their employment, their schools, and even their family life.

If there is any doubt about the reliability of these comparisons, one need only consider the Japanese "student revolt" of the late sixties. It was surely the longest, most disruptive, and most violent of all youth disturbances experienced in advanced nations at that time (Cummings, 1972:632). The intensity of the Japanese revolt is a reflection of the dissatisfaction registered in the Gallup youth survey.

What becomes of youths as they move into the adult institutions? Several possible outcomes can be imagined: (1) the youths once they experience adult society, "convert" to the adult values; (2) the youths stick with their adolescent values, but outwardly conform to the norms of adult society; (3) adult society transforms its structures in order to accommodate the new youth.

Several of the better-known English language studies of the transition from youth to adulthood have minimized the frustration the young experience or have treated this as a passing phenomenon. Abegglen (1958:Ch. 3), in *The Japanese Factory*, devoted detailed attention to the recruitment and training programs of employers without ever seriously investigating the reactions of employees. Rohlen (1974:Ch. 9) devotes more attention to the reactions of young people, but implies that most learn to adjust; however, it should be pointed out that his study focused on a bank, which of all organizations is least likely to recruit rebellious individuals. Azumi (1969), as well as Lifton (1972), are more sensitive to the problems encountered by youths, but still seem to conclude that most youths experience *tenko* (that is, they allow their minds to be changed by adult society).

Whereas these conventional accounts lean toward either the first or second of the alternatives above, the third seems both theoretically plausible and consistent with a considerable body of recent evidence. Thus, the objective in this chapter will be to advance the proposition that the emergence of the new youth has caused a transformation of adult institutions. Particularly egalitarian changes in the structure of work organization and the distribution of rewards and recent political trends and developments will be considered.

FROM SCHOOL TO THE LABOR FORCE

Securing a good job is a major preoccupation of most young people as they plan their last years of schooling. Moreover, the early years of work provide the setting for a dramatic manifestation of the differences between young and old. To provide a background for consideration of this situation, some general features of the labor market for young people in Japan will first be reviewed.

Two distinctive features of this market are (1) the practice of allowing only those youths who are in the final year of their individual educational careers to apply for jobs, and (2) the practice of starting most new jobs in the spring, upon the completion of the school year. As a result of these practices, most youths begin to work only upon graduation from either a junior high school, a senior high school, a college, or a universtiy. Until very recently, there was a strong demand for graduates at each of these levels.

Government statistics collected from 1959 to 1973 on job searches by middle and high school graduates indicate that nine out of ten found a job within three months of their graduation (see Table 9.2).

Of course, the quality of jobs found by young people varies considerably. As in the United States, the particular industry or occupation is a significant determinant of job quality. However, for the

TABLE 9.2
DEMAND–SUPPLY RATIO FOR NEW SCHOOL GRADUATES AND
PROPORTION OBTAINING JOBS

	Number of Openings for New Grads/ Number of New Grads Seeking Employment		New Grads Obtaining Employment within Three Months of Graduation (Percentage)	
	Middle School	High School	Middle School	High School
1959	1.2	1.1	76.4	60.3
1960	1.9	1.5	85.0	68.8
1961	2.7	2.0	85.6	76.0
1962	2.9	2.7	86.5	82.3
1963	2.6	2.7	86.2	82.1
1964	3.6	4.0	90.5	86.4
1965	3.7	3.5	92.1	87.3
1966	2.9	2.6	90.9	87.6
1967	3.4	3.1	92.0	86.8
1968	4.4	4.4	92.2	89.1
1969	4.8	5.7	92.6	88.8
1970	5.8	7.1	99.1	98.7
1971	6.8	8.4	100.0	99.6
1972	5.5	3.2[a]	100.0	99.9
1973	5.8	3.1[a]	99.9	100.0

SOURCE: Japan Institute of Labor, *Japan Labor Statistics*, pp. 58-59.
[a] The lower figures reflect a new system of reporting.

Japanese young person, the specific firms offering jobs are often the
most salient consideration. Over the course of industrialization,
there has emerged an advantaged sector of large businesses and
governmental organizations, which are able to offer workers lifetime employment as well as exceptional fringe benefits and competitive wages. In contrast, there are the more numerous small organizations that use simple technologies and usually offer inferior
working conditions. Traditionally, young people preferred to
become *sarariman* (employees) in the large organizations, and structured their educational careers accordingly. Although contemporary young people are somewhat more critical of large organizations than were earlier generations, the overwhelming majority still
feel that large organizations provide the best opportunities, overall.
Thus, as in the past, their job-seeking behavior is initially oriented
to this sector.

Anticipating that large organizations recruit on the basis of educational qualifications, these young people plan their educational
careers accordingly, striving to attend those high schools and universities that lead to the best jobs. These considerations are behind
the academic competition documented in Chapter Eight. The
placement office of the school in which a youth completes his education serves as the principal intermediary between him and the
labor market.

Necessarily, the large organizations can hire only a fraction of
each year's graduating class. Given the surplus of applicants and the
guarantee of lifetime employment extended to most new hirees,
these organizations go about the process of selection with great
care. In each organization a section headed by a trusted executive
exists for this purpose. In the summer the firm advises the personnel office on the number of new hirees it anticipates. The personnel
office then informs the placement offices of those schools and universities from which it prefers to recruit young people. The government and some firms observe a policy of open announcements
and universalistic evaluation. However, the majority of firms restrict their recruitment to graduates of a small number of educational institutions (*shiteiko*), for this saves costs in evaluating applicants as well as yields a more homogeneous work force.

Individual employers select recruits from the pool of applicants
recommended by the placement offices of approved schools and
invite these youths to take written examinations. The exams primarily test academic achievement; however, these days it is not

uncommon for employers to include some ideological and psychological items in the exams (Azumi, 1969:75 ff.). Following the personnel office's evaluations of these initial results, a small number of semifinalists are invited for interviews to gauge individual poise and character. In addition, corporations hire detective agencies to investigate the past of promising applicants: for example, to determine whether they have run afoul of the law, what types of extracurricular and political activities they engaged in during school, what their families are like, and whether they have had special health problems.

Some corporations reject applicants who have bad records in any of these areas. But, at least in the past, most corporations were likely to employ capable applicants in spite of their deficiencies, because they felt confident of the capacity of their training programs to mold these individuals to the corporate way. This attitude received articulate expression during the period of the recent student revolt. Many personnel officers, admiring the zeal of the student leaders, reported they were eager to harness that energy in the sale of Japanese goods around the world. Government organizations were, understandably, less willing to take these chances.

Large corporations begin to announce their decisions on new hirees by the early fall; government organizations make their decisions by January. Youths who learn they have failed to land a job in a large organization begin examining other alternatives: these include joining a smaller firm or the family business, setting up an independent enterprise, or seeking further education. Of course, for an increasing minority of youth, these alternatives are first choices. In normal times, by March, the month that most schools and universities hold their graduation ceremonies, virtually all graduates of the educational system are committed to one or the other of these alternatives. A few weeks later, those members of the graduating classes who have elected to join the labor force report to their employers.

Receiving the New Employee

Although there are a number of alternatives, the majority of young people begin their work careers as employees of an organization. The promise of lifetime employment is a norm in the organizational world. In return, recruits are expected to devote their energies loyally to their employer.

These norms and expectations, although characteristic of all organizations, are most firmly institutionalized in the large organizations in which employees from both blue- and white-collar ranks
form enterprise unions to protect their interests. Likewise,
employers develop elaborate measures to induce loyal service. One
aspect is the careful process of recruitment just reviewed. Also
employers structure pay increases, pensions, and other fringe benefits so as to reward those who conform to the norm. Finally,
employers maintain educational programs to cultivate the loyalty
and the skills of employees. Especially in the large organizations of
the private sector, new recruits are subjected to an intensive educational experience intended to convert them to the company way.
Their first day of employment often begins with a speech from the
president welcoming the new group. Recruits are then sent off to a
special training camp for anywhere from a few days to a few weeks,
although some firms keep their recruits at these camps for as long
as three months. As in military boot camps, recruits rise early,
exercise, march, sing company songs, and attend workshops extol-
ling their employer and communicating what is expected of them.
Following this camp experience, recruits return to a work place of
their new employer where they are gradually introduced to their
world roles.[1]

One aspect of this introduction is the rotation of employees
through the various organizational sections in order to acquaint
them with the overall work process. In firms that engage in man-
ufacturing or service, it is not uncommon to temporarily assign
fresh white-collar workers to the assembly line or delivery route.
Former prime minister and Nobel Prize winner Eisaku Sato, spent
much of his prepolitical life in the Ministry of Transportation. His
first assignment after joining that ministry was to punch tickets at a
station wicket located in a rural area. New recruits to large organizations, even though they have outstanding academic records, may
be moved from section to section for two years or more without
ever receiving an important assignment.

Another method of introduction is to link each new employee
with a formal *sempai* (a type of older brother), who will listen to the
recruit's problems and offer advice on succeeding in the firm. When

---

[1] This discussion is based on interviews with personnel officers of several large
organizations during the fall of 1973 and the spring of 1976.

problems arise, the *sempai* may either take the recruit out for a drink and console him, or, if necessary, reprimand him.

Individual corporations vary widely in their execution of these programs. Through the mid-sixties, most corporations believed these initiation programs were effective in directing the motivation of young people toward corporate goals. However, from roughly 1965, corporations began to experience a number of problems with their new recruits. For the first time since the Occupation period (1945–1952), the turnover rate among young employees of large corporations began to rise.[2] Worker attitude surveys indicated rising levels of dissatisfaction, especially among young employees. Typical complaints focused on powerlessness and unchallenging work, excessive emphasis on human relations and involvement in the company, long hours, and the inequality in pay (by age and rank). As one executive put it in discussing his recent blue-collar recruits:

> High school graduates come in with strong views about what work they want to do—not like the old days when they were just happy to be part of the company and willing to do whatever job was assigned. After the war, employment in a big company meant security and that was what all strived for. But now with economic prosperity to be experienced everywhere, many young people prefer to work in smaller companies where they feel they can develop their individual talents. And those who do go to work for the major companies are much more demanding—and if they don't get it, they are more likely to quit than in the past (Cole, n.d.:17)

Mizutani (1972), examining the annual employee attitude survey conducted in more than one thousand companies from 1959 to 1972 by the Morale Survey Center, reports that there was a drastic decline in "loyalty to one's employer." A series of surveys conducted by the Productivity Bureau of the Japan Junior Chamber of Commerce (Sorifu, 1975:97) indicates an increasing proportion of young people looking at work as a means to personal goals rather than as

---

[2] According to statistics compiled from the monthly labor survey (Japan Institute of Labor, 1974:65 and 67) the rate of separation from large firms steadily increased from 1966 to 1970. Of greater significance, the proportion of employees leaving work places who indicated they quit for personal reasons slowly increased between the late fifties and 1970.

an end in itself. In addition, this survey reports a significant drop in the level of ambition of youths who take up white-collar work. Between 1970 and 1974, the proportion expressing an interest in becoming an executive declined from 44 percent to 30 percent.

THE RESPONSE OF MODERN SECTOR EMPLOYERS

Alarmed by these trends, employers responded in a variety of ways. No one response predominates, but a few of the more typical are listed below.

1. One widespread response is to improve the techniques for selecting new recruits. Corporations increasingly enlist the aid of such companies as Japan Recruit, Inc., which specialize in the development and administration of personnel testing. Apart from their testing services, these companies have also developed various journals and workshops that corporate personnel managers avidly consult for information regarding the recruitment of the ideal employee.

2. Many corporations attempt to strengthen their recruit training programs. Since the late sixties, corporate expenditures per recruit have substantially increased. At the same time, many corporations have restructured the curriculums of these programs in order to counter directly the new ideas of their recruits. Frager and Rohlen, considering the incidence of corporate-sponsored *seishin* (spirit) oriented training observe that,

> during the sixties many large firms, including about one-third of those enrolled in the Industrial Training Association (*sangyo kun-ren kyōkai*) in 1969, came to institute seishin-related activities as elements in their introductory training programs, particularly those for men. The variation in actual practices from company to company appeared to be large. The bank we studied in detail, for example, featured an extraordinary elaboration of seishin-oriented activities over a three-month training period, yet such intensity is not typical. It is more common to find one or two weeks given over to such activities as *zazen*, a marathon, other endurance tests, or brief training visits to Japan's Self-Defense Force camps (1973:263).

However, it may well be that these training programs, even after being upgraded, have little effect. Research (Lifton, 1961) on intentional adult resocialization indicates the best results are achieved when the subject is placed in unfamiliar, stressful conditions that dispose him to solicit favor from the individuals in charge of the program. Ideally, the subject's daily activities should be structured in a manner that continually confronts the individual with the re-socializing message; diversions must be minimized. The Japanese company training programs, rather than isolating particular recruits for intensive resocialization sessions, allow them to spend most of their time with fellow age-mates who tend to share their values. Moreover, apart from a few hardships such as marching and exercising, the camps avoid generating feelings of stress. After recruits leave the camps for their new work places, the opportunities for resocialization diminish. At the work place, resocialization lessons from supervisors and *sempai* take up only a fraction of each individual's time, the rest being devoted to mastering the work routine and to associating with work mates.

Most recruits rightly feel that developing good relations with fellow age-mates may be more important for their long-term adjustment to the company than getting along with their bosses. Thus, most of their free time is spent with those who share and support their values. Consequently, despite the considerable amounts of money and time a corporation devotes to its company training programs, it is doubtful these have much effect on the values of the young recruits. At best, the programs solidify friendships among recruits and familiarize them with the company and its expectations. A few quit, others endure, and still others complain.

3. Many corporations, recognizing the limitations of any efforts to change the personalities of new recruits, initiated internal reforms to make working conditions more agreeable. Some firms, especially those in high technology industries, curtailed their training camps and job-training programs and tried to move new employees more rapidly into responsible jobs. On the assumption that the apparent loss of ambition of new recruits could be partially attributed to their realistic appraisal of declining opportunities for promotion, some firms increased the ratio of executive and managerial to ordinary staff jobs.

According to Takezawa (1976:36), the mid-sixties witnessed a major movement to introduce various features of job redesign. Two of the most common features were the emphasis on participation in decision making and "small-groupism" (*shoshudan-shugi*). *Shoshudan-shugi* refers to management's effort to foster small, intimate, face-to-face groups among employees. In the case of blue-collar workers, members of a common group may not only work together but also be assigned adjacent rooms in the company dormitory. When the company changes its production routine, the members of particular small groups are transferred as a group to new work assignments (Osako, 1973). Some companies implement group incentive schemes to motivate groups to work together and to increase productivity (Cole, 1971:92). The goal of small-groupism is to combat potential feelings of isolation and atomization by building meaningful social ties. Cole (n.d.:25 ff.) notes how Japanese management increasingly involves work groups in decision making through the encouragement of zero defect and quality control circles. These various reforms are said to have contributed significantly to the improvement of morale and the reduction of turnover (Takezawa, 1976:36).

Throughout the organizational world there has been an effort to reduce the more abrasive aspects of hierarchical authority as well as to eliminate the symbols of executive privilege. One bank president relates that he looked forward to the privileges of being at the top: having a chauffeur, arriving late at the office, golfing in the afternoons, and behaving arrogantly toward subordinates. But by the time he became president, things had changed. He was expected to set a good example by arriving first and leaving last and found that his employees wished to be addressed in a soft and respectful manner. Other executives tell of new limits on their expense accounts and of pressure to ride public transportation to work (as do the mayors and many top officials in Japan's large cities). It seems there has been a substantial transformation of relations in the work place.

With the recent overseas expansion of Japanese firms, Westerners have been able to glimpse Japanese equality. Kraar (1975) in *Fortune* magazine describes a U.S. factory run by "Japanese management," in which all employees through the lower managerial ranks are required to wear identical work jackets; all workers, skilled or otherwise, are expected to clean up their work areas, rather than to leave this work for sweepers and janitors; and most white-collar employees are required to work in large multidesk offices. American workers, accustomed to status distinctions and minute divisions of labor, feel uncomfortable with these practices.

Along with reforms to decentralize authority and to increase the participation of new recruits, corporations attempted to introduce procedures to reward individual ability. Such procedures were developed in the late fifties, when corporate leaders were impressed with America's more rational principles of management. With the support of younger members—although they stood to gain the most from the merit system—employee enterprise unions resisted these reforms because, among other reasons, they were inegalitarian. Another objection was that merit rating would excessively increase the authority of supervisors as well as generate unpleasant rivalries between employees. Although most firms did introduce some form of merit rating into their procedures for determining promotion and salary, there has been little effect. Supervisors feel constrained to give virtually identical ratings to their subordinates or else risk damaging work group harmony. Thus, studies show a steady decline in the proportion of total wages accounted for by incentive rates; in most firms today these account for no more than 5 percent of the variation in individual salaries (Funahashi, 1973:363).

A final area of recent change, promoted by the unions, has been the reduction of wage differentials. Japan's enterprise unions, which include all blue- and white-collar workers of a particular enterprise, were created immediately after World War II. From the beginning, union leaders expressed a strong ideological interest in equality and caused a number of egalitarian changes: blue and white collar came to be designated by a common term (*shain*), and their wage differentials decreased; salary differentials based on university of attendance were abolished; and welfare benefits became more widespread. Over the course of the postwar period, unions have continued to press for greater equality in the treatment of employees.

Recently, perhaps because of a surplus of white-collar and a shortage of blue-collar job applicants, there has been a precipitous decline in white-collar-blue-collar wage differentials. Galenson and Odaka, in a recent survey, conclude "that almost all types of Japanese wage differentials have been declining during the past decade" (1976:605). The egalitarian values of the young dispose them to accept these changes even when it means their relative benefits decrease.

An additional issue in the area of wage differentials is the discrepancy in the wages paid to new workers relative to those with seniority. From a strictly economic view, it is doubtful that the annual seniority increments are justified; at least in the blue-collar ranks, the marginal returns to experience rapidly decline after approximately five years of service. The differentials were intended as a means of curtailing turnover by offering cumulative rewards to loyal employees, and came to be valued by the older workers. Today's youths, on the other hand, are more ambivalent about a lifetime commitment to a single firm and question the justness of paying older workers more. Management, anxious to please young recruits and concerned with the escalating cost of the seniority-based wage system as the labor force ages, has been responsive to the young workers' demands.

4. A final strategy has been to increase investment in sensitivity training programs at lower- and middle-management levels for improving supervisory response to employee problems. According to one survey (Nihon Keieisha Dantai Renmei, 1971), this is currently the most prominent educational program that corporations sponsor. As corporations face the loss of many new recruits despite their resocializing efforts, it makes more sense to invest in management sensitivity programs than in training programs for new workers.

Parallel Developments outside the Modern Sector

In the past, young workers wished to enter the modern large-scale organizational sector because it provided the greatest prestige, security, and income. The majority of today's youths still view the modern sector as a preferred place of employment for these same reasons. The new youth, however, have definite reservations about modern organizational life. Many believe that large organizations are neither sufficiently responsive to their needs for challenge, nor tolerant of their expressions of individualism. Moreover, young people who have internalized the egalitarian sentiment resent working at the bottom of a hierarchy that, in their minds, provides excessive privileges to those with rank and seniority.

Many young people have begun to evaluate seriously the employment opportunities provided by smaller enterprises. Although these firms cannot offer such traditional rewards as prestige or security, such considerations are declining in importance among young people. On the other hand, the smaller firms provide "bigger jobs" with more challenge and responsibility at a much earlier stage of employment. They provide a more personal atmosphere and recently have begun to offer starting wages and salaries competitive with those in the modern sector.

A young recruit is less certain of his future when he joins a small enterprise. If the enterprise falters or goes bankrupt, the young employee may be out of a job. On the other hand, if the firm does well, the young employee can hope for rapid advancement in income and status. Because a small firm offers an employee less security than a large firm, he can feel freer to leave the firm and take up a new job in a work place more to his liking. Also, working in a small firm provides the type of wholistic experience an individual finds useful if he plans to start an enterprise of his own.

Several surveys suggest that young people adjust more easily to small and medium organizations than to large organizations (Sorifu, 1973:207). Quantitative analysis shows that after differences in income are controlled, the young express greater satisfaction with working conditions and other features of smaller organizations (Cummings and Burns). Government labor statistics revealed a net outflow of laborers from small to large enterprises through the early sixties. However, the pattern has since reversed. Growing numbers of workers in the large enterprises, particularly young people in their first jobs, are leaving within two years of joining and are moving to smaller enterprises, in which they hope to find more compatible work (Kiyonari, 1970). The direction of this labor flow can be partially explained by the observation that people go where the jobs are. However, this economic explanation implies that values do not influence the flow. A number of labor market analysts question the economic explanation on this basis. They suggest that one reason why more jobs are being created in the smaller enterprises is that entrepreneurs recognize the compatibility between organizations of small scale and the needs of the new workers. Analyzing the problem of motivation and the implications of new technology, some analysts even claim that the age of the mammoth organization is now passing (Nakamura, 1970).

Generally speaking, small and medium-size organizations cannot afford to spend as much time on labor recruitment or training as large firms. Rather than use formal tests to select personnel, they are more likely to rely on informal means, such as the recommendations of friends. This particularistic mode of selection has the virtue of establishing personal ties between the new recruit and his work place. In the small enterprise, the firm's size facilitates the interaction and the development of close relations between members, who come much closer to becoming a natural community. It might be observed here that it is especially under such diffuse and personalized conditions that members are susceptible to each other's influence. Ironically, although smaller firms devote less time and money to training and resocializing recruits than do large firms, their capacities to exert moral influence on new members are greater. It is partly due to this that young people, after working in smaller organizations, come to espouse somewhat more traditional, less egalitarian values than their age-mates in larger organizations.

OTHER ILLUSTRATIONS OF THE INFLUENCE OF THE NEW VALUES OF YOUNG PEOPLE

Young people also express their values in deciding where to live. For much of the modern period, they have been attracted to the glitter and opportunity of the large cities. However, in the late sixties demographers began to observe a tendency for increasing numbers of people to move back to the smaller towns and rural areas after a few years in the big cities (Tachi, 1970:200 ff.). Behind this trend is the growing interest of young people in living a more fulfilling life. Although rural life may not provide as much excitement, glamour, or fortune, it does allow people to work in smaller and more humanistic work places, to walk or cycle to work, to devote more time to family and community life, and to pursue outdoor hobbies such as mountain climbing and fishing.

Although young people have come to look more favorably on employment in small enterprises, their attitudes toward agricultural employment provide an exception. They rightly estimate that agriculture does not provide as high a standard of living as other jobs, and they doubt that it would provide much intrinsic satisfaction. Those youths who do remain in agriculture are likely to have been less affected by the new egalitarian education and to strongly affirm traditional familial values.

Many of those young people who remain in the rural areas try to introduce new ways of organizing production—combining farms, establishing cooperatives, and so forth—that will promote productivity. Although some are successful in these endeavors, many others leave after a few years to join their classmates in the nonagricultural labor force. The extent to which youth have abandoned agriculture is truly astounding. In 1965, for the first time in modern Japanese history, there was an actual decline in the number of farm households. Some rural areas have experienced serious depopulation, and the local villages are composed almost exclusively of older people (Ibid., p. 207).

THE POLITICAL ORIENTATIONS OF
YOUNG PEOPLE

As already discussed, during the period immediately after World War II, when Japan's conservative forces were powerless, the new "Peace Constitution," the democratic schools, the labor unions, the progressive income tax system, the break-up of the *zaibatsu*, and the universal suffrage were introduced by the American Occupation. To effect its reforms, the Occupation sought the support and counsel of Japan's liberals and others further to the left. Thus, in a sense, the Occupation's reforms were the reforms of the left, a fact that became exceedingly important over the postwar period.

It was not long before the conservative forces regained their strength and began considering steps to dismantle the Occupation's reforms. From 1948, the conservatives obtained a majority of the representatives in both houses of the national Diet and in most of the local governments. Immediately, steps were taken to limit the right to strike of unions, to reduce the autonomy of the schools, and to remove the controls on private enterprise; constitutional amendments were even contemplated. Although the conservative camp was complex and included men with a variety of ideological concerns and interests, it would be fair to say the conservatives were declaring war on the spirit of the Occupation's reforms.

Each attempt by conservatives at counterreform was vigorously opposed by the leftist parties, which received support from such groups as the federated labor unions, the Zengakuren student movement, and the various associations of intellectuals. The confrontation led to a clean split in the Japanese polity between the progressive forces for democracy and equality and the conservative forces of reaction. The critical issue in this struggle was the set of values that the Japanese government should support: Should Japan promote the traditional values of collectivism, national strength, hierarchy, and economic competition or the new values of individualism, participation, and equality? As Watanuki (1967:456) has observed, the fifties was an era of cultural politics.

A political debate focused so heavily on these abstract issues was bound to wane. One of the fundamental problems faced by the conservatives was that their values simply did not appeal to the young. This should be evident from this discussion of the values taught in Japanese schools. Table 9.3 presents the proportion of re-

TABLE 9.3

JAPANESE PREFERRING THE LIBERAL DEMOCRATIC PARTY IN SURVEYS (PERCENTAGES)

Survey	Age Group								60+			Average
	20-24	25-29	30-34	35-39	40-44	45-49	50-54	55-59	60-64	65-69	70+	
1953	30	42	32	31	34	39	37	37		39		41
1958	31	37	38	44			41			37		38
1963	27	38	38	40	51	45	48	55	57	50	52	43
1968	29	24	35	42	43	48	52	48	47	56	52	41
1973	19	25	29	31	39	40	42	45		48		35

SOURCE: National Institute of Mathematics *Nihonjin no Kokuminsei* (The Japanese National Character), vols. 2 and 3.

NOTE: Respondents were asked, "Which political party do you support?"

spondents that prefers the conservative party in each of the five national surveys. In each survey the younger respondents show far
less interest in the conservatives than do the older, and, as we move
from 1953 to 1973, we find declining support for the conservative
party among the youngest (aged twenty to twenty-four) age-
group.

Although this state of youthful disaffection was somewhat disturbing to conservatives, it did not deter them from addressing
their traditional constituencies through the fifties and into the sixties. During this period, the conservatives promoted agricultural
price supports and loan programs for small businesses and attempted to serve the interests of big business. At the same time,
they periodically attempted to challenge the labor unions and other
progressive forces: for example, they supported performance ratings for teachers in 1958, United States-Japan Security Treaty re-
newal in 1959, and achievement tests for students in 1961.

Many within the conservative camp, however, took a dim view
of such confrontations. These critics, often called "doves," felt that
the opposition was in Japan to stay and that the political survival of
the conservatives rested on a Bismarckian approach of promoting
"progressive" legislation. Due to the growing influence of the
doves, the conservatives supported comprehensive health insurance
and social security in 1960 and various other items of welfare legislation since then. This moderate wing worked for a continuation of
some of the Occupation's legislation, such as the progressive income tax, and pursued less militant relations with certain opposition groups, notably the teachers' union and the students. The
doves' accurate perception of the changing values of Japanese
youths has led them to promote more moderate and egalitarian
policies (Cummings, 1976).

Through these tactics, the conservatives have attempted to neutralize value politics and to make themselves more attractive to the
young. In one sense, they have succeeded. Young voters are less
likely than they were in the past to associate the conservatives with
traditional values and more likely to view the socialists and other
progressive parties in a critical light. Although the conservatives'
new moderation has not been rewarded by any increase in support
from young people, neither has the Liberal Democratic party's
principal rival, the Socialist party, made any gains. Instead, the
most pronounced trend among new voters is away from politics in
general. Whereas in 1953 only 15 percent of the twenty to twenty-

four year olds said they were undecided, the proportion rose to 51 percent in 1973. When asked in 1953 how determined they were to vote, 54 percent of the young age-group said they would make every effort; in 1973 this proportion declined to 23 percent. Most of the young people said they would at least try to vote, but a growing proportion (up from 4 percent in 1953 to 17 percent in 1973) flatly stated that they were disinterested (National Institute of Mathematics, 1975:571).

Clearly, many young people will begin voting as they grow older, and many will lean to the left. The days of Japan's conservative party thus may be numbered. It is still too early to predict the future of Japanese politics if the conservatives fall, or join in a coalition government, but one thing is certain: future regimes will pay more attention to the new generations.

The Government's Youth Policy

Japan's progressive political parties devote considerable energy to reaching out to the young. The socialists rely on their contacts with the teachers' union and other party-affiliated unions to reach youths in the schools and the work places. The communists devote much time and money to reaching youth in the universities: on many campuses their student affiliates, the *minsei*, control the local self-government associations. As a contribution to the party, youths deliver the party paper, *Akahata*, to some four million homes daily. Similarly, the Komeito (Fair Play Party) sponsors a youth group as does its kindred religion, the Sokka Gakkai.

Relative to these opposition groups, the conservative political organization assumes that its influence in so many of the formal organizations of education and work provides sufficient contact with young people: thus, the conservatives make no special effort to create youth associations, especially in the urban areas. It may well be that the more vigorous efforts of the peripheral parties have influenced the anticonservative trends in youth values and voting observed in this study. One might also surmise that the left's efforts to mobilize youths are an important ingredient underlying the relative equality of political participation in Japan.[3] By and large, the left

---

[3] Several surveys reviewed by White (1975) indicate "that the socioeconomic 'have nots' are much less handicapped in their political participation in Japan than in the U.S."

tries to mobilize youths, housewives, and other marginal groups that have lower social status; in recent years these efforts have been particularly successful. People's movements are a significant political force in the Japan of the seventies. In contrast, the conservatives tend to rely on traditional groups, such as local Rotary clubs, farmers' associations, and each politician's *koenkai* (support group); but these groups, which are mainly located in rural areas, have weakened in recent years. Equality in Japanese political participation, then, stems from the upsurge of youthful support for the left and the decline of support for the conservatives from older groups.

Over the past few years, however, it appears that the conservatives have begun to reorient their policy toward youth. One new tactic is the effort to strengthen their influence over youth in those formal areas they control. For example, they have pressured the Ministry of Education to intensify its censorship of school textbooks; the well-known Ienaga case is a reminder. The main thrust of the censor's judgment was that Ienaga's Japanese history textbook placed too strong an emphasis on the people's role in building the Japanese nation and did not show enough respect for the emperor or the nation. In addition, the conservatives have devoted considerable effort toward formalizing the post of head teacher in the schools. The conservatives' underlying expectation is that the position will enable them to exert more pressure on teachers to adhere to government educational policy. In the Ienaga case, the government met with a surprising judicial setback, and in the struggle over head teachers, less than one third of Japan's prefectures have thus far implemented the order.

Another tactic of conservatives is to construct youth recreation centers throughout the country. The most conspicuous of these is located near the Nakano station of the Chuo Train Line in Tokyo. The center stands some twenty stories tall and includes a main gymnasium, an Olympic-size swimming pool, facilities for a great variety of indoor sports, reading rooms, banquet halls, wedding rooms, an active club system, and a small hotel service; the total cost was upwards of $25 million. Eto (1974) has observed that no other government outside the socialist camp has devoted so much money and organizational effort to contain and direct the energies of its youths. However, despite the attractions of Nakano and other centers, they are only one among many outlets where youth seek recreation. It is thus doubtful that such youth programs will have much bearing on Japan's future.

OTHER EGALITARIAN TRENDS

As new cohorts of young people inculcated with egalitarian and individualistic values move into society, they initiate changes in several other areas deserving of note.

1. *Language usage.* The traditional Japanese language included at least five different levels of honorifics, which were to be used according to one's status, the person to whom one talked, and the person or situation discussed. Today, most Japanese have a working command of no more than three levels, and they often fail to use even these properly. Thus, employees are only mildly deferential to their bosses, wives treat their husbands as equals, and children demean their fathers. Without a doubt, social relations as conveyed through language have been leveled.

2. *Family formation and structure.* In Chapter Four it was observed that young people are increasingly assertive in the exercise of mate selection and that family structures are more egalitarian compared to earlier periods. These changes have been strongly influenced by the new values of postwar youths. As with other changes, a "feedback process" is operative: new youths mature to form egalitarian families with children who, because of their early family experiences, develop even stronger egalitarian and individualistic orientations than did their parents.

3. *Occupational prestige.* Chapter Seven described how young people are developing a more egalitarian view of occupations than their parents. This new orientation helps to explain their willingness to enter jobs that traditionally were considered low in prestige—for example, jobs in the small and medium enterprises. In that chapter it was also noted that young people tend to make fewer sharp distinctions when rating the prestige of occupations. As the adult population comes to consist of more young people with egalitarian perspectives, one can anticipate a gradual leveling of the occupational prestige hierarchy. A definite trend in that direction is already evident.

The first occupational prestige survey in Japan was conducted in 1955 by the Japan Sociological Association. Twenty years later a replication survey was performed (see Table 9.4). Comparing the two sets of prestige scores, it can be noted that the higher prestige occupations have declined several points, whereas the lower prestige occupations have risen. The only other society in which a simi-

[4] See Chapter Three for more detail on these issues.

TABLE 9.4
SELECTED OCCUPATIONAL PRESTIGE SCORES, 1955 AND 1975

	1955	1975	1975 less 1955
University professor	90	83	− 7
Doctor	83	83	0
City department chief	71	60	−11
Company department chief	70	61	− 9
Civil engineer	69	63	− 6
Mechanical engineer	69	61	− 8
Temple priest	66	59	− 7
Teacher	66	63	− 3
Employee in large organization	52	49	− 3
Policeman	51	54	+ 3
Manager of small shop	50	49	− 1
Owner farmer	49	45	− 4
Railway station employee	46	45	− 1
Barber	42	45	+ 3
Joiner	40	43	+ 3
Auto mechanic	40	43	+ 3
Truck driver	40	41	+ 1
Carpenter	39	45	+ 6
Lathe operator	39	37	− 2
Insurance agent	38	35	− 3
Typographer	38	47	+ 9
Fisherman	36	36	0
Worker in bread factory	35	37	+ 2
Clerk in small shop	35	35	0
Spinner	33	33	0
Tenant farmer	29	30	+ 1
Coal miner	23	28	+ 5
Road construction	22	27	+ 5
Street salesman	22	28	+ 6
Coal dealer	22	23	+ 1

SOURCE: For 1955, reported in Shigeki Nishihira, "Le Prestige Social des differentes professions—l'evaluation populaire au Japon," p. 554; for 1975, see *1975-Nen SSM Chosa: Kiso Tokei* (Report of Basic Statistics from the 1975 SSM Survey). 1976; pp. 70-71.

lar leveling has been reported is Poland; in Poland's case, the shift from a capitalist to a communist regime was an important conditioning factor (Sarapata, 1974).

4. *Income equality*. Much of the recent discussion of equality in advanced Western societies has focused on income. It thus seems appropriate to conclude the analysis of social change by providing some summary of the situation in Japan. Several of the developments discussed in this chapter—the decreasing occupation- and

age-based wage differentials, the improved social welfare benefits, the progressive taxation system—imply a trend toward increased income equality.

National statistics on personal income distribution are difficult to compare. However, economists who have worked with this data seem to agree that contemporary Japan has one of the most egalitarian distributions of all advanced societies (Boltho, 1975:161–187; Ishizaki, 1967; Hicks and Nosse, 1974:264–287; Thurow and Lucas, 1972). Gini indexes, computed by Boltho for selected countries, are presented in Table 9.5. After considering the effects of unreported property income and entertainment allowances, the differential effects of income tax systems, and the impact of unreported cases, Boltho concludes:

> On balance, some upward adjustments of Japan's figures in Table 9.5 may be warranted. But a number of points militate in an opposite direction. . . . Impressionistically assessing the various considerations set out above, therefore, a tentative conclusion might not be very different from the one originally proposed. Assuming that the international data assembled are reasonably reliable, Japan's personal income distribution, while not necessarily the

TABLE 9.5
GINI COEFFICIENTS FOR PERSONAL INCOME
DISTRIBUTION IN SELECTED COUNTRIES

	Year	All Incomes	Wage and Salary Incomes
Japan	1965	0.32	0.21
Japan	1970	0.28	0.19
France	1962	0.52	0.35
Germany	1964	0.47	0.28
Italy	1966	0.37	—
United Kingdom	1963/4	0.40	0.27
United States	1964	0.40	—
Australia	1967/8	0.34	—
Canada	1969	0.38	—
Finland	1962	0.47	—
Netherlands	1962	0.44	0.40
Norway	1963	0.36	—
Sweden	1963	0.40	0.36
Czechoslovakia	1965	0.24	0.19
Hungary	1967	0.26	0.25

SOURCE: Andrea Boltho, *Japan: An Economic Survey*, p. 166.

most equal in the world, is among the more equal ones in developed countries, despite the "dualism" of the economy. And Japan's degree of equality is particularly evident at the bottom of the income scale. The share of income obtained by the top 5 or 10 per cent of households is not very different from that in other relatively "egalitarian" market economics like Australia or Norway (1975:165-167).

Boltho observes that the Gini indexes for Japan were quite large in the 1950s, but have declined steadily since that time. Table 9.5 shows the downward trend between 1965 and 1970. This trend has continued through the seventies. Ishizaki (1967:356) and the Economic Planning Agency of Japan (Keizai Kikakucho, 1975:12 ff.) also find that income has become more evenly distributed (allowing for cyclical fluctuations) over the postwar period. They observe the progress toward equality immediately after the war, the slow reversal through the mid-fifties, and the continuous trend toward equality since the late fifties.

THE EFFECTIVENESS OF RESOCIALIZATION EFFORTS

Many political and economic leaders are concerned about the values of the young and the social changes these values are precipitating. Through corporate training programs, the national youth program, and curricular reforms in the schools, these leaders are attempting to control and even reverse the trend of value change. But, as already noted, the effectiveness of these efforts is limited. First, the well-entrenched teachers' union acts as a buffer against the intrusions of conservatives in the schools. Second, the strength of peer relations wards off the objections of parents. Finally, the company training programs, because of their competing goals of fostering peer friendships and company loyalty, fail to alter the new values of young people. Thus, although for particular individuals and subgroups there is undoubtedly some drift away from egalitarianism, in general there is little reason to expect that the postwar generations will abandon these values as they proceed into adult life.

THE PERSISTENCE OF THE NEW VALUES

In Chapter Seven three clusters of values that are particularly significant in considering postwar social change were identified: the egalitarian orientation to jobs, the individualistic orientation, and the participatory orientation. With respect to these clusters, it was shown that the young are consistently more progressive than adults and that new cohorts of young people have progressively stronger tendencies to affirm these new values.

The review of the early adult experience of these same young people indicates a further hypothesis: once they adopt these new values, they will not abandon them.

Several questions from the national character survey of the National Institute of Mathematics enable a test of this hypothesis. This survey has been replicated every five years since 1953. Although each replication has interviewed a new sample of individuals, it is possible to follow an imaginary cohort through its life cycle by focusing on particular age-groups over successive surveys. For example, starting (at the upper left-hand corner of Table 9.6) with the youngest age group (twenty to twenty-four years old) of the first survey, their cohort will be twenty-five to twenty-nine years old at the time of the second survey, thirty to thirty-four at the time of the third, and so on diagonally toward the bottom-right corner. As an indication of the cohorts' tendency to retain values, the manner in which they answer designated questions should remain constant over time.

Chapter Seven used the question on life goals as a measure of the emerging orientation toward individuation. Table 9.6 is based on the same question. Starting with the cohort aged twenty to twenty-four in 1953, 43 percent selected one of the two alternatives

TABLE 9.6
SURVEY RESPONDENTS AFFIRMING AN ORIENTATION TOWARD
INDIVIDUATION (PERCENTAGES)

| | Age Group | | | | | Total Age |
	20-24	25-29	30-34	35-39	40-44	20-70+
1953	43	32	45	33	28	32
1958	50	51	54	38	44	45
1963	60	54	52	49	51	49
1968	67	61	56	51	54	52
1973	76	72	66	62	57	62

SOURCE: National Institute of Mathematics *Nihonjin no Kokuminsei* (The Japanese National Character), vols. 2 and 3.

NOTE: In the successive national surveys, respondents were asked about their attitudes toward life. This table represents those who chose "suit one's tastes" or "live each day as it comes."

indicative of more private or individualistic goals—"suit one's own tastes," and "live each day as it comes." In the survey five years later, 51 percent of this cohort gave these same responses. Following the cohort through each successive period, one finds roughly the same proportions: 52 percent in the 1963 survey, 51 percent in 1968, and 57 percent in 1973. Thus, for the imaginary cohort aged twenty to twenty-four in 1953, an essentially stable proportion affirm the individualistic life goal as they grow older.[5] Similarly, for the imaginary cohort that was twenty to twenty-four years old in 1958, 50 percent selected an individualistic alternative; following this cohort, the respective proportions are 54 percent in 1963, 56 percent in 1968, and 62 percent in 1973. For the imaginary cohort that was twenty to twenty-four years old in 1963, the successive proportions are 60 percent, 61 percent and 66 percent. Comparing, one sees that each successive cohort contains a slightly larger proportion affirming the individualistic response, and each maintains its edge over the preceding cohort. The table thus provides powerful evidence that postwar youths not only persist in but even intensify their individualism.

Turning to the cohort trends for the two questions selected in Chapter Seven to measure the antiauthority-participatory orientation, one finds roughly the same pattern. Table 9.7 presents the results for "parents should inform the child of teacher's wrongdoing." The percentages for the imaginary cohort aged twenty to twenty-four in 1953 who agreed that parents should tell are 50 percent in 1953, 50 percent in 1958, 52 percent in 1963, 53 percent in 1968, and 59 percent in 1973. The percentages for the cohort aged twenty to twenty-four in 1958 are 45 percent (the only figure notably out of line) in 1958, 55 percent in 1963, 58 percent in 1968, and 59 percent in 1973. For the youngest cohort in 1963, the figures are 58 percent, 54 percent, and 56 percent.

Table 9.8 presents the trends for the proportion disagreeing that "one should leave everything to leaders." Again, there is considerable stability within a given cohort over time. For example, for the cohort aged twenty to twenty-four in 1953, the proportions who disagree range between 50 percent and 58 percent. For the youngest cohort beginning with the 1958 survey, the proportions fluctuate between 52 percent and 64 percent.

[5] More precisely, as the imaginary cohort grows older, an increasing rather than a stable proportion select individualistic goals. Ike (1973:1199) refers to this tendency as adult change.

TABLE 9.7
SURVEY RESPONDENTS AFFIRMING AN ANTIAUTHORITY
ORIENTATION (PERCENTAGES)

| | Age Group | | | | | Total Age |
	20-24	25-29	30-34	35-39	40-44	20-70+
1953	50	49	44	42	36	42
1958	45	50	38	44	31	41
1963	58	55	52	53	50	50
1968	55	54	58	53	49	52
1973	64	59	56	59	51	54

SOURCE: National Institute of Mathematics *Nihonjin no Kokuminsei* (The Japanese National Character), vols. 2 and 3.

NOTE: In the successive national surveys, respondents were asked about their attitudes toward authority. This table represents those who answered "tell him it is true" to the following question: "Suppose that a child comes home and says that he has heard a rumor that his teacher has done something to get himself into trouble, and suppose that the parent knows this is true. Do you think it is better for the parent to tell the child that it is true, or to deny it?"

CHANGE IN VALUES AND CHANGE IN BEHAVIOR

The main interest here has been the enduring effect of egalitarian socialization on several value clusters of the new generations. Even though adult institutions have made various efforts to induce young people to abandon their new values, it appears that these efforts have been unsuccessful. Cohorts raised in the postwar era continue to affirm the values learned in school. Although it is likely that some social settings are more conducive to resocialization than others—for example, small enterprises are probably most conducive, professions least—the available evidence suggests no major value shifts in any of the postwar cohorts.

On the other hand, there is good reason to suspect that these resocialization efforts have greater impact on behavior. Krauss (1974), for instance, observes that large organizations discourage overt political activity by employees, especially among white-collar ranks; insofar as young employees feel compelled to protect their career prospects, they are likely to follow these guidelines. Thus, Krauss finds that young radicals who take jobs in large organizations terminate their participation in public protest marches. One might say they become silent radicals, restraining their behavior yet retaining their values.

The proportions voting for the Liberal Democratic party (see Table 9.3) provide another indication of behavioral change within

TABLE 9.8

SURVEY RESPONDENTS AFFIRMING A PARTICIPATORY
ORIENTATION (PERCENTAGES)

| | Age Group | | | | | Total Age |
	20-24	*25-29*	*30-34*	*35-39*	*40-44*	*20-70+*
1953	54	48	46	38	28	38
1958	60	50	51	45	46	44
1963	58	54	52	46	51	47
1968	63	58	52	54	57	51
1973	74	61	66	64	58	60

SOURCE: National Institute of Mathematics *Nihonjin no Kokuminsei* (The Japanese National Character), vols. 2 and 3.

NOTE: In a national survey, respondents were asked about their attitudes toward participation. This table represents those who disagreed with the following proposition: "Some people say that if we get outstanding political leaders, the best way to improve the country is for the people to leave everything to them, rather than for the people to discuss things among themselves."

cohorts. Ignoring the results for 1973 (when Liberal Democratic support plummeted across all age-groups), support for the party within cohorts increases with age. For example, only 30 percent of the cohort aged twenty to twenty-four in 1953 supported the LDP; five years later, 37 percent of this cohort preferred the LDP; ten years later, 38 percent; and fifteen years later, 42 percent. Somewhat similar results are observed for the other imaginary cohorts.

This disjunction between value and behavioral change helps to explain why a virtual revolution in postwar values has not brought about even greater social changes than those already enumerated. Confronted with the cool reception of adult society, many young people fail to act on their new values and instead adjust their behaviors to conform to established roles. The contradictions between outward behavioral conformity and inward value-based opposition generate a comparatively high level of tension and frustration in Japan's young adults.

CONCLUSION

Much of the conventional literature suggests that Japan's schools teach youths those values and orientations that facilitate rapid adjustment to the demands of adult society. For example, schools teach youths discipline and responsibility, they sensitize youths to the needs of others, and they orient youths to the world of work and citizenship. Because the schools teach these lessons, they are said to be well integrated with adult institutions.

However, there is another aspect of the school-society link, which the conventional perspective neglects. Schools also teach youths several lessons that conflict with adult experience—in particular, the three lessons identified here that form the egalitarian sentiment: the egalitarian orientation to work, the individuated disposition, and the critical orientation to structures of authority. Because Japanese young people learn these inconsistent lessons, they feel immensely dissatisfied upon their initial encounters with adult institutions. Indeed, the international youth survey cited in Table 9.1 suggests that Japanese young people are the most dissatisfied youths in the advanced world.

Is it possible that these young people gradually forget their egalitarian lessons and adjust to the institutionalized inequalities of adult institutions? The conventional perspective answers in the affirmative. The objective in this chapter has been to present the opposite view. A number of recent changes in Japanese society that appear to have been precipitated by the demands of the new youth have been identified. Because youths are taught their egalitarian lessons in the schools, it can be concluded that education is transforming society. There are two major counterarguments to this conclusion.

One common counterargument goes as follows: the egalitarian sentiment is not unique to Japanese youths, but, rather, is shared by the youths of all advanced industrial societies. The sentiment emerges from the common set of structural changes these advanced societies are experiencing—for example, occupational and educational upgrading, the shift to a postindustrial economy, the maturation of the baby-boom cohort, and the unprecedented situation of sustained mass affluence. Youths throughout the world, in response to these changes, have developed a united movement that both opposes established ways and is adaptive to the projected demands of the coming postindustrial social order. A surprising number of contemporary observers ascribe to this postindustrial explanation and discount the role of the schools. However, this grand explanation seems to beg too many questions: (1) Are youths in the various societies responding to identical changes? (2) Is there a worldwide youth movement? (3) Do youths in the various societies experience common levels of difficulty in adjusting to adult institutions? (4) Where do youths acquire their critical orientations to the adult world? In our opinion, none of the expositors of the postindustrial explanation has provided a satisfactory answer to these questions. As the postindustrial explanation is elaborated, we anticipate it will recognize the contribution of contemporary education. For we suspect that the educational institutions of all advanced societies, in greater or lesser degree, teach values that are inconsistent with the demands of the adult world. The postindustrial explanation, rather than being a counterargument, is a generalization of our thesis.

It can also be argued that the changes documented here are best accounted for by other forces. For example, it is clear that the new values of young people are no more than a secondary factor in the postwar trend of declining occupational and work-place size wage-differentials. Likewise, the shift of youths away from the conservative political party is, at least in part, a function of that party's failure to recognize the needs of this group. These explanations are certainly relevant. Yet, given the complexities of modern social organization, one should not expect a single explanation to be sufficient to account for a particular change. Education's egalitarian impact supplements these other forces. Perhaps the strongest support for the argument advanced here is the fact that Japan's conservative politicians and business leaders, whose interests are threatened by these changes, attribute egalitarian education with the blame for the postwar egalitarian transformation.

THE LESSONS OF JAPANESE
EDUCATION

This book illustrates how education can transform the adult institutions of an advanced industrial society. The focus on the Japanese case has highlighted several issues that are neglected by the mainstream of contemporary writing on education. The differences in emphasis are important, and thus in the first section of this final chapter they will be made explicit. By so doing, it is hoped that a new approach to educational research will be encouraged. However, the central concern here is with the impact of education on children and society. Japanese education has exceptional potency in several areas: (1) the strong public interest in education; (2) the relative equality in the cognitive achievement and motivation of school children; (3) the high average level of cognitive achievement; (4) the transmission of an egalitarian moral sentiment; (5) egalitarian social change; and (6) the equalization of social opportunity. Over the course of the book an attempt has been made to explain how Japanese education generates these outcomes. In the second section of this chapter these conclusions and their practical and theoretical implications will be summarized. Finally, a few of the problems that trouble contemporary Japanese education and some future possibilities will be considered.

NEW QUESTIONS

The traditional commitment of advanced capitalist states to the meritocratic approach has led to the development of a standard set of procedures for its description and evaluation, but these are largely irrelevant to the transformationist approach. A new set of questions needs to be asked.

Why Only Cognitive Effects?

Educators recognize that their pupils undergo remarkable growth during the school years. In Japan, teachers welcome this growth and attempt to influence it in all its diversity. Their ideal is "whole-person education."

The notion of promoting the development of the whole person is not alien to the American educational tradition. Yet, reviewing the conventional American evaluative studies, one finds that most focus exclusively on the "cognitive outputs" of schools and on the educational system's function of conferring certification. The evaluative studies acknowledge that the schools may have effects on other faculties. For instance, Jencks et al. (1972:134), choosing to label these other effects as "noncognitive traits," go so far as to say that they are the most important. However, these same authors demur from a serious analysis of noncognitive growth, positing that little is or can be known about it as the methodology of social science lacks adequate procedures for categorizing and measuring noncognitive traits.

The same consideration guides most of the conventional research. In a few studies, attitudinal and motivational variables are used as predictors of cognitive achievement, but in no instance are they treated as outcomes. The potentially important question of the noncognitive effects of schooling is avoided because it cannot be handled with the most advanced methodology. By default, research focuses on the possibly trivial but measurable alternative of cognitive growth.[1]

This research into the Japanese situation has provided convincing evidence of the severe handicaps any evaluative study encounters if it focuses exclusively on cognitive outcomes. Society cannot be changed simply by making people smarter. To bring about change, the objects people value and the amounts of energy they are prepared to expend to realize their values have to be altered.

Why Only Short-run Effects?

Each person's development occurs over a long period, with individual idiosyncrasies in rates and stages. At some points in an individual life cycle, development may proceed quite rapidly, whereas at other points there may be a long slump. Thus, meaningful trends in individual development cannot reliably be ascertained over a short period of time.

---

[1] This situation seems a perverse reversion of Lord Kelvin's famous dictum "When you cannot measure, your knowledge is meager and unsatisfactory."

A carefully planned evaluative study of the effects of school reforms on individual growth would review individual change at
several points over a sufficient time span. Although this research
design is generally acknowledged as ideal, most conventional
American evaluative studies have not followed it.

The research for the much-publicized Coleman report (1966) of
the mid-sixties was far removed from this design. Measurements of
children's performance and of variables thought to be influential on
performance were taken at only one point in time. Despite the in-
appropriateness of the design, the Coleman report liberally drew
policy inferences. For instance, the report forcefully argued that the
increased integration of schools through busing and other means
would lead to improvements in the cognitive achievement of both
the black and white groups participating in these changes. Several
years later Coleman himself criticized this inference as unjustified.
Despite the limitations of the one-shot survey approach, most
American evaluative studies rely on it.

A design that considers development over a long period is pref-
erable to the one-shot model. One strong impression gained from
the experience of this study is that schools and teachers take a
longer perspective. The principal at one of the primary schools visited urged parents not to worry if their children were not performing well after the first semester or even after the first year. For, as he
explained, primary school lasted six years, and throughout this period, the teachers would be making efforts to read the child.
Teachers often maintain relations with individual students long
after these children graduate, and for these teachers the real satisfaction derives from watching their former students cope with the
adult world. These teachers view education as a lifetime process
and are inclined to evaluate their efforts accordingly.

The importance of a long-term perspective on educational
achievement cannot be discounted. Hence, in this report, an attempt has been made, within the limits of available data, to relate
the postwar emergence of the new education to several long-term
changes in Japanese culture and society.

Does School Achievement Result in
Status Attainment?

The conventional American studies relate features of school structure to trends in the personal development of children from different socioeconomic and racial backgrounds. Underlying these

studies is the assumption that once school reforms can be identified that lead to a narrowing of racial and ethnic differentials, the wider implementation of these reforms will contribute to greater equality in educational and social opportunities. Educational achievements are assumed to be related to educational attainment and in turn, educational attainment is associated with socioeconomic achievement.

The Japanese situation points to a number of problems in these assumptions. Even if the reforms that might reduce the effect of background on cognitive achievement could be identified, unexpected problems at the stage of implementation would be encountered. One of the special problems in the Japanese case is the large number of schools that lie outside the public sector. Moreover, there is only a modest association between the educational attainment and the cognitive achievement that the traditional evaluative studies measure. Yet it is educational attainment that has the major effect on an individual's occupational career. In addition, at least in the Japanese context, in which different schools at the same level open up distinctive social opportunities, it becomes necessary to question what is meant by educational attainment. Simple measures that merely identify number of years of schooling do not even approximate the complexity of the school system. All of these insights can be profitably applied to the American experience.

A second body of research evaluates the effects of educational status on social mobility and status attainment. As with the school effects research, the status attainment tradition is guided by the norm of equal opportunity. Two guiding propositions are derivable: (1) to the extent that the relation between indicators of the social background and the educational attainment of individuals weakens, equality of educational opportunity has increased; and (2) to the extent the relation between the educational attainment and the occupational status of individuals strengthens, social opportunity has increased.

Compared to the research on school effects, the status attainment tradition is in a better position to evaluate changes over time. Some research in this tradition dates back forty years and comparisons between studies conducted at different points in time are meaningful. These comparisons (Hauser and Featherman, 1976) provide some indication of progress toward greater equality of educational opportunity, but little indication that the more equitable distribution of educational opportunities is related to the better distribution of social opportunities. According to Hauser et al. (1975), who have conducted the most detailed analysis of this situation, over the past forty years social opportunities have become more open, but this is due solely to changes in the occupational structure. These authors maintain that the same conclusion would apply to all of the advanced societies. However, this generalization from the single case of the United States is not justified.

Education as a Constant

There was a time when social scientists carried out their analyses with simple analytical techniques. In recent years, however, this situation has radically changed. Many of today's significant works make assumptions and utilize complex procedures beyond the grasp of the ordinary layman. In the education field the Coleman report was the first major official document evaluating school effects that used regression techniques. Jencks et al.'s *Inequality* relied on the even more complex technique of structural equations, and nearly one third of the latter report was devoted to explaining the methodology.

The rapid advances in analytical techniques have created a situation in which most readers are unable to follow the data analysis underlying social science investigations and, hence, have to rely on the investigator's literal summation. The research for this study identified two potential areas in which readers may misunderstand the conclusions of current research.

The first concerns the difference between a variable and a constant and the implication of this distinction for interpreting negative findings on school effects. School effects studies generally identify a large number of school or educational characteristics that can be quantified—the ratio of students to teachers, the expenditures per student, the number of library books per student, and so forth. Researchers visit a large number of schools and determine each school's score with respect to these characteristics. Insofar as the schools differ widely in their traits, it is said that the characteristics have statistical variance. From among those characteristics with variance, the researchers then select a limited number to enter into an equation used to predict such educational outcomes as performance on an achievement test or satisfaction with school. These selected characteristics are said to be important to the extent that the variances in their distributions manifest a statistical association with the variance in the distribution of achievement test scores.

As it is almost second nature for the current generation of researchers to equate importance with statistical association, the following implications should be considered: those school characteristics that have small variances are, by this criterion, deemed unimportant. Yet this leads to a disturbing anomaly. One of the goals of public sector educational reform throughout the advanced world has been to reduce the variance in the distribution of school characteristics. In the effort to realize equal educational opportunity, educators have attempted to equalize interschool student-teacher ratios, student expenditures, and a host of other factors. Their efforts have transformed many school characteristics from variables to constants and thereby made these factors useless as predictors of variations in schooling outcomes.

A typical research report using today's techniques might conclude that these equalized school characteristics are unimportant. When one considers what schooling would be like without these constants of school buildings, teachers, and library books, one begins to recognize how an evaluative interpretation that relies only on degree of association as the criterion of importance can be misleading.

The possibility for this kind of misinterpretation is most likely in a system such as Japan's in which school reforms have made outstanding progress toward equalizing facilities. Combers and Keeves, who compiled the International Association for the Evaluation of the Educational Achievement's study *Science Achievement in Nineteen Countries*, observed that: "The small or zero correlations reported for several variables from Japan may arise from the high degree of uniformity across the schools of the country in the provisions made for science teaching" (1973:257).

It is no surprise to discover that for the Japanese case school variables contribute absolutely nothing to the explanation of variance in science echievement, whereas in other societies these variables explain anywhere from 2 percent to 8 percent of science achievement variance. Yet this does not mean Japanese schools are relatively unimportant.

Not only have reformers been concerned with equalizing school facilities but in recent years they have shown a keen interest in equalizing educational results. Between countries there are wide variations in the degree of success achieved, but Japan is among the leaders. As school systems narrow the performance distribution, it becomes increasingly difficult with the standard regression method to determine what is contributing to differential performance. As with equal facilities, to the extent a school system realizes equal results it becomes difficult to interpret the dynamics of the schooling process.

Thus, to study the Japanese case, in which school facilities and outcomes are relatively equal, it is necessary to put aside the standard analytical strategies that emphasize variance, and instead, to ask what is constant between schools. Whereas the standard approach focuses on variables to explain variables, the approach here tried to identify the constants that explained other constants. Particularly when we considered the emergence of new values among Japanese students, we were concerned with the constants of that nation's schooling experience.

Insofar as the individuals of a given cohort share certain values, it can be said that they are "constant" with respect to these values. Focusing on the values that comprise the egalitarian sentiment, we found that for the immediate postwar period it was primarily the highly educated young people who were in possession of these values. As successive cohorts passed through the postwar schools, educational attainment steadily declined as a predictor for acceptance of the egalitarian complex. Increasing proportions of each new cohort, regardless of educational attainment, came to affirm these values. Educational attainment as a predictor of this egalitarian complex has shifted over time from a variable to a constant while the schools have been the principal instructor in egalitarianism.

Is the Family First?

The prominent educational role attributed to the family in conventional studies raises another set of issues. There are various reasons for attributing importance to the family in developmental processes. Children spend most of their early years in a family setting, and many parents appear to be zealous cultivators of their children's development. Freudian theory, as well as other socialization theories, argues that the events of early childhood have profound significance for subsequent development. But in fact, there are few studies that demonstrate that internal family dynamics lead to personality consequences. The principal support in the United States for the family primacy assumption derives from studies in which status proxies for familial impact link with developmental outcomes. However, a growing body of research (Prewitt, 1975; Maccoby,

1968; Luecke and McGinn, 1976) suggests that these conventional procedures may yield spurious correlations. Studies in Japan that use status variables as proxies for family child-rearing practices report modest "family effects." However, are these status variables acceptable proxies? As discussed in Chapter Four, in postwar Japan there is virtually no relation between the social status of a family and its child-rearing practices. In addition, Japanese studies find virtually no relation between child-rearing practices and personality consequences—at least through the preschool years. A review of American studies might produce a similar conclusion. In sum, although there are theoretical grounds for expecting that family interaction has an important impact on personality development, the supporting evidence is weak. In view of this situation, it is possible to propose a theoretical reformulation that grants that family processes are important providing they are reinforced by processes in the school and community. Such a reformulation would account for the complex pattern of value transmission that has evolved in postwar Japan. On the one hand, Japanese youths continue to affirm many of the values and to observe many of the same customs as their parents. On the other hand, there are certain areas in which Japanese youths are departing from their parents. It is impossible to explain this value discontinuity within the limited framework of the family primacy model. Moreover, although Japanese families are becoming increasingly similar in their structure and child-rearing patterns (that is, in those features that are related to value acquisition according to the family primacy model), there is no evidence that the adult Japanese population is becoming more homogeneous in its value commitments. Convergence in some areas is balanced by divergence in others. As suggested by the reinforcement model, socialization experiences outside the family must be considered if one is to provide a full explanation for these complex trends.

The Political Economy of Schools

This list of questions concludes with the most complicated one: what is the relation between schools and the broader political economy? Most of the American evaluative studies have avoided this topic altogether, restricting their attention to a technically sophisticated but limited analysis of the association between school characteristics and school outcomes. Failing to find strong school effects, these studies turn to technical discussions concerning measurement error, the inadequacy of cross-sectional designs, and the need for more research.

In reaction to these technical excuses, an exciting body of radically oriented analysis has emerged that accepts these negative findings and attempts to explain them by reference to processes in the broader political economy. The earliest radical statements were primarily schematic in nature, pointing to the control that the corporate ruling class exerts over the national and local governments in which school policy is established. From these observations, a *correspondence principle* was advanced, which states: "The activities and outcomes of the educational sector correspond to those of the society generally. That is, all educational systems serve their respective society such that the social, economic, and political relationships of the educational sector will mirror closely those of the society of which they are a part" (Levin, 1976:26).

Among the several empirical studies that have sought to validate the correspondence principle, Bowles and Gintis's *Schooling in Capitalist America* provides the richest examination of the American situation. These authors point to several control mechanisms the corporate class has instituted to realize its goals.

1. The corporate class manufactures a meritocratic ideology so as to induce the common people to contribute their labor without resistance to corporate purposes.

2. Through its labor market decisions, the corporate class ensures a permanent reserve army of labor so as to control the influence of labor organizations.

3. By the way it organizes production, the corporate class ensures that work will retain a significant influence over the lives of workers and the way they raise their children. Thus, families will unwittingly cooperate in reproducing the class system.

4. Through its infiltration of the central political institutions, the corporate class guarantees the implementation of educational policies favorable to its interests, such as the post-Sputnik upgrading of the curriculum and the current emphasis on vocationalism.

5. Through its influence over local governments, the corporate class ensures the selection of school administrators and teachers who will support the corporate ideology. To further this end, the corporate class opposes the organization of teachers into unions and encourages their passive white-collar mentality on matters relating to school authority.

Bowles and Gintis marshal convincing evidence that these mechanisms operate to fulfill the correspondence principle in the United States. The Japanese corporate class is just as determined to institutionalize these mechanisms as is its American counterpart, and in certain areas, the Japanese corporate class may even be more successful: its control over government, its articulation of ideology, its ability to shape the labor market and to command the loyalty of its workers are the envy of corporate elites throughout the advanced capitalist world.

There is, however, a major flaw in the attempt of the Japanese ruling class to dominate the reproductive process that has compromised its success on the other fronts. Since World War II, most of the teachers have been organized in a strong labor union that is firmly committed to the realization of a socialist society. Although unable to circumvent corporate influence at the central and local government levels, the teachers' union has succeeded in mobilizing the majority of teachers in campaigns to prevent the implementation of several unwanted government policies. In addition, the union has articulated an egalitarian philosophy and a diffuse body of educational principles that have exercised a profound influence on the daily conduct of education in Japan.

Japan's ruling class has vigorously opposed the teachers' union by depriving the union of its legal right to collective bargaining, imprisoning numerous union leaders, attacking the union in the mass media, and providing career incentives to those teachers who resist union membership. Significantly, these ploys have failed. The union has persisted throughout the postwar period, and its influence on the actual events in classrooms has steadily increased. This flaw in the corporate class's efforts to reproduce the prevailing social order has been fatal. In our view, the union is the principal source of postwar change. A study of the schools that fails to take account of their broader socio-political context would not provide a meaningful evaluation of the transformation model.

The Determinants of Japan's Educational Achievements

In the body of this discussion, six arguments were developed to explain the achievements of Japanese education. The first of these, the exceptional concern manifested in Japan vis-à-vis education, provides a background for the other five. These arguments can be summarized as follows:

1. *The determinants of concern with education.* (*a*) The old-system nationalistic and utilitarian tradition of education is respected by important elements of the ruling class. (*b*) The centralization of educational and economic institutions enables industrial and business elites to advance the educational system as a supplier of scarce manpower. Moreover, it helps to focus popular attention on the link between educational success and the attainment of prestigious social positions. (*c*) The postwar constitution and the educational laws legitimate an educational system with humanistic and democratic goals. The nationalistic and utilitarian orientations of conservative elites often seem to contradict these ideals. (*d*) The broad sense of public confusion with the appropriate goals for child socialization results in the public's demand that the schools play a key role in moral education. (*e*) The rising affluence of the population enables a growing number of parents to consider sending their children on for higher education and, hence, heightens their concern with their children's educational performance. (*f*) The emergence of a strong ideological teachers' union, which champions the constitution's educational ideals, results in articulate opposition to the traditional and utilitarian policies of conservative groups. The union's objections are generally reported in the national news media, thereby continually bringing educational issues to the attention of the general public.

2. *Cognitive and motivational equality.* (*a*) Given Japan's rapid urbanization, most young people live in cities. There is much less socioeconomic segregation in the city than is typical for the United States. Thus, public schools, especially at the primary level, tend to be composed of students with diverse class and family background characteristics. (*b*) Adhering to its constitutional obligation to "provide equal education to all according to their ability," the central government has developed an impressive program to ensure equality of educational facilities during the years of compulsory education. It also promotes a standard curriculum for the entire nation. (*c*) The schools are organically organized with a minimum of internal differentiation. For example, at the primary level there are no specialty teachers, and ability tracking is not practiced. (*d*) Many of the teachers are ideologically committed to equality. They try to bring all the students up by creating a positive situation in which all pupils receive rewards. This is facilitated by adjusting the classroom pace to the learning rates of students and by relying on students to tutor each other. (*e*) Teachers find that their best response

to parental concern is to provide equal education to all students irrespective of ability or family status.

3. *The determinants of the achievement effect.* (*a*) The general concern with education places pressure on students to excel. (*b*) Equal education minimizes the incidence of exceptionally low achievers. (*c*) The centrally prepared curriculum is demanding geared to the learning rate of the better-than-average student. (*d*) Students spend far more hours at school than do their counterparts in most other advanced societies. (*e*) According to the norm of an orderly classroom, a relatively large proportion of classroom time is devoted to actual instruction, as contrasted with efforts by teachers to maintain order. (*f*) Students perceive school as interesting (especially in the primary years) and generally have a positive attitude toward learning. (*g*) Teaching tends to be a lifetime occupation. In addition, Japanese teachers are relatively active in government- and union-sponsored workshops which introduce new teaching techniques. Their experience commitment contribute to effective instruction and teaching habits.

4. *Egalitarian moral orientations.* (*a*) In the realm of actual instruction, teachers are relatively free from external influence. Neither parents nor their local government has the power to dismiss a teacher who engages in "biased" instruction. (*b*) Many teachers approve of egalitarian values, and a few are committed to using the educational system as a vehicle for revolutionizing the "consciousness" of young people. (*c*) The schools approach "total" institutions. (*d*) The schools are organically organized. (*e*) Particularly during the early years of primary education—that is, those years in which children begin to develop the higher stages of moral reasoning—the Japanese system stresses moral education. (*f*) The relative equality in cognitive performance moderates the propensity of children to rank each other in terms of performance. Instead, the children are disposed to see themselves as working together to master the curriculum. The lack of hierarchy within the classroom is consistent with the egalitarian moral messages conveyed by the teacher. (*g*) Until children leave school for the work place, most of their experiences reinforce the early egalitarian moral instruction.

5. *Education's contribution to egalitarian social change.* (*a*) The schools teach certain moral orientations that promote continuity and harmony. (*b*) At the same time, they inculcate egalitarian and humanistic values that are inconsistent with the role expectations institutionalized in many adult social structures. (*c*) Although repre-

sentatives from key institutional areas oppose this "subversive" type of education, they find that the political balance underlying the school system is difficult to overturn. (*d*) Most of the social networks to which young people belong tend to support the values learned in school. Employers are the major critics of the egalitarian values of young people, but the employers' efforts at desocialization are neutralized by the support young people find in their peer groups. (*e*) The strains that the new generations of young people experience as they attempt to fit into adult society lead them to exert pressure for various changes of a broadly egalitarian nature. (*f*) The relatively equal levels of ability and motivation fostered by the Japanese schools facilitate the adaptation of young workers to more egalitarian social structures.

6. *The equalization of educational and social opportunities*.[2] (*a*) Egalitarian education has provided increasing proportions of successive cohorts of young people with the cognitive skills and motivation necessary for advanced education. (*b*) As a result, increasing proportions of young people have sought and attained advanced education. With the decreasing variance in educational attainment, social background variables decline as predictors of individual attainment. (*c*) Egalitarian education has taught young people to recognize the intrinsic rewards of occupations, and has modified the traditional value placed on secure high status occupations of the modern sectors. (*d*) As a result, young people have become more flexible in their occupational choices, and social background appears to have a decreasing influence on individual status achievement.

Practical Implications of the Central Arguments

It is not unusual to hear arguments for Japan's educational achievements that begin with the premise that the Japanese people value education highly. The first argument above indicates this concern with education is not simply a reflection of personal values. Instead, concern emerges because actors believe that education has an instrumental effect on their interests. Concern is also generated through conflict over educational goals and practices.

---

[2] In a final report to the National Institute of Education, several regression analyses of the data from Japan's 1965 and 1975 social mobility surveys were included. Comparisons were made of overall 1965 and 1975 coefficients, of age-groups within each survey, and of imaginary cohorts constructed through combining the results from the two surveys. These various analyses provide the empirical background for these generalizations.

In the United States, educational issues are among the most important issues in local elections, and few nations spend as large a proportion of national income on education. However, in recent years one senses that large segments of the American people have lost faith in public education. The United States requires a more penetrating and positive debate on educational matters. The Japanese case suggests the important role a teachers' union can play in provoking creative dialogue, provided the union devotes attention to educational goals and processes along with typical trade union issues. The teachers' union, in its attempt to gain the respect of parents as well as to maintain the allegiance of teachers, has been forced to focus on educational issues. Most American teachers' unions are still at the stage of struggling for bargaining rights and better working conditions.

The second argument concerns the conditions leading to equal cognitive outcomes. It was noted how many of the educational strategies that Japanese teachers have developed resemble the theory of mastery learning advocated by Benjamin Bloom and his colleagues. There are, however, several differences that should be recognized. This account devoted more attention to the external conditions that facilitate egalitarian education. Widespread parental concern is one of these. A standardized curriculum and equal educational facilities are also included in the list. However, of even greater importance are the ideological sensitivity of teachers and their sense of security. These latter conditions enable teachers to resist the selfish influences of individual parents. Thus, although the children in many Japanese classrooms come from homes that vary widely in socioeconomic status, these status differences have little effect on teacher-student interaction.

The third argument identifies several factors behind Japan's high level of cognitive achievement. It has often been suggested that Japanese children perform well in school because their families provide an exceptional level of support. As discussed earlier, however, family support becomes an important factor only in the later stages of schooling: at that level it does help some children raise their achievement levels above their age-mates. Through the early years of middle school, this support is not so critical. Rather, the demanding curriculum, the quality of teachers, and above all, the concern teachers show for pupil motivation are the important factors. The Japanese teacher during the early years focuses the major part of his attention on motivation, even at the expense of covering the curriculum. The teacher moves forward in the curriculum only when all of the young pupils are ready. Throughout these early school years, the teacher tries to reward and encourage each and every pupil. As a result, the Japanese school inculcates basic academic skills in virtually all of its pupils. The initial stress on motivation and mastery results in the small incidence of low scores on achievement tests.

The emphasis in the Japanese schools on moral education is perhaps its most outstanding characteristic. It is responsible for a wide variety of other educational and social outcomes: the orderliness of the classroom and of society, the comparatively harmonious social interaction characteristic of Japan, and the unity and cohesiveness of the Japanese nation. American schools, particularly at the primary level, have steadily retreated from the firm moral emphasis favored by the Puritans. Students languish in classrooms, chewing gum and talking while teachers blithely ignore these improprieties. The courts have forbidden bible lessons, spankings as a disciplinary technique, and a host of other particulars that made up the school's traditional moral curriculum. Teachers are so fearful of exceeding the authority of their role that they adhere resolutely to the academic curriculum. Only in America's colleges do we hear educators speak of the need for moral education. Yet, by the time children reach college age, it is difficult for educational institutions to achieve a moral impact. Japanese educators have wisely shaped an educational system that emphasizes moral education at an early age.

Moral education in the Japanese school is not simply another course in the curriculum. The entire faculty of a school develops a comprehensive vision of the morality it wishes to convey to its pupils, and then the entire school program is shaped so as to reinforce this vision. School assemblies, excursions, school events, daily lunches, and an array of other perfunctory activities serve as vehicles for achieving moral education.

Procedures that break up the organic integrity of the school and of its constituent classroom groups are believed to detract from moral education. Thus, in the Japanese primary school, the same instructor teaches all the subjects, and subject specialists are rarely employed. In normal times, the same teachers and pupils stay together for two consecutive years. Ability tracking is avoided. In the middle schools, students are placed in homerooms, which teachers visit instead of having the students parade from classroom to classroom. The totality of the Japanese educational experience—the more numerous school days, the heavier assignments, the extensive extracurricular program—enhances the impact of moral education.

It would require a major commitment on the part of American education to approximate the Japanese approach to moral education, perhaps more than Americans can muster. Local government budget directors and teachers' unions would resist the lengthening of the school year. Teachers would experience difficulty in achieving a consensus on the moral traits to be emphasized. Parents of particular ethnic and class groups represented in the schools might challenge the moral education program in the courts.

Finally, it is the Japanese school's emphasis on morality that enables it to promote change. American neoradical theorists insist that the schools are subordinate to the ruling class, and insofar as the schools teach values, these values correspond to the prevailing social order. Hence, the schools are unable to promote change. In the Japanese case, school budgets and curricula are controlled by the ruling class, but the teachers, acting through their unions, have managed to buffer classroom activities from external control. Many teachers do not accept the vision of the ruling class for Japanese society. Rather than follow the ruling class's guidelines for moral education, these teachers identify with the task of building a more equalitarian society in which the people participate in the organizations that shape their lives. The teachers build this egalitarian sentiment into their instruction, and their success in this "inconsistent" education invalidates the correspondence principle.

Although this thesis of social change is not addressed directly to the traditional liberal emphasis on equality through opportunity, it does carry resounding implications. The liberal position has always stressed the school's role in imparting cognitive skills, whereas the Japanese experience highlights the importance of moral education. Whereas the liberal position is content with the prevailing hierarchical order, the Japanese case indicates the efficacy of leveling these hierarchies. Reducing basic inequalities contributes to the dissolution of inequalities in educational and social opportunity.

STRAINS IN JAPANESE EDUCATION

Because of a concern in this discussion with lessons for the United States, the positive side of Japanese education has been stressed. However, the Japanese parent who sends his child to school is much more likely to emphasize the problems of Japanese education—the lack of individual attention in the schools, the stress-provoking preparation for examinations, and the inequality of opportunity. Teachers are dissatisfied with the inadequate public educational expenditures, the excesses and inconsistencies in the official curriculum, and the long school year. Established elites complain that the schools fail to produce the ideal Japanese, that too few children select vocational courses, and that those who go on to college are not as knowledgeable nor as creative as they should be. Each of the constituencies of Japanese education has a long list of complaints, and since the student revolt of the mid-sixties, many of these groups have drafted reform proposals.

The entrance examination system, which monitors the movement of youths into elite secondary schools and universities, may well be the most severely criticized institution in the educational system. Many of the problems of the school system stem from the need to prepare students for these entrance exams. For example, the school curriculum, rather than responding to the diverse interests of students, is standardized so that all children can benefit from an equal educational background when they compete for university entrance. The public school curriculum is demanding so that the typical student will not be placed at a great disadvantage relative to the fortunate few who are able to attend expensive exam-oriented private schools. Young people are said to lose their vitality and creativity because they have to apply themselves with such singular discipline to prepare for the exams.

Although Japan's leaders are aware of these problems, it is only since the student revolt of the late sixties that they have devoted extensive attention to educational reform: the government, in preparation for what it hoped would become a wholesale reconstruction of the existing system, asked the Central Council for Education to prepare a series of reform proposals. Among the various problems considered by the council was the troublesome examination system. The council's final report concluded: "Because the student selection system has an undesirable effect on the whole system of education in Japan, we must try to improve it. . . . Qualified students should be able to gain admission to higher educational institutions suited to their individual abilities without special provision for entrance examinations" (1972:43). The council urged the central government to take decisive action to reform the examination system, and if the government had been determined, it had several available strategies. It could have taken more serious steps to level the hierarchy of universities, both in the national sector (through leveling the extreme differentials in government support) and in the private sector (through large government subsidies). It could have also eliminated the attached schools to national universities, or at least reduced their level of subsidy to that received by ordinary public schools and insisted that the national schools admit students on a random basis or some other means designed to obtain an ordinary student body. More intense moral persuasion could have been directed at the private employment sector to promote a more flexible consideration of job applicants irrespective of their academic degrees. Laws or regulations could have been introduced to control the activities of the private sector's best schools—for example, compulsory education could have been extended through high school, thus placing these schools under official influence. However, the government has been reluctant to take the initiative in reforming the competitive examination system.

Critics of competition say the conservative government is actually a silent supporter of the competition—and there may be some truth in this. A recent platform statement of the Liberal Democratic Party stated that "competition is the basic principle of life—it brings the best out of men" (Toyama, 1976:27). Government and business leaders make no secret of their belief in the efficiency of educational competition. They say it helps them to select the nation's most able youths for their organizations. They may differ on some of the details: the government continues to rely on the University of Tokyo as its principal supplier of higher civil servants, for it feels the products of this school will be the most intelligent and disciplined and their common school tie will add to the civil service's esprit de corps; in contrast, some businesses prefer the graduates of other schools, feeling they have more vigor and personality. In general, government and business leaders are not impressed with the quality of education or the personal values that the competitive school system teaches their recruits, and they would like to see some changes in these areas, but they are confident of the transformative power of their on-the-job training programs. These leaders also appreciate the role of academic competition in maintaining social order.

Needless to say, there are many other groups that have a vested interest in the competitive system. Those universities that receive the most outstanding students and thereby maintain their prestigious position stand to lose if the competition is significantly altered. Tokyo University reacted with obvious disinterest to the proposal that it abandon undergraduate education and become Japan's first graduate school university. The university's representatives have played a significant role in sabotaging the National University Assocation's effort to develop a meaningful reform of existing procedures for selecting entrants to the respective institutions of the national system.

The demand to reform the examination system is strongest among public school teachers and parents as represented in their parent-teacher organizations and other groups. Yet at the same time, many of these teachers earn money from the competition by moonlighting as *juku* teachers and private tutors. The concerned parents, although they can agree in principle that competition should be curbed, are not prepared to pull their own children out until everyone else does. Often the most articulate parents in opposition to competition are those devoting the greatest private effort toward pushing their children forward. A prize example is a principal of one of the middle schools visited for this study who constantly complained about the pressure that parents placed on his school to stress academic over other school activities; yet this principal had guided his son to success in the entrance exam to Kyoto's most famous private school, Rakusei. There is also the story of several Kyoto principals who, upon retirement, joined hands in opening a large *juku*. Thus, there are many who silently support Japan's elite groups in their preference for maintaining the competitive system.

Public Policy and Private Schools

Although the central government and the universities have floundered in their attempts to reform the examination system, several local governments have in recent years imitated the Kyoto "democratic" high school system, which has a reputation for reducing many of the pressures associated with preparation for entrance examinations. The Kyoto system was originally developed during the Occupation period in conformity with the "neighborhood school" principle. In contrast to the traditional hierarchy of secondary schools, each institution was to be equal in quality. Qualified students who wished to go to a high school would enter their neighborhood high school, rather than worry about competing for entrance to a "best" school. The uniform high quality of the high schools would in theory enable all high school students to receive adequate college preparation while participating in a well-rounded program of extracurricular activities.

At the beginning of the postwar period all of Japan's prefectures were encouraged to institute a system similar to the Kyoto arrangement. However, from the mid-fifties, most reverted to some variation of the traditional hierarchical system. In extreme cases, a prefecture placed all of its high school students in a single "large competitive system." Students who achieved the highest scores on an entrance exam were admitted to the best high schools and those who did not do as well were required to attend lesser high schools, or, if they preferred, those of the latter group could sit out for a year of exam preparation and compete again for entry to the best high schools. From the point of view of maximizing student prospects for success in the elite university entrance exams, the large district system appears to be superior. It concentrates a prefecture's best-qualified youths in a superior high school, where, in an environment of mutual stimulation, they cover material at an accelerated pace. In contrast, the neighborhood principle places bright students in classrooms with others who learn at a slower pace and who offer less academic stimulation. However, the large district system leads to an explicit ranking of students and also fosters adolescent anxieties over the prospects of getting into the best high schools. Kyoto educators, influenced by the egalitarian ideology of the teachers' union, have maintained that these costs of the large district system are too great to justify its theoretical benefit of providing a favorable setting for outstanding youths. To buttress their position, Kyoto educators have periodically compiled reports purporting to show that their system enables Kyotoites to do well in the exam competition while avoiding its costs. For example, Kyoto youths have one of the highest rates of college attendance of all prefectures and a disproportionate number of Kyoto high school graduates have succeeded in the entrance exams for Tokyo University and Kyoto University, Japan's two most prestigious higher educational institutions. At the same time, Kyoto's suicide rate for youths and its rate for "hate-schoolers" (long-term school absentees known as *gakuo kirainin*) are low.[3]

For over a decade the Kyoto government stood alone as the de-

[3] When the number of graduates from each prefecture who in 1975 and 1976 gained entrance to either the University of Tokyo or Kyoto University is divided by the total number graduating from high schools in each prefecture, it is found that Kyoto graduates achieve the highest rate for entrance to these two elite institutions. For basic data, see *Shukan Asahi*, April 16, 1976, pp. 158-159.

fender of the so-called democratic neighborhood system. However, radical educators throughout the nation were impressed with the Kyoto example and anxious to see it adopted in their areas. Since the late sixties, progressive parties have won elections in several of the local areas in which radical educators are numerous. Responding to the educators' preference, several of these newly constituted progressive governments have abandoned their large systems and reintroduced the democratic model. Yet, contrary to the Kyoto experience, students have not responded to these reforms as anticipated. In far too many cases, the brightest students of these districts have shown their distrust for the public sector reform by refusing to attend a public high school. Instead, these youths have elected to attend the more expensive and exclusive private schools that provide instruction specifically designed for exam preparation.

Tokyo provides the most dramatic example. Prior to the reforms, Tokyo practiced the large district system, and several of Tokyo's public high schools were among the nation's leaders in sending graduates to elite universities. In 1970, immediately following Tokyo's shift to the neighborhood model, the competition for well-known non-public schools increased significantly, and these schools were able to recruit the best students. By 1972 Hibiya and Koishikawa, two public high schools the students of which had always excelled in the exam competition, were displaced from the top ten high schools supplying students to Tokyo University. By 1976 only one public high school was among the top ten, and this school was in the neighboring prefecture of Saitama, which uses the large district system. The top school was the private, exam-oriented Nada Koko of distant Hyogo prefecture. The next three were attached schools to national universities in the Tokyo area, and the remainder were private exam-oriented schools. Among Tokyo's formerly strong public schools, only Nishi was in the top twenty ("Toritsuko," 1976). Although some from the public schools gained entrance into well-known universities, these schools were now largely sending their graduates to second- and third-rank universities. Because the educational planners tried to limit the geographical areas from which students might compete to enter the outstanding public schools, they ruined the special climate of these schools. Moreover, they probably increased inequality of opportunity: whereas prior to the reforms the best schools were in the comparatively inexpensive public sector, after the reforms the best schools were located largely in the more costly private sector.

Shocked by the failure of its democratic experiment, Tokyo is now attempting a slow retreat. Other progressive-controlled prefectures are uncertain what to do. Whereas they oppose the elitist large district system, they fear a repetition of Tokyo's mistake and of Kyoto's possible fate. The Tokyo experiment points out the difficulty of achieving an educational policy goal through reform of the public sector when a large number of equivalent institutions are in the private sector, protected from the influence of public sector planners. This is perhaps the biggest dilemma now being confronted by the Japanese school system.

The Future of Egalitarian Education

The problems encountered in alleviating the strain of the examination system illustrate the complexity of the educational system. In the face of this complexity it is impossible to make precise projections for the system's future. However, a few observations can be made on forces that influence the egalitarian character of the system's educational outcomes.

First, the implications of the exam system should be considered. Despite its failings, the examination competition as currently structured actually reinforces certain of the effects of Japan's egalitarian education. Most Japanese youths are not exposed to the competition until the latter part of middle school. By that time they have already internalized egalitarian values that dispose them to react negatively toward the competitive pressures. Egalitarian values seem to draw youths together, even as the examination system seeks to pull them apart and to send them on diverse paths to adulthood.

In the future, however, if the examination system is not reformed, it is conceivable that the examination competition will begin to affect more youths at earlier stages in their socialization. Although most youths will continue to attend public primary schools, these schools may decline as a central life interest. Even in the primary school years, youths will become involved in the world of *juku*, private tutors, and intensive study. If increasing numbers of private school youths are caught up in the pressure to prepare for exams, they may become oblivious to the egalitarian lessons of their primary schools. Although parents and teachers will react to this with dismay, there are other groups in the society who, believing education should do more to nurture individual abilities and practical skills, will welcome this trend.

A second threat to the future of egalitarian education is the prospect of political victory by progressive political forces. Most political observers believe it is only a matter of time before the conservative Liberal Democratic Party will be displaced by a government reflecting progressive forces. In the past, a key ingredient in the ability of the teachers' union to influence classroom teaching was its position as a critical and mistreated outsider. The union's continuing battle with the government has enabled it to generate a creative vision of egalitarian education that has appealed to the rank-and-file teacher. In the absence of conflict with government, it is not known whether the union would be able to continue to generate new pedagogical insights or to excite the ordinary teacher with the need to persist in the conscientious practice of egalitarian education. It is possible that the union would become preoccupied with promoting a series of practical demands—better salaries, a five-day work week, and a less demanding curriculum. It would be difficult for a progressive government to resist these demands. Yet if a future regime makes these concessions, it will be weakening several of those distinctive characteristics of Japanese education that are most central to its egalitarian achievements.

In the event of a progressive victory, Japan's radical educators would have to face up to the problems inevitably encountered by those who rule. Throughout the postwar period, radical teachers have carried on a vigorous campaign of protest against the conservatives' utilitarian and meritocratic policies. The radicals have charged that the conservative policies underlie the exam competition and most of the other problems that trouble Japanese education. As the radical forces gain control of local governments and increase their participation in the central government, they will be under pressure to remedy these deep-seated problems. Yet it is not at all clear that they are armed with viable solutions. One of the policies that radical educators have persistently urged is Kyoto's democratic high school system, yet the difficulties that were encountered when this system was imitated by the Tokyo metropolitan government have already been noted. Recently, in Aichi prefecture, a progressive government assumed office and began to reform the educational system. Although it affirmed its ideological commitment to equal opportunity, this government found it had to treble the tuition for public kindergartens as well as increase fees in the public high schools in order to pay for its reform programs. The Japanese public is carefully watching the new progressive governments that have already gained office in several local areas, but these regimes show little promise of alleviating the problems that their political spokesmen formerly blamed on the conservatives. Insofar as progressive regimes fail to make headway on these problems, the public is likely to withdraw its respect for these regimes and for their political ally the teachers' union. If this occurs, egalitarian education will be threatened.

Contemporary Japanese society faces a condition never before encountered by an advanced society. Over the course of industrialization, educational systems were relied upon to place young people in the social system: those who did well in school learned that they were bright and deserved social status; others learned that they should settle for less. Postwar Japanese education has failed to teach its pupils these lessons. It has encouraged all to do well in school, and a large proportion have responded admirably. In Japan today, nearly all youths attend high school, and the vast majority wish to go on to college. These youths, although they appreciate their individual strengths and weaknesses, are not inhibited by deep feelings of elitism or inferiority. They feel equal to each other and ask society to treat them accordingly.

Adult society is dismayed by these demands. Given rapid growth and a need for the labor and commitment of young people, however, adult society has attempted a modest accommodation. Thus, traditional hierarchies are not as steep as they once were, and young people are given responsibility and challenge at an earlier age than were their predecessors. In certain respects, Japan may be ahead of other advanced societies in its concessions to youths. But will these trends continue, or will a backlash set in? The egalitarian experiment is still in its infancy.

Abegglen, James C. *The Japanese Factory*. New York: Free Press, 1958.

Akuto, Hiroshi, Kenichi Tominaga, and Takao Sofue. *Hendoki no Nihon Shakai* (Changing Japanese Society). Tokyo: Nihon Hoso Shuppan Kyokai, 1972.

Anderson, Ronald S. *Education in Japan: A Century of Modern Development*. Washington, D.C.: U.S. Government Printing Office, 1975.

Asahi Shinbunsha. *Ima Gakkode* (Now in the Schools), Vols. 1-5. Tokyo: Asahi Shinbunsha, 1973-1976, a.

—————. *Nihon Kyosanto* (Japan's Communist Party). Tokyo: Asahi Shinbunsha, 1973, b.

—————. "Teachers, Children, and School," *Japan Interpreter* 9, No. 1, (Spring, 1974 c.): 1-14.

Aso, Makoto. *Erito to Kyoiku* (Elites and Education). Tokyo: Fukumura Shuppan, 1967.

Aso, Makoto, and Ikuo Amano. *Education and Japan's Modernization*. Tokyo: Ministry of Foreign Affairs, 1972.

Asu no Kyoiku o Kangaerukai. "Kokka 100-Nen no tame no Shi-Kyoiku Sen" (Proposal for a New Educational Approach on the Nation's 100th Anniversary). *Bungei Shunju* 53 (August 1975): 92-126.

Azumi, Koya. *Higher Education and Business Recruitment in Japan*. New York: Teachers College Press, 1969.

Banks, Olive. *The Sociology of Education*. 2d ed. London: B. T. Batsford, 1971.

Beckmann, George M. *The Modernization of China and Japan*. New York: Harper and Row, 1962.

Befu, Harumi, *Japan: An Anthropological Introduction*. San Francisco: Chandler Publishing, 1971.

Bell, Daniel. *The Coming of Post Industrial Society*. New York: Basic Books, 1973.

Bennett, George K., et al. *Differential Aptitude Tests Manual*. 2nd ed. New York: Psychological Corporation, 1952.

Bereday, George Z. F., and Shigeo Masui. *American Education through Japanese Eyes*. Honolulu: University Press of Hawaii, 1973.

Bidwell, Charles E., and Rebecca S. Vreeland. "College Education and Moral Orientations: An Organizational Approach." *Administrative Science Quarterly* 8 (September 1963): 166-191.

Blau, Peter M., and Otis Dudley Duncan. *The American Occupational Structure*. New York: John Wiley & Sons, 1967.

Blood, Robert D. *Love Match and Arranged Marriage*. New York: Free Press, 1967.

289

Bloom, Benjamin S. *Human Characteristics and School Learning*. New York: McGraw-Hill, 1976.

———. *Stability and Change in Human Characteristics*. New York: John Wiley & Sons, 1964.

Boltho, Andrea. *Japan: An Economic Survey: 1953-1973*. London: Oxford University Press, 1975.

Boudon, Raymond. *Education, Opportunity, and Social Inequality*. New York: John Wiley & Sons, 1973.

Bourdieu, Pierre, and Jean-Claude Passeron. "Dependence Through Independence." In Bourdieu and Passeron, *Reproduction in Education, Society and Culture*, tr. Richard Nice. London: Sage Publications, 1977.

Bowles, Samuel, and Herbert Gintis. *Schooling in Capitalist America*. New York: Basic Books, 1976.

Bowman, Mary Jean, et al. "Schools and the Future in Japan." Manuscript.

Brameld, Theodore. *Japan, Culture, Education and Change in Two Communities*. New York: Holt, Rinehart and Winston, 1968.

Brown, Roger. *Social Psychology*. New York: Free Press, 1965.

Burnstein, Ira J. *The American Movement to Develop Protestant Colleges for Men in Japan, 1868-1912*. Comparative Education Dissertation Series, No. 11. University of Michigan, 1967.

Carnoy, Martin. *Education as Cultural Imperialism*. New York: David McKay Company, 1974.

Carnoy, Martin, and Henry M. Lewin. *The Limits of Educational Reform*. New York: David McKay Company, 1976.

Caudill, William, and David W. Plath. "Who Sleeps by Whom? Parent-Child Involvement in Urban Japanese Families." *Psychiatry* 29 (1966): 344-366.

Caudill, William, and Helen Weinstein. "Maternal Care and Infant Behavior in Japan and America." *Psychiatry* 32 (1969): 12-43.

Central Council for Education. *Basic Guidelines for the Reform of Education*. Tokyo: Ministry of Education, 1972.

Cole, Robert E. *Japanese Blue Collar*. Berkeley and Los Angeles: University of California Press, 1971.

———. "Work Redesign in Japan: A Macro View." Manuscript.

Coleman, James S. *The Adolescent Society*. New York: Free Press, 1961.

Coleman, James S., et al. *Equality of Educational Opportunity*. Washington, D.C.: U.S. Government Printing Office, 1966.

Collins, Randall. "Some Comparative Principles of Educational Stratification." *Harvard Educational Review* 47, No. 1 (February 1977): 1-27.

Comber, L. C., and John Keeves. *Science Achievement in Nineteen Countries*. New York: John Wiley & Sons, 1973.

Cummings, William K. "The Conservatives Reform Higher Education." *Japan Interpreter* 8, No. 4 (Winter 1974): 421-431.

———. "The Crisis of Japanese Higher Education." *Minerva* 10, No. 4 (October 1972): 631-638.

————. "The Effects of Japanese Schools." In *Education in a Changing Society*. Edited by Antonina Kloskowska and Guido Martinotti. London: Sage Publications, 1977.

————. "The Japanese Private University." *Minerva* 1, No. 3 (July 1973): 348-371.

————. "The Problems and Prospects for Japanese Higher Education." In *Japan: The Paradox of Progress*, edited by Lewis Austin. New Haven: Yale University Press, 1976.

Cummings, William K., and Atsushi Naoi, "Social Background, Education, and Personal Advancement in a Dualistic Employment System." *Developing Economics* 12 (September 1974): 245-274.

Cummings, William K., and Robert Burns. "Organizational Size and Job Turnover." Manuscript.

Cummings, William K., Ikuo Amano, and Kazayuki Kitamura, eds. *Changes in the Japanese University*. New York: Praeger, 1979.

Cummings, William K., and Osamu Kusatsu. "Shokugyo Taikei to Shokugyo Bunka" (Occupational Structures and Occupational Culture). In *Shokugyo Seikatsu no Shakaigaku*, edited by Ryoichi Iwanchi. Tokyo: Gaku bunsha, 1975.

Doi, Takeo. *The Anatomy of Dependence*. Tokyo: Kodansha International, 1973.

Dore, Ronald. *British Factory—Japanese Factory*. Berkeley and Los Angeles: University of California Press, 1975, a.

————. *City Life in Japan*. Berkeley and Los Angeles: University of California Press, 1958.

————. *The Diploma Disease*. Berkeley and Los Angeles: University of California Press, 1976.

————. "The Future of Japan's Meritocracy." In *Social Structures and Economic Dynamics in Japan up to 1980*, edited by Gianni Fodella. Milan: Institute of Economic and Social Studies for East Asia, Luigi Bocconi University, 1975, b.

————. *Land Reform in Japan*. London: Oxford University Press, 1950.

————. "Textbooks Censorship in Japan: The Ienaga Case." *Pacific Affairs* 43 (Winter 1970-1971).

Dreeben, Robert. *On What is Learned in School*. Menlo Park: Addison-Wesley, 1968.

Duke, Benjamin C. "The Image of an Ideal Japanese." *Educational Forum* 32 (November 1967): 31-37.

————. *Japan's Militant Teachers*. Honolulu: University Press of Hawaii, 1973.

————. "The Textbook Controversy." *Japan Quarterly* 13 (July-September 1972): 337-352.

Dunkin, Michael J., and Bruce J. Biddle. *The Study of Teaching*. New York: Holt, Rinehart and Winston, 1974.

Economic Planning Agency. *White Paper on National Life 1974*. Tokyo: Overseas Data Service Company, 1975.

Eto, Jun. "Japanese Youth: Their Fears and Anxieties," *Japan Quarterly* 21, No. 2 (April-June 1974): 152-159.

Evans, Robert. *The Labor Economics of Japan and the United States*. New York: Praeger, 1971.

Featherman, David L., F. Lancaster Jones, and Robert M. Hanser. "Assumptions of Social Mobility Research in the U.S.: The Case of Occupational Status." *Social Science Research* 4 (1975): 329-360.

Foster, Philip, and James R. Sheffield, eds. *Education and Rural Development*. London: Evans Brothers, 1973.

Frager, Robert, and Thomas P. Rohlen. "The Future of a Tradition: Japanese Spirit in the 1980's." In *Japan: The Paradox of Progress*, edited by Lewis Austin. New Haven: Yale University Press, 1975.

Freedman, Richard B. *The Over-Educated American*. New York: Academic Press, 1976.

Fujishiro, Motoko. "The Changing Aims of the Japanese Elementary Curriculum as Reflected in the Moral Education Course." Master's thesis, University of South Carolina, 1967.

Fujita, Hidenori. "Education and Status Attainment in Modern Japan." Ph.D. dissertation, School of Education, Stanford University, 1978.

Fujita, Taki. "The Higher Education of Women in Japan." In *Education in Japan*, papers presented at the World Federation of Educational Associations Seventh Biennial Conference, Tokyo, 1937. Tokyo: Tokyo Printing Co., 1938.

Fujinaga, Tamotsu, and Aso Makoto. *Noryoku, Tokusei, Sentaku to Kyoiku* (Ability, Individuality, Selection and Education). Tokyo: Daiichi Hōki Shuppansha, 1975.

Fukaya, Masashi, and Kazuko Fukaya. *Gendai Kodomoron* (Perspectives on Today's Children). Tokyo: Yukikaku, 1975.

Fukui, Haruhiro. *Party in Power: The Japanese Liberal Democrats and Policy Making*. Berkeley and Los Angeles: University of California Press, 1974.

Fukutake Tadashi. *Japanese Society Today*. Tokyo: University of Tokyo Press, 1974.

Funahashi, Naomichi. "The Industrial Reward System: Wages and Benefits." In *Workers and Employers in Japan*, edited by Kazuo Okochi et al. Tokyo: University of Tokyo Press, 1973.

Galenson, Walter, and Konosuke Odaka. "The Japanese Labor Market." In *Asia's New Giant*, edited by Hugh Patrick and Henry Rosovsky. Washington, D.C.: The Brookings Institute, 1976.

Giddens, Anthony. *The Class Structure of the Advanced Societies*. New York: Harper & Row, 1973.

Goffman, Erving. "The Characteristics of Total Institutions." In *Sym-

posium on Preventive and Social Psychiatry. Washington, D.C.: Walter Reed Army Institute of Research, 1957.

Goodman, Mary Ellen. "Values, Attitudes, and Social Concepts of Japanese and American Children." *American Anthropologist* 59 (December, 1957): 979-999.

Gump, Paul V. "What is Happening in the Elementary Classroom." In *Research into Classroom Processes,* edited by Arno A. Bellack and Ian Westbury. New York: Teachers College Press, 1971.

Grusen, Hiroko. *Parent-Adolescent Relationships in Japan: Patterns of Dependency.* Ann Arbor: University Microfilms International, 1971.

Hachiya, Kei, ed. *Ningen no Tame no Kyoiku 2: Shonen* (Humanistic Education for Young Children). Tokyo: Nihon Hoso Shuppan Kyokai, 1973.

Hall, Ivan. *Mori Arinori.* Cambridge, Mass.: Harvard University Press, 1973.

Hall, Robert K. *Shushin: The Ethics of a Defeated Nation.* New York: Teacher's College Bureau of Publications, 1949.

Hanushek, Eric A. "An Insider's View of Educational Production Functions." *Educational Research,* forthcoming.

Hauser, Robert M., and David Featherman. "Equality of Schooling: Trends and Prospects." *Sociology of Education* 49 (April 1976): 99-120.

Hauser, Robert M., et al. "Structural Changes in Occupational Mobility among Men in the United States." *American Sociological Review* 40 (October 1975): 585-598.

Hicks, J. R., and Nobuko Nosse. *The Social Framework of the Japanese Economy.* Tokyo: Oxford University Press, 1974.

Honna, Nobuyuki. "A Note on Social Structure and Linguistic Behavior." In *Language in Japanese Society,* edited by Fred Peng. Tokyo: University of Tokyo Press, 1975.

Husén, Torsten, ed. *International Study of Achievement in Mathematics: A Comparison of Twelve Countries.* 2 vols. New York: John Wiley & Sons, 1967.

Hutchins, Robert Maynard. *The Learning Society.* New York: Praeger, 1968.

Huthwaite, Motoko. *An Analysis of Contemporary Children's Literature with a Focus on Values.* Ann Arbor: University Microfilms International, 1974.

Ienaga, Saburo. *Shin Nihonshi* (A History of Modern Japan). Tokyo: Sanseido Press, forthcoming.

Ike, Nobutaka. "Economic Growth and Intergenerational Change in Japan." *American Political Science Review* 67 (December 1973): 1194-1203.

Inglehart, Ronald. *The Silent Revolution: Changing Values and Political Styles among Western Publics.* Princeton: Princeton University Press, 1977.

Ishizaki, Tadao. "The Income Distribution in Japan." *Developing Economies* 5, No. 2 (June 1967): 351-370.

Ito, Kei. "Kyoin no Senmon Ishiki no Kozo" (The Professional Consciousness of Teachers). *Kyoiku Shakai Kenkyu* 26 (1971): 152-167.

Iwai, Hiroaki. "Delinquent Groups and Organized Crime." In *Japanese Culture and Behavior*, edited by Takie Sugiyama Lebra and William P. Lebra. Honolulu: University Press of Hawaii, 1974.

Iwauchi, Ryoichi. "Industrial Training in Japan, 1890-1930." *Bulletin of the Tokyo Institute of Technology* 111 (March 1972): 41-49; 114 (March 1973): 63-86.

Japan Institute of International Affairs. *White Papers of Japan: 1969-70.* Tokyo: Japan Institute of International Affairs, 1971.

Japan Institute of International Affairs. *White Papers of Japan: 1973-74.* Japan: Cepres, 1975.

Japan Institute of Labor. *Japan Labor Statistics.* Tokyo: Japan Institute of Labor, 1974

Japan Research Center. *Wakamono Ishiki Chosa* (Analysis of the Psychology of Youth in Japan). Tokyo: Japan Research Center, 1972.

Jencks, Christopher, et al. *Inequality.* New York: Basic Books, 1972.

Jichitai Mondai Kenkyusho, ed. *Kyoto Minshu Seifu* (Kyoto's Democratic Government). Tokyo: Jichitai Kenkyusha, 1974.

Kajita, Eiichi. "Cross-National Study of the Vocational Values of Children." *Research Bulletin of the National Institute for Educational Research* 13 (1975): 21-32; 14 (1976): 27-43.

Karabel, Jerome, and A. H. Halsey, eds. *Power and Ideology in Education.* New York: Oxford University Press, 1977.

Kato, Masaaki. "Self-destruction in Japan: A Cross-Cultural Epidemiological Analysis of Suicide." In *Japanese Culture and Behavior*, edited by Takie Sugiyama Lebra and William P. Lebra. Honolulu: University Press of Hawaii, 1974.

Katsuda, Kichitaro. *Zetsubo no Kyoiku Kiki* (The Hopeless Educational Crisis). Tokyo: Nihon Keizai Tsushinsha, 1974.

Katsuta, Shuichi and Nakauchi Toshio. *Nihon no Gakko* (The Japanese School). Tokyo: Iwanami Shinsho, 1964.

Katz, Michael B. *Class, Bureaucracy and Schools.* New York: Praeger, 1971.

Kawai, Kazuo. *Japan's American Interlude.* Chicago: University of Chicago Press, 1960.

Kawakami, Fujiko. "Nencho Kyoinzo no Shokumu Ishiki ni Mirareru Gakko Soshiki no Niju Kozosei" (The Dual Structure of Schools as Reflected in the Attitudes of Teachers and Their Supervisors). *Kyoikugaku Kenkyu* 44, No. 1 (March 1977): 59-70.

Kawashima, Takeyoshi, and Kurt Steiner. "Modernization and Divorce Trends in Japan." *Economic Development and Cultural Change* 9, No. 1, Part 2 (October 1960): 213-239.

Keniston, Kenneth. *Young Radicals: Notes on Committed Youth.* New York: Harcourt Brace & World, 1968.

Keizai Kikakucho. *Kokumin Seikatsu Hakusho 1975* (1975 White Paper on People's Livelihood). Tokyo: Okurasho Insatsukyoku, 1975.

Kerckhoff, Alan C. *Socialization and Social Class.* Englewood Cliffs, N.J.: Prentice-Hall, 1972.

Kiefer, Christie W. "The Psychological Interdependence of Family, School and Bureaucracy in Japan." In *Japanese Culture and Behaviour*, edited by Takie Sugiyama Lebra and William P. Lebra. Honolulu: University Press of Hawaii, 1974. Originally published in *American Anthropologist* 72 (1970): 66-75.

Kiyonari, Tadao. *Nihon Chusho Kigyo no Koza Hendo* (The Changing Structure of Small and Medium Enterprises). Tokyo: Shinhyoron, 1970.

Kobayashi, Tetsuya. *Society, Schools, and Progress in Japan.* Oxford: Pergamon Press, 1976.

Kobayashi, Victor. *John Dewey in Japanese Educational Thought.* Ann Arbor: University of Michigan Comparative Education Dissertation Series, 1964.

Kojima, Kazuto. *Sengo Seronshi* (Postwar Trends in Public Opinion). Tokyo: NHK Bukkusu, 1975.

Kokuritsu Kyoiku Kenkyusho. *Shunendo Chosa: Chugakko Sotsugyo Jikki no Jokyo* (Initial Survey: The Situation at the Time of Graduation from Middle School), Vols. 1-10. Tokyo, Kokuritsu Kyoiku Kenkyusho. 1966-1968.

Kondo, Sumio. "Off We Go to Our Lessons." *JAPAN Interpreter* 9 (Spring 1974): 15-24.

Kotschnig, Walter. *Unemployment in the Learned Professions.* London, 1937.

Koyano, Shogo. "Sociological Studies in Japan." *Current Sociology* 24, No. 1 (1976): 55-57.

Kraar, Louis. "The Japanese are Coming—With Their Own Style of Management." *Fortune* (March, 1975): 116-121 and 160-164.

Krauss, Ellis S. *Japanese Radicals Revisited.* Berkeley and Los Angeles: University of California Press, 1974.

Kusatsu, Osamu. "Ego Development and Socio-Cultural Process in Japan." *Asia Daigaku Keizai Kiyo* 3, No. 1 (December 1977): 41-109; No. 2 (February 1978): 74-128.

Levin, Henry M. "Educational Reform: Its Meaning." In *The Limits of Educational Reform*, edited by Martin Carnoy and Henry Levin. New York: David McKay Company, 1976.

Lifton, Robert J. *Thought Reform and the Psychology of Totalism: A Study of "Brain Washing" in China.* New York: Norton, 1961.

Lifton, Robert J. "Youth and History: Individual Change in Postwar Japan." *Daedalus* 91 (Winter 1972): 171-197.

Lockwood, W. W. *The Economic Development of Japan.* Expanded edition. Princeton: Princeton University Press, 1968.

Lortie, Dan C. *School Teacher: A Sociological Study.* Chicago: University of Chicago Press, 1975.

Luecke, Daniel F., and Noel F. McGinn. "Regression Analyses and Education Production Functions: Can They be Trusted?" *Harvard Educational Review* 45 (August 1976): 325-350.

Maccoby, Eleanor E. "The Development of Moral Values and Behavior in Childhood." In *Socialization and Society*, edited by John Clausen. Boston: Little, Brown, 1968.

McClelland, David C. "Values in Popular Literature for Children." *Childhood Education* 3 (November 1963): 135.

McFarland, David D., and D. J. Brown. "Social Distance as a Metric: A Systematic Introduction to Smallest Space Analysis." In *Bonds of Pluralism*, edited by E. O. Laumann. New York: John Wiley & Sons, 1973.

Makieda, Motofumi. *Nihon no Kyoshitachi* (Japan's Teachers). Tokyo: Sanshodo, 1975.

Masanori, Horie. *Nihon no Rodosha Kaikyu* (Japan's Labor Class). Tokyo: Iwanami Shinsho, 1962.

Massey, Joseph A. *Youth and Politics in Japan.* Lexington: D. C. Heath, 1976.

Matsumoto, Yoshiharu Scott. *Contemporary Japan: The Individual and the Group.* Vol. 50, pt. 1. Transactions of the American Philosophical Society. Philadelphia, 1960.

Merelman, Richard M. *Political Socialization and Educational Climates.* New York: Holt, Rinehart and Winston, 1971.

————. "Social Stratification and Political Socialization in Mature Industrial Societies." *Comparative Education Review* 19, No. 1 (February 1975): 13-30.

Meyer, John W. "The Effects of Education as an Institution." *American Journal of Sociology* 83 (July 1977): 55-77.

Ministry of Education. *Educational Standards in Japan.* Tokyo: Government Printing Office, 1970.

Ministry of Education. *Education in Japan 1971: A Graphic Presentation.* Tokyo: Government Printing Bureau, 1971.

Ministry of Education, Science and Culture. *Course of Study for Elementary Schools in Japan.* Tokyo: Ministry of Finance Printing Bureau, 1976.

Ministry of Education, Science and Culture. *Course of Study for Lower Secondary Schools.* Tokyo: Ministry of Finance Printing Bureau, 1976.

Mitchell, Richard H. *Thought Control in Prewar Japan.* Ithaca: Cornell University Press, 1976.

Mizutani, Eiji. "The Changing Picture of Lifetime Employment in Japan." *Japan House Newsletter* 19 (May 1, 1972).

Mohachi Motegi. "A Problem of Cross Culture Between Japan and

U.S.A.: Findings in a Study of McCarthy Scales of Children's Abilities." *International Newsletter* 18 (October 1977): 12-13.

Mombusho. *Gakusei Hyakunenshi* (One-Hundred-Year History of Japanese Education). 2 vols. Tokyo: Teikoku Chiho Gyosei Gakkai, 1972.

———. *Kotogakko Sotsugyosha no Shinso Jokyo* (The Situation of High School Graduates). Tokyo: Mombusho, 1970.

———. *Showa 50-Nendo Hakusho: Wagakuni no Kyoiku Suijun* (1975 White Paper: Educational Standards in Japan). Tokyo: Okurasho Insatsu Kyoiku, 1975.

———. *Zenkoku no Gakushu Juku Kayoi no Jitsuyo* (National Pattern of Juku Attendance: Interim Report of the 1976 Survey). Tokyo: Gyosei, 1977.

———. *Wagakuni no Kyoiku Suijun, Showa 50 Nendo Hakusho* (Educational Standards in Japan: The 1975 White Paper). Tokyo: Government Printing Office; 1976.

Moore, Ray. "Adoption and Samurai Mobility in Tokugawa Japan." *Journal of Asian Studies* 29, No. 3 (May 1970): 617-632.

Morioka, Kiyomi. *Kazoku Shakaigaku* (Family Sociology). Tokyo: Yukikaku, 1967.

Mosteller, Frederick, and Daniel P. Moynihan, eds. *On Equality of Educational Opportunity*. New York: Vintage Books, 1972.

Mussen, Paul H., John J. Conger, and Jerome Kagen. *Child Development and Personality*. 4th edition. New York: Harper and Row, 1974.

Nagai, Michio. *Japanese Higher Education: Its Take-off and Crash*. Tokyo: University of Tokyo Press, 1971.

Nagoshi, Kiyoka. "Gendai Kyoshi no Kaikyu Kizoku Ishiki to Kyoshi o Meguru Shomondai" (Class Consciousness and other Opinions of Contemporary Teachers). *Osaka Daigaku Ningen Kagakubu Kiyo* 2 (1976): 186-217.

Nakamura, Hideichiro. *Daikibo Jidai no Owari* (The End of the Era of Large Companies). Tokyo: Daiyamondosha, 1970.

Nakane Chie. *Kinship and Economic Organization in Rural Japan*. New York: Humanities Press, 1967.

Nakano, Takashi. *Shoka Dozokudan no Kenkyu: Noren o Meguru Ie no Kenkyū* (A Study of Merchant Dōzoku groups). Tokyo: Miraisha, 1964.

Nakano, Yumiko. "Kaikyu to Gengo" (Social Class and Language). *Nihon Shakaigaku Kenkyu* 29 (1974): 146-160.

National Institute of Mathematics (Kokuritsu Tokei Suri Kenkyusho). *Nihonjin no Kokumensei* (The Japanese National Character). Vols. 2 and 3. Tokyo, 1969, 1975.

Nihon Keieisha Dantai Renmei. *Sangyo Kunren Hakusho* (Industrial Training White Paper). Tokyo: Nihon Keieisha Dantai Renmei, 1971.

Nihon Kodomo o Mamorukai. *Kodomo Hakusho 1975* (White Paper on Children). Tokyo: Koyo Insatsu, 1975.

Nihon Koto Gakko Kyoshokuin Kumiai, ed. *Gakuryoku Mondai to Koko*

Kyoiku (The Problem of Academic Ability and High School Education). Tokyo: Minshusha, 1975.

Nikkyoso (Nihon Kyoshokuin Kumiai). "Kyoiku Katei Kaizo no tame no Gakuryoku Jittai Chosa Hokoku" (Report on a Survey of Student Achievement as a Background for Reforming Education). *Kyoiku Hyoron* 338 (July 1976): 16–110.

1975-Nen SSM Chosa: Kiso Tokeihyo (Report of Basic Statistics from the 1975 SSM Survey). Tokyo: 1975-Nen SSM Zenkoku Chosa Iinkai Jimukyoku, 1976.

Nishihira, Shigeki. "Le Prestige social des differentes professions— l'evaluation populaire au Japon." *Revue française sociologie* 9, No. 4 (1968): 550–558.

OECD Education Committee. *Reviews of National Policies for Education: Japan.* Paris, OECD, 1971.

Ogburn, William F., and Meyer F. Nimkoff. *Technology and the Changing Family.* Boston: Houghton Mifflin, 1955.

Ohashi, Ryuken. *Nihon no Kaikyu Kosei* (The Composition of Japan's Classes). Tokyo: Iwanami Shinsho, 1971.

Oki, Ken, et al. *Nihon no Kyoshi* (Japanese Teachers). Nihon no Kyoiku Koza 7. Tokyo: Shin Nihon Shuppansha, 1975.

Orihara, Hiroshi. "Test Hell and Alienation, A Study of Tokyo University Freshmen." *Journal of Social and Political Ideas in Japan* 5, Nos. 2-3 (December 1967): 225–250.

Osako, Masako. "Auto Assembly Technology and Social Integration in a Japanese Factory: A Case Study." Ph.D. dissertation, Northwestern University, 1973.

Oyama, Ryu. *Gendai Kazoku no Yakuwari Kozo* (Functional Differentiation of the Contemporary Family).

Parsons, Talcott. *Social Structure and Personality.* New York: Free Press, 1964.

Passin, Herbert. *The Legacy of the Occupation—Japan.* Occasional Papers of the East Asian Institute. New York: Columbia University, 1968.

―――. *Society and Education in Japan.* New York: Teachers College Press, Columbia University, 1965.

President's Commission on Higher Education. *Higher Education for American Democracy.* Vols. 1-4. Washington, D.C.: U.S. Government Printing Office, 1947.

Prewitt, Kenneth. "Some Doubts About Political Socialization Research." *Comparative Education Review* 19, No. 1 (February 1975): 105–114.

Riesman, David, et al. *The Lonely Crowd.* New York: Doubleday, Anchor Books, 1953.

Rohlen, Thomas P. *For Harmony and Strength.* Berkeley and Los Angeles: University of California Press, 1974.

―――. "Is Japanese Education Becoming Less Egalitarian? Notes on High

School Stratification and Reform." *Journal of Japanese Studies* 3, No. 1 (1977): 37-70.

Sarapata, Adam. "Occupational Prestige Hierarchy Studies in Poland." Paper delivered at Eighth World Congress of Sociology, Toronto, August 1974.

Sasaki, Susumu. *Koko Kyoiku Ron* (Thoughts on High School Education). Tokyo: Daimeishoya, 1976.

Shimbori, Michiya, et al. *Nihon no Kyoiku Chizu: Taiiku Spootsu* (Sports and Japanese Schools). Tokyo: Gyosei, 1975.

Shimizu, Yoshihiro. *Shiken* (Examinations). Tokyo: Iwanami Shinsho, 1957.

"Shiritsu Koko wa 40-manen Jidai" (Costs at Private High Schools Above 400,000 Yen). *Asahi Shimbun*, May 26, 1976.

"Shiritsu Yumeiko no Fukei Shirabe" (Investigation of the Parental Background of Children in Famous Private Schools). *Shukan Asahi*, March 23, 1976.

Silberman, Charles E. *Crisis in the Classrooms*. New York: Vintage Books, 1970.

Simmons, John, and Leight Alexander. "The Determinants of School Achievement in Development Countries: A Review of the Research." *Economic Development and Cultural Change* 26 (January 1978): 341-357.

Singleton, John. *Nichu: A Japanese School*. New York: Rinehart and Winston, 1967.

Smith, Robert J. "Pre-Industrial Urbanism in Japan: A Consideration of Multiple Traditions in a Feudal Society." *Economic Development and Cultural Change* 9, No. 1, Part 2 (October 1960): 241-257.

Sorifu Seishonen Taisaku Honbu. *Gendai no Wakamono Tachi* (Contemporary Youth). Tokyo: Okurasho Insatsukyoku, 1970.

―――. *Seikai Seinen Ishiki Chosa Hokokusho* (International Youth Survey). Tokyo: July 1973.

―――. *Seishonen Hakusho 1969* (1969 White Paper on Youth). Tokyo: Okurasho Insatsukyoku, 1969.

Sorifu Tokei Kyoku. *Kokusei Chosa Hokoku* (Population Census of Japan). Tokyo: Okurasho Insatsu Kyoku.

―――. *Kokusai Tokei Yoran 1975* (1975 International Statistics). Tokyo: Okurasho Insatsukyoku, 1975.

Stoetzel, Jean. *Without the Chrysanthemum and the Sword*. New York: Columbia University Press, 1955.

Sumiya, Mikio. "The Emergence of Modern Japan," and "Contemporary Arrangements." In *Workers and Employers in Japan*, edited by K. Okochi et al. Tokyo: University of Tokyo Press, 1973.

―――. "The Functions and Social Structure of Education: School and Japanese Society." *Journal of Social and Political Ideas in Japan* 5, Nos. 2-3 (December 1967): 117-138.

Sumiya, Mikio. *Social Impact of Industrialization in Japan.* Tokyo: Japanese National Commission for UNESCO, 1963.

Suzuki, Shuichi, et al. *Noryoku Shugi no Jyugyo to Gakuryoku* (Ability-Oriented Teaching and Academic Achievement). Tokyo: Hato no Mori Shobo, 1973.

Tachi, Minoru. *Mirai no Nihon Jinko* (The Future Japanese Population). Tokyo: NHK Bukkusu, 1970.

Takahashi, Akira. "Nihon Gakusei Undo no Shiso to Kodo" (Thought and Behavior of the Japanese Student Movement). *Chuo Koron*, May, June, August, September 1968.

Takashima, Hideki. "Tokyo Shuhen Toshi no Kyoiku Kozo to Jyumin no Kyoiku Ishiki" (Educational Attitudes of the People and Teachers in a Tokyo Satellite City). *Meisei Daigaku Jinbun Gakubu Kenkyu Kiyo* 12 (January 1976): 21-52.

Takezawa, Shinichi. "The Quality of Working Life: Trends in Japan." *Labour and Society* 1 (January 1976): 29-48.

Tawney, R. H. *Equality.* 4th edition. New York: Barnes and Noble, 1965.

Teichler, Ulrich, and Friedrich Voss. *Bibliography on Japanese Education: Postwar Publications in Western Languages.* Munich: Verlag Dokumentation, 1974.

Thayer, Nathaniel B. "Elections, Coalitions, and Prime Ministers in Japan, 1965-1985." In *Japan: The Paradox of Progress*, edited by Lewis Austin. New Haven: Yale University Press, 1976.

Thurow, Lester C., and Robert E. B. Lucas. *The American Distribution of Income: A Structural Problem.* Study prepared for the use of the Joint Economic Committee, U.S. Congress. Washington, D.C.: Government Printing Office, March 17, 1972.

Thurston, Donald R. *Teachers and Politics in Japan.* Princeton: Princeton University Press, 1973.

"Todai no Ova-Dokuta Jokyo" (The Situation of Over-Doctors at the University of Tokyo). *Shukan Asahi*, February 1977.

"Todai 50-Nendo no Fukei no Shokugyo to Kazoku no Kyoiku Kankyo" (The Family Background and Educational Preparation of Students Who Passed the 1975 University of Tokyo Entrance Exam). *Shukan Gendai*, April 8, 1976.

Tokyo Daigaku Koseika. *Keizai Seikatsu no Ryunen Henka: 1958-1970* (Trend Analysis of the Economic Conditions of Student Life: 1958-1970). Tokyo: Tokyo Daigaku Koseika, 1971.

Tominaga, Kenichi. "Studies of Social Stratification and Social Mobility in Japan: 1955-1967." *Rice University Studies* 56 (1970): 133-149.

Tomoda, Yasumasa. "Occupational Aspirations of Japanese High School Students." *International Journal of Educational Sociology* 2 (1968): 217-222.

"Toritsuko de yonko dake ga Todai Riisu in Kachi nokotte-iru" (Only

Four Public High Schools Remain among the Top Ten Training Entrants for the University of Tokyo). *Shukan Asahi*, April 9, 1976.

Toyoama, Kei. *Kyoso Genri o Koete* (Moving Beyond Competition). Tokyo: Taro Jirosha, 1976.

Tsuneichi, Warren, et al. *Sources of Japanese Tradition*. New York: Columbia University Press, 1958.

Tsuru, Hiroshi. *Kokosei no Seikatsu to Shinri* (Life and Psychology of High School Students). 4th edition. Tokyo: Dainipon Tosho, 1969.

Ugai, Shinsei. *Atarashii Shakai* (A New Society). Tokyo: Tokyo Shoseki Kabushiki Gaisha, 1975.

Umene, Satoru. *Nihon no Kyoiku* (Japanese Education). Tokyo: Horobu Gyosho, 1975.

———. *Nihon No Kyoiku Do Arubeki Ka?* (What Should Be Done with Japanese Education?). Tokyo: Keisoshobo, 1972.

United States Education Mission to Japan. *Report*. Mimeographed. Tokyo, March 30, 1946.

Ushiogi, Morikazu, et al. "Koko Fushingakusha Hassei no Mekanizumu: Gifu-Ken no Jikkei Kenkyu" (The Factors Stopping Middle School Graduates from Seeking Further Schooling in Gifu-Ken). *Nagoya Daigaku Kyoiku Gakubu Kiyo* 19 (1972): 15-43.

Vidich, Arthur J., and Joseph Bensman. *Small Town in Mass Society*. Princeton: Princeton University Press, 1968.

Vogel, Ezra. *Japan's New Middle Class*. Berkeley and Los Angeles: University of California Press, 1963. 2nd ed. 1975.

Wagatsuma, Hiroshi. "Some Aspects of the Contemporary Japanese Family: Once Confucian, Now Fatherless." *Daedalus* 106 (Spring 1977): 181-210.

Watanuki, Joji. "Pattern of Politics in Present Day Japan." In *Party Systems and Voter Alignment*, edited by S. M. Lipset and Stein Rokkan. New York: Free Press, 1967.

White, James E. "Status Differences in Political Participation in Tokyo." Paper delivered at the American Political Science Association Meeting, San Francisco, September 1975.

Whyte, William Foote. *Street Corner Society*. Chicago: University of Chicago Press, 1943.

Yamamura, Yoshiaki. *Nihonjin to Haha* (The Japanese and Their Mothers). Tokyo: Toyokan Shuppansha, 1971.

Yasuda Saburo, ed. *Gendai Nihon no Kaikyu Ishiki* (Class Consciousness in Contemporary Japan). Tokyo: Yukikaku, 1973.

———. *Shakai Ido no Kenkyu* (Research on Social Mobility). Tokyo: Tokyo Daigaku Shuppankai, 1971.

Yuzawa, Yawahiko. *Kazoku Mondai* (Problems of the Family). Tokyo: NHK Bukkuzu, 1973.

Library of Congress Cataloging in Publication Data

Cummings, William K
    Education and equality in Japan.

    Bibliography: p.
    Includes index.
    1.   Education—Japan—History—1945-   2.   Educa-
tional equalization—Japan—History—20th century.
I.   Title.
LA1311.82.C85   370'.952   79-3199
ISBN 0-691-09385-7
ISBN 0-691-10088-8 (pbk.)